T0301710

DIGITAL ECONOMY AND THE SUSTAINABLE DEVELOPMENT OF ASEAN AND CHINA

Series on Asian Regional Cooperation Studies

Print ISSN: 2717-5456
Online ISSN: 2717-5464

Chief Editor: GAO Fei *(China Foreign Affairs University, China)*
Deputy Chief Editor: GUO Yanjun *(China Foreign Affairs University, China)*

Track II Diplomacy usually refers to an unofficial process with a government background. It plays an important role in promoting regional cooperation in Asia. The main tasks of Track II Diplomacy are to analyze problems, make policy recommendations, and provide intellectual support for official cooperation. Participants are mainly experts and scholars engaged in policy research as well as the government officials participating in their private capacities. The Institute of Asian Studies (IAS) at China Foreign Affairs University is China's focal point for three most influential Track II mechanisms of this region, namely the Network of East Asian Think-tanks (NEAT), the Network of ASEAN-China Think-tanks (NACT) and the Network of Trilateral Cooperation Think-tanks (NTCT). IAS is proud to launch Series on Asian Regional Cooperation Studies jointly with the World Scientific Publishing, the most reputable English academic publisher in Asia. The purpose of this series is not only to motivate more scholars to get involved in Track II Diplomacy of Asia, but also to increase the recognition of the three networks by reaching out to a wide audience. Based on the platforms of NEAT, NACT and NTCT, this series will invite outstanding scholars to conduct in-depth research on significant and challenging issues in Asian regional cooperation, through conference proceedings, scholarly monographs, textbooks and translations with high academic standards and strong policy relevance.

Published

The complete list of the published volumes in the series can also be found at
http://www.worldscientific.com/series/sarcs

Series on Asian Regional Cooperation Studies—Vol. 9

DIGITAL ECONOMY AND THE SUSTAINABLE DEVELOPMENT OF ASEAN AND CHINA

Edited by

YANG Yue

China Foreign Affairs University, China

World Scientific

EW JERSEY · LONDON · SINGAPORE · BEIJING · SHANGHAI · HONG KONG · TAIPEI · CHENNAI · TOKYO

Published by

World Scientific Publishing Co. Pte. Ltd.

5 Toh Tuck Link, Singapore 596224

USA office: 27 Warren Street, Suite 401-402, Hackensack, NJ 07601

UK office: 57 Shelton Street, Covent Garden, London WC2H 9HE

Library of Congress Cataloging-in-Publication Data
Names: Yang, Yue, 1976– editor.
Title: Digital economy and the sustainable development of asean and china /
    edited by Yue Yang, China Foreign Affairs University.
Description: Hackensack, NJ : World Scientific, [2023] | Series: Series on
    asian regional cooperation studies, 2717-5456 ; Vol. 9
Identifiers: LCCN 2022020997 | ISBN 9789811254475 (hardcover) |
    ISBN 9789811257896 (ebook) | ISBN 9789811257902 (ebook other)
Subjects: LCSH: Information technology--Economic aspects--Southeast Asia. |
    Sustainable development--Southeast Asia. | Information technology--
    Economic aspects--China. | Sustainable development--China.
Classification: LCC HC441.I55 D54 2023 | DDC 338.900285095--dc23/eng/20220713
LC record available at https://lccn.loc.gov/2022020997

British Library Cataloguing-in-Publication Data
A catalogue record for this book is available from the British Library.

Sponsored by ASEAN-China Cooperation Fund

Disclaimer: The views expressed in the papers in the book are those of the individual authors and do not necessarily reflect the views of the editor or the views of the Institute of Asian Studies, China Foreign Affairs University.

For any available supplementary material, please visit
https://www.worldscientific.com/worldscibooks/10.1142/12783#t=suppl

Desk Editors: Nimal Koliyat/Lixi Dong

Typeset by Stallion Press
Email: enquiries@stallionpress.com

Printed in Singapore

Foreword

This book is the major outcome of "Digital Economy and Sustainable Development of ASEAN–China Relations" project sponsored by ASEAN–China Cooperation Fund (ACCF). The project was incubated and planned before the outbreak of COVID-19 pandemic and aimed at enhancing ASEAN–China cooperation on the industrial transformation. However, it comes with an unfortunate surprise that the global public health crisis broke out when the project was about to be implemented and has been ravaging every corner of the world still in the severe manner till the project is completed. The COVID-19 pandemic injects new perspective into the project. More importantly, many contributing researchers touch upon this new element and give insightful analysis in their chapters which will shed the light on the digital technology development, its impact on economic recovery and its implications for the sustainable development of ASEAN–China relations.

The global public health crisis of COVID-19 highlights the importance of digital technology which not only helps people cope with the infectious disease in terms of case investigation, contact tracing, and long-distance diagnosis and treatment and so on and so forth, but also makes people's communication more instant and accessible instead of being blocked by the pandemic. Digital economy is also boosting during the pandemic, which becomes one of the major driving forces of economic recovery. However, "digital divide" has been laid bare at the same time. Before the pandemic, AMS and China have formulated national strategies of their own and carried out bilateral and regional cooperation to better prepare each of their state and the region for the fourth industrial revolution. Given the vital importance of digital technology and digital economy, this book provides an in-depth understanding of their implications for the sustainable development of ASEAN–China relations from various perspectives. In addition, authors also contribute their resourceful insights on the sustainable development of both China and AMS through the lens of eco-tourism, carbon neutrality, and social inequality, and among others.

Thirteen chapters are incorporated in this book and written by excellent researchers from China, Indonesia, Lao PDR, Malaysia, the Philippines, Singapore, and Vietnam. Both Chapter 1 by Feng Xingyan and Chapter 13 by Cao Xiaoyang focus on ASEAN–China digital cooperation. Feng Xingyan employs regional and global approaches to examine the implications of digitalization and industrial transformation for ASEAN–China digital cooperation in the pandemic era. The key issues explored in Feng's chapter include recent trends in rapidly digitalizing global economy in the pandemic era, technological revolution and scope for digital transformation and industrialization, digital strategy and industrial transformation in China and ASEAN, challenges in achieving digitalization and industrial transformation in China and ASEAN, and policy recommendations for strengthening ASEAN–China digital cooperation. In her chapter, Cao Xiaoyang takes stock of ASEAN–China digital cooperation thereby pointing out the opportunities facing bilateral cooperation and peering into the future pathway of cooperation. Chapters 2, 7, 9, 11 and 12 dwell upon the specific questions regarding digital economy from both national and regional perspectives, namely management of digital platforms and ASEAN–China cross-border e-commerce on medical devices. In the rest of book, the authors discuss the means by which ASEAN–China relations can be sustained in a healthy manner such as fostering ecotourism in Chapter 3, reducing the gap of inequality through ASEAN–China trade relations in

Chapter 4, fighting against the pandemic and digital cooperation in Chapter 5, poverty alleviation in Chapter 6, ASEAN–China cooperation in achieving carbon neutrality goal in Chapter 8, and Malaysia's efforts on localizing SDGs in Chapter 10.

The book would not have been possible without the wisdom and research efforts of all the contributing authors. They are Prof. Feng Xingyan from China Foreign Affairs University, Dr. Cao Xiaoyang from Chinese Academy of Social Sciences, Prof. Lee Anyu from Sichuan University, China, Yulida Nuraini Santoso and Tunggul Wicaksono from Universitas Gadjah Mada, Indonesia, Bounphieng Pheuaphetlangsy from Institute of Foreign Affairs Lao PDR, Anthony Tan from the All-Party Parliamentary Group Malaysia on SDG (APPGM-SDG) Secretariat, Farlina Md Said from Institute of Strategic and International Studies, Malaysia, Francis Mark A. Quimba from Philippine Institute for Development Studies, the Philippines, Eylla Laire M. Gutierrez from Asian Institute of Management, the Philippines, Tai Wei LIM and Bojian LIU from National University of Singapore, Yu Hong from National University of Singapore, Chu Minh Thao from Diplomatic Academy of Vietnam, and Nguyen Dinh Sach from Institute for Foreign Policy and Strategic Studies, Vietnam.

Thanks also to my colleagues Prof. Guo Yanjun, Dr. Li Fujian, Dr. Li Tianhui and Ms. Zhang Yingjin who have provided enormous support and contributed resourceful ideas to the project. I am also deeply indebted to the editor in editing this book. Last but not least, my deep thanks go to ACCF team for their project review, supervision and generous funding.

This collection of works will attract academics, think tankers, practitioners, and Ph.D. candidates interested in ASEAN–China relations, ASEAN–China cooperation in digital economy and sustainable development.

About the Editor

YANG Yue is Professor and Deputy Director of the Institute of Asian Studies at China Foreign Affairs University. Dr. Yang received her PhD in International Relations from Chinese Academy of Social Sciences in 2013. She was a Fulbright Scholar at Georgetown University in the US from 2006 to 2008. Her research focuses on American politics and foreign policy, ASEAN–China relations, East Asia Regional Cooperation, and cultural diplomacy. Her latest books include *Theory and Practice of China's Cultural Diplomacy — An Empirical and Country-specific Study, The Belt and Road Initiative: ASEAN Countries' Perspectives,* and *ASEAN-China Cooperation for Environmental Protection and Sustainable Energy Development.* Her latest articles include "ASEAN's Perception of and Response to China–US Competition," "Theoretical Analysis and Practical Approaches of Cultural Diplomacy: A Perspective of the 'Civilization Dialogue Theory,'" and "Major Power Competition and the Trump Administration's Policy toward Southeast Asia." As a member of NACT China (Network of ASEAN–China Think-tanks), Dr. Yang has been actively engaging in Track II diplomacies focusing on ASEAN–China relations.

Contents

Chapter

1

Digitalization and Industrial Transformation: Implications for China–ASEAN Digital Cooperation

Feng Xingyan

China Foreign Affairs University, Beijing, China

fengxingyan@cfau.edu.cn

Introduction

The COVID-19 pandemic crisis created opportunities for innovative solutions to cope with the pandemic. Many countries are aiming for speedy recovery from pandemic through the promotion of digital economy. Meanwhile global industrial and supply chains are undergoing a new round of profound adjustments. The momentum of regionalization is steadily growing in the post-COVID era. The development of the digital infrastructure, including the Fourth Industrial Revolution has opened new opportunities and has brought new challenges for digitalization of industries in the developing countries.

In China and ASEAN, during the last few decades, the trend of the advancement of technology has built an innovative pathway to the digital economy for sustainable development. Adoption of digital technologies in traditional industry sectors (agriculture, manufacturing and services) as well as in emerging digital industries is contributing to new and innovative ways of economic cooperation. With the establishment of China–ASEAN digital economy partnership and the designation of 2020 as the China–ASEAN Year of Digital Economy Cooperation, China and ASEAN are pursuing to improve connectivity by synergizing common priorities in the Master Plan on ASEAN Connectivity (MPAC) 2025 and the Belt and Road Initiative (BRI) for the goal of high-standard, people-oriented, people-centered and sustainable development.[1] The era of Fourth Industrial Revolution is also calling for further integration of regional production networks.

Recent Trends in a Rapidly Digitalizing Global Economy in the Pandemic Era

Onset of the COVID-19 pandemic has brought to forefront the vulnerability of the international production networks and the importance of digital industrial transformation. This originates from the ability to reduce distance and entry costs for firms by facilitating greater ease in communication and access to foreign markets.[2] The World Economic Forum noted that firms with stronger digital infrastructure have tackled COVID-19 pandemic disruptions better (Hedwall, 2020).[3] The World Trade Organization also stated that digital preparedness is an important factor in mitigating supply chain disruptions (WTO, 2020).[4]

---

[1] ASEAN–China Joint Statement on Synergizing the MPAC 2025 and the BRI.
[2] Cassetta, E., U. Monarca, I. Dileo, C. Di Berardino and M. Pini, "The relationship between digital technologies and internationalisation," *Industry and Innovation*, 2020, 27(4), pp. 311–339.
[3] Hedwall, M., The ongoing impact of COVID-19 on global supply chains. *World Economic Forum*, 2020. https://www.weforum.org/agenda/2020/06/ongoing-impact-covid-19-global-supply-chains/ (accessed 15 September 2021).
[4] World Trade Organization (WTO). World Trade Report 2020: Government Policies to Promote Innovation in the Digital Age, Geneva, 2020.

The global digital economy is characterized by wider digital divides

Despite continuing efforts of the Economic and Social Commission for Asia and the Pacific (ESCAP) and its member states, the digital divide is still significant and there remain obstacles in the current paradigm of digital infrastructures that prevent a sustainable inclusive recovery. The digital divide within countries and between countries at the regional level has been widened, which has created new development inequalities as COVID-19 drags on.[5]

Access to and use of Internet remains uneven

According to the estimation of International Telecommunication Union (ITU), there are great cross-country differences in access to Internet (Figures 1 and 2). Fixed-broadband subscriptions have nearly doubled over the last decade, while remaining low in developing countries, at just over 11.2 per 100 people in 2019, compared to 33.6 in developed countries. The developing countries had only a third of that number of developed countries. Least developed countries (LDCs) had almost no fixed-broadband connections owing to

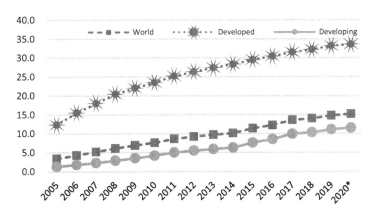

Figure 1:   Fixed-Broadband Subscriptions
Note: *June-2020 estimate.

---

[5] ASEAN Digital Master Plan 2025.

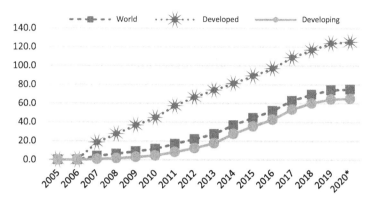

Figure 2:   Active Mobile-Broadband Subscriptions
Note: *June-2020 estimate.

the high cost and lack of infrastructure. In contrast, mobile broad-band subscriptions have risen rapidly, reaching nearly 124 active sub-scriptions per 100 people in 2019 in developed countries and 64 in developing countries.

Furthermore, within countries, there are significant divides between rural and urban areas. Globally, about 72% of households in urban areas had access to the Internet at home in 2019, almost twice as much as in rural areas (nearly 38%). Only 20% of people in LDCs use the Internet, typically at relatively low download speeds and with a relatively high price tag attached. In particular, the penetration rates of urban and rural areas in developing countries are 65.1% and 28.8%, respectively.[6]

Significant Internet usage gaps also remain between different countries (see Figure 3). ITU estimates that 51.4% of the global population, or 4 billion people, are using the Internet at the end of 2019, as compared to only 17% in 2005. In developed countries, 86.6% of the individuals are using the Internet, and Europe is the region with the highest Internet usage rates (82.5%). However, the Internet usage rate in the developing countries is 46%. The LDCs are the least connected with only 19% of their population and only 40%

---

[6] UNCTAD: Digital Economy Report 2021.

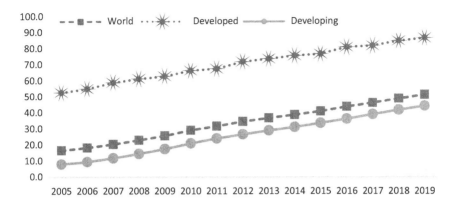

Figure 3: Individuals Using the Internet
Source: ITU World Telecommunication/ICT Indicators database. Updated: November, 2020.

have access to a high-speed mobile broadband network.[7] Installing traditional broadband connections is costly, and countries often face difficulties in financing the fiber-optic cables required. As to 4G network coverage, between 2015 and 2020, the rate doubled globally and almost 85% of the global population were covered by 4G network at the end of 2020. 4G network coverage in developed and developing countries are respectively 97% and 87%.[8]

Developed countries continue to dominate global e-commerce market

Many European countries and the US are at the digital-economy frontier. They make big technological investments, develop many digital innovations, trade a large number of digital goods and services, and dominate the global e-commerce market. According to UNCTAD estimates, global e-commerce jumped to US$26.7 trillion globally in 2019, equivalent to 30% of global gross domestic product (GDP). Among the top 10 countries of e-commerce sales, developed

---

[7] ITU World Telecommunication/ICT Indicators database, Updated: November 2020.
[8] ITU-D: ICT facts and figures.

countries remain in the dominant position, while China is the only developing country ranking third.[9] The United States continued to dominate the overall e-commerce market, ahead of Japan and China. Among the top 13 Business-to-Consumer (B2C) e-commerce firms, 9 are from the developed countries.

E-commerce developments greatly depend on a country's capacity to engage in the digital economy. Developed countries are in many ways better prepared to respond to challenges associated with the growing role of digital platforms than developing countries that have limited resources and capacities. According to the 2020 edition of the UNCTAD B2C E-commerce Index, European nations continue to dominate the top 10 list, of which 8 are in Europe. The LDCs take up 18 of the 20 bottom positions in the index. All of the top 10 developing economies in the 2020 index are from Asia, and all are upper middle-income or high-income economies.

Data divide leaves developing countries behind

Moreover, data-related digital divide has emerged in connection with the "data product value." Data are a special resource and can be processed into digital intelligence — in the form of statistics, databases, insights, information, etc. These data products contribute to moving up in the development process. Developed countries have greater advantages associated with the growing role of digital platforms. The result is that many developing countries have become providers of raw data to global digital platforms but they have to pay for the digital intelligence generated from their data. The US and China are the frontrunners in harnessing data, with 50% of the world's hyperscale data centers, the world's highest rates of 5G adoption, 70% of the world's top artificial intelligence (AI) researchers and 94% of all funding for AI startups.

The digital divide has been highlighted as a critical barrier to mitigation of the impact of the COVID-19 pandemic. COVID-19 has reversed steady declines in global poverty for the first time in three

---

[9] UNCTAD, Global e-commerce jumps to $26.7 trillion, COVID-19 boosts online retail sales. https://unctad.org/press-material/global-e-commerce-jumps-267-trillion-covid-19-boosts-online-retail-sales, UNCTAD/PRESS/PR/2021/009.

decades (United Nations 2020) and precipitated the "deepest recession since World War II" (World Bank 2020). In particular, the world's poorest and most vulnerable people, especially those without access to digital services and Internet access are likely to be the hardest hit. They cannot benefit from successful remote learning, telecommuting, e-commerce and healthcare. Unsurprisingly, digital and broadcast remote learning have the potential to reach more students in wealthier countries than in poorer ones. Globally, three out of four students who cannot be reached by remote learning opportunities come from rural areas and/or poor households. Lack of access to computers and the Internet at home as well as a low level of computer-related skills put many already marginalized students at a further disadvantage. It has exposed severe inequalities in our societies and is further exacerbating disparities within and among countries.[10]

Digitalized industrial strategy toward the Sustainable Development Goals

The COVID-19 pandemic abruptly disrupted implementation toward many of the Sustainable Development Goals (SDGs) and, in some cases, turned back decades of progress. However, crisis is also an opportunity for change. Developed countries accelerated digital transformation and prompted changes in industry structures to address pandemic challenges. They put the SDGs Agenda 2030 at the center over GDP growth rebound (see Table 1).

The surge of the COVID-19 crisis has accelerated the use of AI and other forms of automation. Indeed, investing in automation can help ensure the continuity of production in a crisis and can prevent disruptions in supply chains. Digitally developed countries tend to focus on basic and applied research, talent attraction and development. In contrast, digitally developing economies focus on public sector reform and infrastructure creation. The results also confirm that both digitally developed and developing economies have focused on using digital transformation as a tool for economic growth.[11]

---

[10] United Nations: The Sustainable Development Goals Report 2020.

[11] Jang, Yungshin, "Digitalization in Asia-Pacific region: Ready for growth, but ready for inclusion," *World Economy Brief*, June 14, 2021, 11(32).

Table 1:   Main Digital Strategies and Policies in the United States, EU and Japan

Areas	Contents of strategies and policies
Increase in the quality and coverage of digital infrastructure	(1) *National Strategy to Secure 5G of the United States of America.* (2) *National Industrial Strategy 2030: Strategic Guidelines for German and European Industrial Policy.* Industrial production with the use of the Internet (Industry 4.0) is able to realize the digitization and intellectualization of information of manufacturing, supply and sales. (3) The EU issued *2030 Digital Compass: The European Way for the Digital Decade* in March 2021, setting a number of advanced technology development objectives. (4) *Action Plan for Coordinated Development of "Dual-gigabit" Networks 2021–2023.* (5) Japan issued *The Master Plan for Regional Expansion of ICT Infrastructure 2.0* to speed up the construction of 5G and optical fiber.
Develop advanced manufacturing, and facilitate digital transformation in manufacturing sector	*Advanced Manufacturing Partnership Plan* and *Strategy for American Leadership in Advanced Manufacturing. The United States Innovation and Competition Act of 2021* proposes to implement "made in America plan" and promotes innovative application of frontier digital technology in manufacturing. *A Vision for the European Industry until 2030, European Union's New Industrial Strategy, Industry 5.0 Strategy* increase digital technology capabilities and build efficient and advanced manufacturing industry chain system. *2021 White Paper on Manufacturing Industries in Japan* promotes implementation of digital transformation strategy of manufacturing with "scene driven + project" model. Germany *Industry 5.0 strategy* emphasizes digitalization and intelligentization of manufacturing, supply and sales information. The United Kingdom *Digital Economy Strategy 2015–2018*, and *National Digital Strategy 2020*.
Digital transformation of small and	(1) Germany *Small and Medium Enterprises — Action Plan* in 2016 has taken the digital transformation of small and medium-sized enterprises as 1 of the 10 action fields.

medium-sized enterprises	(2) Germany *Digital Strategy 2025* proposes a Digital Investment program for SMEs with a volume of €1 billion. In 2019, Digital Investment program implemented investment subsidies and set up digital experimental spaces for SMEs. In 2020, the new funding program "Digital Jetzt — Investment Funding for SMEs" will last until the end of 2023 with a total support fund of €203 million to improve digital business processes.
Collaboration of digitalization and sustainable green growth	(1) The EU announced *2020 Commission Work Programme* to promote the ecological and digital transitions of the EU economy and society. In 2021, the EU issued *Sustainable and Smart Mobility Strategy* to increase the application of emerging technologies and reduce CO_2 emissions in the next 30 years. (2) *Japan's National Comprehensive Strategy on Science, Technology and Innovation 2020* proposes to formulate and implement a scientific and technological innovation roadmap aimed at sustainable development.

Dominant position of developed countries in frontier digital technologies

The evolution of the digital economy is closely associated with progress in several frontier technologies, including blockchain, data analytics, AI and other software-oriented technologies. Other emerging technologies include Internet of Things (IoT), automation, robotics and cloud computing, user-facing devices to 3D printers as well as other specialized machine-oriented hardware technologies.[12] The main technology trends which will be important over the next decade are set out in Table 2.

There is a race for leadership in digital technological developments, as the leader may gain economic and strategic advantages. Progress of countries in using frontier technologies greatly depends on their national capacities related to physical investment, human capital and technological effort, particularly in areas such as next

---

[12] UNCTAD: Technology and Innovation Report, 2021.

Table 2:   Key Technology Trends Over the Next 10 Years

Important existing trends	Future trends
Internet will continue to be there in its current form and evolve to provide a wide range of Cloud services.	AI will be a very powerful solution in specific problem areas.
Connectivity has mostly delivered all we need where it is geographically available.	Big Data will be valuable in manufacturing process and data analytics.
Virtual Reality and Augmented Reality will remain niche but AR might play a larger role.	Robotics will bring more automation.
Robotics has been widely used in manufacturing.	Autonomous vehicles will evolve slowly.
IoT delivers productivity gains and better working devices.	3D printing will substantially reduce time to develop new products.

Source: ASEAN Digital Master Plan, 2025.

generation infrastructure, including fifth generation (5G) mobile and cloud services. The top seven providers of the frontier technologies are the United States, followed by China, Japan, Germany, Republic of Korea, France and the United Kingdom. They are mainly developed countries except for China. Fifth generation (5G) wireless technology is expected to be critical for IoT due to its greater ability to handle massive volumes of data. It is estimated that by 2025, the United States, followed by Europe and Asia-Pacific will be leaders in 5G adoption.[13]

The new frontier technologies are generally biased toward skills and related capabilities, which might reduce the comparative advantage of developing countries in traditionally labor-intensive manufacturing activities. In addition, GVCs make it harder for low-income countries to use their labor-cost advantage to offset their technological disadvantage.[14] Meanwhile policymakers in developed countries are

---

[13] International Telecommunication Union (ITU), "Setting the Scene for 5G: Opportunities & Challenges," Geneva, 2018. https://www.itu.int/en/ITU-D/Documents/ITU_5G_REPORT-2018.pdf.

[14] Rodrik, D., "New technologies, global value chains, and developing economies," NBER working paper No. 25164, 2018.

aiming at reshoring manufacturing activities by using robots in production to compensate labor-cost disadvantages.

Developing countries also face great challenges in harnessing the benefits of frontier technologies, due to digital divide and shortage of skills. Many frontier technologies rely on steady, high-speed fixed Internet connections and require at least literacy and numeracy skills. Regards to shortage of skills, in developing countries the basic and standard skills are on average 10–20 percentage points lower than in developed countries. Around 46% of the population have basic computer skills in developing countries, while in developed countries the number is 65%.

Fragmented approach to data governance hinders global interconnection and digital competitiveness

In digital economy, the functioning of international production networks and international trade becomes increasingly interacted with data flows. Both global trade in digital products and services and the resultant movement of information and data across borders have risen significantly. Policymakers from all countries are aware of the key importance of data in a digital world. Despite a growing number of trade agreements addressing data flows, disagreements continue to exist among the main players.

As shown in Table 3, only few countries have adopted a light-touch or restrictive/guarded approach, while most countries have adopted some form of prescriptive regulatory frameworks on cross-border data flows. Singapore's adoption of a light-touch approach to cross-border data flows is expectedly due to its open, liberal economy. The dependence of the economy of the Philippines on the outsourcing industry may explain its light-touch approach.

Except for private data protection, enabling the physical flow of data is important and the efficiency and effectiveness of the data economy is dependent on advancement of regional production network and e-commerce. A divided approach to data governance could eventually lead to reduced opportunities for digital innovation and development across the world.[15] This fragmentation would also lead

---

[15] *Ibid.*

Table 3: Mapping of Regulations on Cross-Border Data Flows

Strict data localization	Partial data localization	Conditional transfer: Hard	Conditional transfer: Intermediate/ soft	Free flow of data
Restrictive (R) or guarded (G) approach		Prescriptive approach		Light-touch approach
China (R) Indonesia (R/G) Vietnam (R) India (G) Russian Federation (R)		Malaysia Thailand Japan Republic of Korea European Union New Zealand Brazil		Philippines Singapore United States

Source: UNCTAD, Digital Economy Report, 2021.

to a reduced ability to participate in the dynamics of global interconnection. Most small and developing economies will lose opportunities if they fail to raise their digital competitiveness.

Technological Revolution and Scope for Digital Transformation and Industrialization

Economic development was traditionally associated with the process of structural transformation. Much of the high value-added pre-production (research and development (R&D), and design) and post-production (marketing, logistics and distribution) segments are located in developed countries, while developing countries specialize in the lower value-added production segment, and focus on mass production (World Bank *et al.* 2017).[16] Countries like China, Mexico, Brazil and some Asian countries moved up the income ladder by transferring labor and capital from relatively lower-productivity agriculture to higher-productivity manufacturing and services.

---

[16]World Bank *et al.*, *Global Value Chain Development Report 2017: Measuring and Analyzing the Impact of GVCs on Economic Development*. Washington, DC: World Bank, 2017. https://openknowledge.worldbank.org/handle/10986/29593.

The recent development of information and communications technology (ICT) and digitalization has triggered changes in the development strategy. A new type of industrialization is possible through digitalization of traditional sectors without structural change. New technologies can re-invigorate traditional production sectors and speed up industrialization and economic structural transformation.

Technological revolution and the dynamism of digital transformation strategy

Technological changes are combined with financial capital to create new techno-economic paradigms — the cluster of technologies, products, industries, infrastructure and institutions that characterize a technological revolution. At present, the world is reaching the end of the deployment phase of the "Age of ICT" and starting the installation phase of a new paradigm that involves frontier technologies and is known as Industry 4.0 (see Table 4).[17] Many developed countries are in the beginning stage of the third unbundling, while most of the developing countries are in the beginning or middle stage of the second unbundling. The third stage unbundling highlights the importance of digital economy and development in services sector.

Leapfrogging and feedback strategy can work as part of the development process related to the three stages of unbundling. The leapfrogging development strategy might include export-oriented commercial agriculture; service outsourcing; plantations and mining controlled by artificial intelligence. Examples of a feedback strategy might include smartphone use in agriculture; 3D printing in the manufacturing industry; and the Internet of Things on manufacturing floors. It is imperative to use new ICT in a wider range of industries. It represents a historical chance for developing economies to leapfrog to a more advanced-economy status. More attention should be paid to the ability of poor countries to compete in world economy in

---

[17] Industry 4.0 is also referred to as smart factory, industrial Internet of Things, advanced manufacturing and supply chain 4.0.

Table 4:   Industrial Dynamism with Key Technology Trends

Step	Pre-globalized world	The first unbundling	The second unbundling	The third unbundling
Key technologies	Self-subsistence	Steam revolution, mass production	ICT revolution, fractionalization and offshoring	Fourth industrialization-telepresence and telerobotic; Digital platforms
International specialization	Production/consumption clusters	Industrial clustering (Core–periphery)	Global value chain: North deindustrialized and south industrialized	
Representative industries	Subsistence agriculture	Labor-intensive industries	Machine industries	Digital economy
Leapfrogging: Skip some stages and catch up				
Feedback: Frontier technology changes traditional industries				

Commercial agriculture

Service outsourcing

Full automation by artificial intelligence

Internet of things

3D printing

Smartphone use in agriculture

Supply chain management

Food value chains

Source: Author's edition of footnote [13] and Kimura, F., "'Unbundlings' and development strategies in ASEAN: Old issues and new challenges," *Journal of Southeast Asian Economies*, 2018, 35(1), pp. 13–21.

which others have much greater capacity to capitalize on new technologies.

The scope for industrial transformation in developing countries

Reconsidering the role of digitalization in manufacturing

The rapid spread of digital technologies is affecting the manufacturing process and there has been a tendency of manufacturing servicification. The new digital technologies, especially ICTs associated with the Internet of Things significantly raise the importance of the post-production segment for the entire manufacturing process. Much of value addition that used to happen in fabrication stages before the second unbundling has been transferred to the pre- and post-fabrication stages that are dominated by service inputs. This means that manufacturing and services activities are to be more closely interwoven.[18]

Digitalization in manufacturing would tend to reduce the value added by workers in the production stage and the share of value-added accruing in developing countries. Combined with the possibility that digitalization might remain largely confined to developed countries, it would make the smile curve deeper and further increase developed countries' share in high value added.[19]

New opportunities for industrial upgrading in developing countries

Moving toward a digital economy may hold greater potential for industrialization in developing countries than often thought. By leveraging their national innovation systems, developing countries can

---

[18] Baldwin, R., *The Great Convergence: Information Technology and the New Globalization*, Cambridge: Belknap Press of the Harvard University Press, 2016.

[19] Mayer, Jörg, Digitalization and industrialization: Friends or foes, UNCTAD Research Paper No. 25 (accessed July, 2018). https://unctad.org/system/files/official-document/ser-rp-2018d7_en.pdf.

skip some development stages and introduce advanced technologies into traditional industries to become more competitive (Kimura, 2018).[13]

While low-value positions may be associated with limited productivity gains in the short term, such activities may provide a means of entry into networks and ecosystems of production, which in turn would provide a source of learning, technology access and better value over time. Some start-ups in developing countries have also been able to move up in the value chain from simple to higher value-added service provision.[20]

Using the new digital technologies may also allow developing countries to engage in the higher value-added activities in the value chain and benefit from the income-generating potential of digitalization. Cloud computing and big-data analysis reduce the need for hard digital infrastructure, as well as the cost of computing and using software. All of this has the potential to make both access to market-related information and its analysis more easily affordable for developing countries. Using digital technologies in the pre-production phase would most likely help compensate part of the lack of skilled designers in developing countries. As a result, the pre-production segment of the manufacturing process may at least in part move to developing countries. This move could accelerate if the pre- and the post-production segments are integrated.

Digital Strategy and Industrial Transformation in China and ASEAN

The development of ICT and digitalization has triggered changes in the development strategies of developing countries and enables high-quality growth in the era of new industrialization. China and ASEAN have adopted strategies to utilize the fourth industrial revolution

---

[20] UNCTAD, Digital Economy Report 2019 — Value creation and capture: Implications for developing countries, 2019, Geneva: United Nations Conference on Trade and Development, p. 194.

technologies and to make their economies and industries more value-added through digitalization. In the post-COVID era, digitalization and digital transformation are prioritized to speed the recovery from COVID-19.

ASEAN's digital strategy in the era of new industrialization

Starting with the e-ASEAN Framework Agreement in 2000, ASEAN has been promoting the digital economy centered upon ICT promotion policies. There are various policy frameworks such as the ASEAN Economic Community (AEC) Blueprint, ASEAN e-Commerce Work Programme, ASEAN Digital Integration Framework, etc. (see Table 5). The importance of digital economy has been further revealed in the context of COVID-19. ASEAN has adopted Digital Masterplan 2025 to accelerate the inclusive digital transformation for speedy recovery from the pandemic.

For instance, Indonesia's digital economy is the largest among Southeast Asian countries followed by Thailand and Vietnam. The Indonesian government emphasizes e-commerce, digital finance, and especially focuses on the start-up ecosystem that serves as a foundation of digital transformation. The digital economy of Vietnam has achieved a 29% growth rate backed by the government's high commitment for the digital economy. In Thailand, digital economic policy takes a comprehensive industry-wide approach. Thailand 4.0 seeks to innovate the economy as a whole and promote the high value-added industries based on the "smartization" of society aimed at realizing a Smart Industry, Smart City and Smart People. The strategy is centered on "S-Curve" industries (next-generation automobiles, smart electronics, medical well-being tourism, agricultural bio, and future food) and New S-Curve industries (robotics, aviation logistics, bio-fuel chemistry, digital technology and medical hub). ICT manufacturing bases in Vietnam and Thailand have grown into global manufacturing bases. Meanwhile, Laos, Myanmar and Cambodia are the countries with the weakest bases of the digital economy among the ASEAN member countries.

Table 5:   Major Digital Framework and Related Promotion Policies in ASEAN

Year	Framework agreements	Major contents and action plan
2000	e-ASEAN Framework Agreement	e-Society
2009	ASEAN ICT Masterplan 2010–2015	Toward an empowering and transformational ICT
2015	ASEAN Economic Community Blueprint 2025	AEC implemented initiatives
2015	ASEAN ICT Masterplan 2016–2020	Eight interconnected Strategic Thrusts
2016	ASEAN E-Commerce Work Programme 2017–2021	ICT infrastructure, e-legal and regulatory framework, trade facilitation education and technology competency, electronic payment and settlement, online consumer protection, cybersecurity, and logistic to facilitate e-commerce
2018	ASEAN Digital Integration Framework	ASEAN Digital Integration Framework Action Plan 2019–2025
2018	ASEAN Framework on Digital Data Governance	Identifies four strategic priorities of digital data governance that support the ASEAN digital economy and initiatives
2019	ASEAN E-Commerce Agreement	Regional e-commerce trade facilitation and SME promotion
2021	ASEAN Digital Masterplan 2025	To build ASEAN as a leading digital community and economic bloc, powered by secure and transformative digital services, technologies and ecosystem
2021	ASEAN Data Management Framework 2021	Data governance and protection throughout the data lifecycle
2021	Work Plan on the Implementation of the ASEAN Agreement on Electronic Commerce 2021–2025	A coherent and harmonized approach that guide AMS in implementing the Agreement, taking into account different level of development among ASEAN member states

Source: Compiled by author based on ASEAN's documents.

China's digital strategy and industrial transformation

According to the China Academy of Information and Communications Technology (CAICT), the digital economy accounts for nearly 40% of China's GDP in 2020.[21] China first provided active support for big data development as a national strategy in 2012, and is developing the digital economy by fostering data-related technologies and industries, such as AI, IoT, cloud computing, 5G, etc. Digital development is also a key component of the Made in China 2025 initiative, which intends to boost technological innovation, and promotes break-throughs in 10 key sectors, including information technology and emerging and next-generation digital technologies.

Along with "Made in China 2025," China's Internet Plus strategy is an important strategy to realize innovation as a new growth engine for China. The strategy will be responsible for promoting industrial advancement and formulating an effective response to the 4th Industrial Revolution. Particularly, China is promoting the innovation of software in the 4th Industrial Revolution and the transition toward "smart" processes in existing industries such as distribution, logistics and manufacturing.

China also aims to increase investments in digital and telecommunications infrastructure, such as digital trade zones and smart city projects. China seeks to contribute to South–South cooperation under the BRI, which brings together traditional infrastructure with digital technologies such as the Digital Silk Road (DSR). DSR not only promotes the development of the digital service sector, such as cross-border e-commerce, smart cities, telemedicine and Internet finance but also accelerates technological progress including computing, big data, Internet of Things, artificial intelligence, etc. China is formulating a national plan on IT application for the 14th Five-Year Plan period (2021–2025) and is determined to enhance Closer Partnership of Science, Technology and Innovation for Future.

---

[21] Digital economy includes platform services, manufacturing and services related to digital devices, as well as application of digital technology in non-digital sectors like agriculture and finance.

Regional supply chain and China–ASEAN digital cooperation

The global production network is characterized by a few larger hubs connected with other economies. At the aggregate level, the global production network appears to be relatively spread out, and the United States, China and Germany appear to be larger hubs connected with other economies. Moreover, there might be greater long-term consequences as firms re-shore or near-shore certain production steps. The expansion of GVCs halted after the 2008–2009 global financial crisis, so that supply chains have become more domestic, with fewer production stages located abroad (Miroudot and Nordström, 2019; OECD, 2020).[22] Due to the pandemic crisis, the shocks and disruptions in international production networks have led businesses to consider diversification of investments and restructuring of supply chains. In the medium and longer terms, investments in manufacturing and research and technical cooperation will encounter structural and geographical changes.

In fact, global value chain trade is far more regionalized than trade in final goods in the three main regional supply networks — Factory Asia, Factory North America, and Factory Europe.[23] China's reliance on inputs from the US, Germany and Japan have been falling, not rising — especially for inputs from Japan. The asymmetric evolution means, for example, that in 2015 about 9% of U.S. manufacturing output comprised inputs made in China, while inputs imported from

---

[22] Miroudot, S. and Nordström, H., Made in the World revisited, EU Working Paper RSCAS No. 2019/84, Florence: Robert Schuman Centre for Advanced Studies Global Governance (RSCAS), 2019; OECD, Shaping Government Interventions for a Faster and More Resilient Economic Recovery, Statement from the OECD Secretary-General, 8 June 202, Paris, 2020.

[23] Baldwin, Richard and Rebecca, Freeman, Supply chain contagion waves: Thinking ahead on manufacturing "contagion and reinfection" from the COVID concussion, CEPR (accessed April 1, 2020). https://www.g20-insights.org/related_literature/supply-chain-contagion-waves-thinking-ahead-on-manufacturing-contagion-and-reinfection-from-the-covid-concussion/.

the U.S. amounted to only 2% of Chinese manufacturing output. China is emerging as a central player in international supply chains.[24]

China and AMS are now striving to achieve economic and industrial leaps by implementing digitalized transformation strategies. Seeing each other's development as crucial opportunities, China and ASEAN have promoted integrated and interconnected development by synergizing development strategies and boosting infrastructure development and transformation in this field. China and ASEAN both reaffirmed their commitment to leveraging opportunities brought by the Fourth Industrial Revolution and expanding cooperation in relevant areas including innovation, digital economy, digital supply chain and work force, AI, big data, Internet of Things, ICT, e-commerce and so on.[25]

Challenges in Achieving Digitalization and Industrial Transformation in China and ASEAN

The progress of digital transformation in the Asia-Pacific region differs across different countries depending on the stage of economic development and the types of digitalization, while digitalization in the region proceeds more rapidly compared to the average speed of world economy. More specifically, more challenges remain due to the widening digital divide for digital transformation and sustainable development.

Connectivity-related digital divide remains large

Digital access is a precondition for any individual, firm or organization to use the emerging technologies, and to benefit from opportunities in digital economy. The traditional digital divide among China and AMS countries remains high in terms of their levels of ICT development such as Internet connectivity, access and use (see Table 6).

---

[24] Baldwin, R. and R. Freeman, Trade conflict in the age of COVID-19 (accessed May 22, 2020). https://voxeu.org/article/trade-conflict-age-covid-19.
[25] China–ASEAN Joint Statement on Synergizing the MPAC 2025 and the BRI.

Table 6:   Digital Infrastructure and Access, Internet Use in China and ASEAN: 2019

	Mobile-cellular subscriptions[a]	Fixed-telephone subscriptions[a]	Active mobile-broadband subscriptions[a]	Fixed-broadband subscriptions[a]	ICT prices[b]
Brunei Darussalam	133	20	148	13	0.95
Indonesia	126	4	81	4	2.43
Malaysia	140	23	127	9	1.19
Philippines	155	4	n.a.	5	2.90
Singapore	156	33	156	26	0.37
Thailand	186	8	87	15	2.66
Vietnam	141	4	72	15	1.87
Lao PDR	61	21	49	1	9.43
Cambodia	130	0	96	1	10.99
Myanmar[c]	114	1	93	0	2.52
China	122	13	97	31	1.08
Japan	147	49	203	34	1.42
Korea	134	48	115	43	0.80

Notes: [a]per 100 inhabitants; [b]mobile data and voice basket (high consumption) as a percentage of GNI p.c. in 2020; [c]2018 available.

Source: ITU, World Telecommunication/ICT Indicators Database, August, 2021.

Affordable connectivity remains a major challenge in many developing countries, especially in their rural and remote areas. The development of ICT-related infrastructure is uneven with large development gaps between and within countries. Singapore is a world leader in the supply of digital infrastructure. Other AMS such as Cambodia, Lao PDR, Myanmar and Indonesia continue to experience lower fixed-broadband subscriptions than other countries in the region. Active mobile-broadband subscription in Singapore is three times that of Lao PDR. In the LCMs, however, the average number of fixed broadband subscriptions per 100 people was virtually nil in the 2005–2020 period, as these countries have leapfrogged with increasingly efficient and accessible mobile connectivity. Moreover, poorer people are spending much larger percentages of their income on data. Mobile data and voice basket (high consumption) as a percent of GNI p.c. in Cambodia is 10.99, while the ratio in Singapore is 0.37, reflecting huge infrastructure and technological gaps.

Insufficient human resources are big obstacles to benefit from digital technologies

There will be an urgent need for external cooperation to increase the capabilities to promote digital economy in developing countries. The digital divide means that only those privileged with internet access will be able to continue remote learning. The most vulnerable students face a double burden of the pandemic and the lack of access to technology to support remote learning.[26] The disruption to schooling could lead to a drop in human capital accumulation. A UNICEF report showed that around a third of schoolchildren in Asia could not access remote learning during school closures. At least about 150 million schoolchildren in South Asia and 80 million in East Asia and the Pacific could not be reached by digital and broadcast remote learning programs, accounting for about half of the world's total. Some children or young people, especially those in financially distressed families, could permanently drop out when schools reopen.[27] In addition, the CLM countries lag far behind in terms of individuals with ICT skills. Individuals with standard ICT skills also range greatly in ASEAN where the ratio in Singapore (40%) is 8 times larger than in

---

[26] United Nations ESCAP, Asia and the Pacific SDG progress report 2021. https://www.unescap.org/sites/default/d8files/knowledge-products/ESCAP_Asia_and_the_Pacific_SDG_Progress_Report_2021.pdf.
[27] UNCTAD, Digital Economic Report 2019 (accessed September 4, 2019). https://unctad.org/system/files/official-document/der2019_en.pdf.

Cambodia in 2020. The gaps in individuals with advanced ICT skills is ever more serious.[28]

Underdeveloped policy and regulatory infrastructure for e-commerce

Despite the progress of digital trade and e-commerce, doing business across borders remains difficult in many developing countries. There is great need in various policy areas to increase the capacity of countries to participate effectively in e-commerce. The UNCTAD B2C E-commerce Index shows the existing differences among China and AMS. Singapore, Malaysia and Thailand are among the top 10 developing economies in the B2C E-commerce index 2020.[29] The biggest improvement in the index value was noted for Lao PDR, which saw its scores surge by at least five points largely due to significant improvements in postal reliability (see Table 7). According to UNCTAD 2021, Cambodia, Lao PDR and Myanmar have benefited from an e-Trade Readiness Assessment.

Ensuring efficient cross-border digital flow is a prerequisite to the creation of a single China-ASEAN digital market and to enabling that digital market to be globally competitive. Regulatory and logistical obstacles to cross-border trade would leash huge business opportunities and better digital ecosystems are in great need.[30] So far, ASEAN countries have no common position on regulating cross-border data flows and some are far more advanced in domestic rule-setting. Indonesia, Malaysia, the Philippines and Singapore have recently passed new laws; Thailand is considering such rules; and Brunei

---

[28] ITU, World telecommunication/ICT indicators database (accessed July, 2021). https://www.itu.int/en/ITU-D/Statistics/Pages/publications/wtid.aspx.

[29] UNCTAD, The UNCTAD B2C E-commerce Index 2020 (accessed December, 2019). https://unctad.org/system/files/official-document/tn_unctad_ict4d17_en.pdf.

[30] Since 2016, UNCTAD has conducted Rapid eTrade Readiness Assessments in LDCs covering seven key policy areas to help them improve their e-commerce capabilities.

Table 7:   UNCTAD B2C E-commerce Index 2020

2020 Rank	Country	Share of individuals using the Internet (2019 or latest)	Share of individuals with an account (15+, 2017)	Secure Internet servers (normalized, 2019)	UPU postal reliability score (2019 or latest)	2020 Index value	Index value change (2019–2020 data)	Rank 2019
4	Singapore	89	98	94	97	94.4	-0.4	3
18	Korea	96	95	68	100	89.8	0.4	19
20	Japan	85	98	79	93	88.7	2.4	21
30	Malaysia	84	85	71	85	81.3	-2.1	31
42	Thailand	67	82	59	97	76.0	2.0	48
55	China	61	80	54	85	70.1	0.0	55
63	Vietnam	69	31	64	83	61.6	0.8	66
83	Indonesia	48	49	60	43	50.1	0.0	85
96	Philippines	65	35	39	40	44.7	-5.1	86
101	Lao PDR	26	29	30	78	40.6	5.4	112
117	Cambodia	40	22	42	21	31.1	0.3	121
130	Myanmar	31	26	22	17	24.0	-2.9	128

Note: UPU-universal postal union.

Source: UNCTAD B2C E-commerce Index, 2020.

Darussalam and the CLM countries have no personal data protection laws or regulations. Because of the differences of the AMS' positions and paces in the related rule settings, the 2018 ASEAN Agreement on E-commerce had to leave room for member states to develop their own frameworks to regulate the use of computing facilities and ensure the safety of communications.

Growing concentration of new digital technologies

Differences in digital readiness hamper the ability of many developing countries to benefit from these frontier digital technologies. "Country readiness index" assesses the progress of countries in using frontier technologies, based on their digital capacities related to physical investment, human capital and technological effort, particularly in next generation infrastructure, such as 5G and cloud services.[31]

As shown in Table 8, Singapore is the best prepared for frontier technologies. The top overall performers have well-balanced performances across all building blocks of the index. The Philippines, Vietnam and China are among the top five overperforming countries in using frontier technologies relative to per capita GDP, while with lower rankings for ICT connectivity and skills. The Philippines has a high ranking for industry, reflecting high levels of foreign direct investment in high-technology manufacturing, particularly electronics. Multinational corporations are attracted by the country's strong supply chains and solid base of parts manufacturing. The Philippines also has pro-business policies along with a skilled, well-educated workforce and a network of economic zones. Vietnam also does well with supportive government policy.

---

[31] It scores countries on their readiness for frontier technologies based on five building blocks, including ICT deployment, skills, research and development (R&D), industry activity and access to finance.

Table 8: The Readiness for Frontier Technologies Index Score Ranking

Country	Total score	Total ranking	Score group	ICT ranking	Skills ranking	R&D ranking	Industry ranking	Finance ranking
Singapore	0.95	5	High	4	9	18	4	18
Korea	0.93	7	High	19	27	3	9	8
Japan	0.87	18	High	9	49	7	14	4
China	0.76	25	High	99	96	1	7	6
Malaysia	0.71	31	High	29	65	33	12	19
Philippines	0.60	44	Upper-middle	76	88	46	2	52
Thailand	0.59	46	Upper-middle	57	91	40	34	9
Vietnam	0.49	66	Upper-middle	74	111	66	22	15
Indonesia	0.40	82	Lower-middle	101	113	49	51	91
Cambodia	0.26	113	Lower-middle	109	122	140	95	26
Myanmar	0.22	121	Low	104	144	83	94	118
Lao	0.19	127	Low	127	129	133	52	127

Source: UNCTAD, Technology and Innovation Report, 2021.

Policy Recommendations for Strengthening China–ASEAN Digital Cooperation

To promote an equitable sharing of the benefits from digitalization in line with the SDGs, government should ensure that everyone has safe and affordable access to the Internet and meaningful use of digitally enabled services. Two criteria should be considered to strengthen China–ASEAN digital cooperation. First, the different interests of the economies in various economic development stages on digitalization and digital inclusion can be synchronized and balanced. Second, considering convergence is a prevalent feature of the digital economy, collaboration within AMS should be emphasized in digital inclusion cooperation in various areas and projects.

Building a more resilient and robust digital infrastructure

Improved digital infrastructure enables better connectivity with international suppliers, distribution networks and customers, providing firms with a foundation to integrate themselves into and upgrade in global value chains.[32] Reducing the digital divide and improving the quality and access of ICT infrastructure and services are key to building economic resilience and supporting digital transformation. China and ASEAN should work together and promote policy measures and technical means to increase the quality and coverage of digital infrastructure.

China and ASEAN should ensure adequate international Internet connectivity. In order to accelerate access to adequate ICT services, efforts should be made to increase access to fast, affordable and reliable Internet services, as well as to last-mile connectivity. A substantial amount of data traffic is international and hence there needs to be excellent international fiber-optic connectivity. The demand for bandwidth continues to grow and it is important to continually review and upgrade international fiber links.

China and ASEAN should launch a project to identify connectivity gaps and detail how this might evolve in future investment in digital and ICT. It is desirable to launch the China–ASEAN Information Superhighway project to reduce the digital divide and expand broadband facilities across and within countries. Considering that local 5G is a service that is expected to increase efficiency in smart manufacturing and AI services, commitment should be made to address urban and regional gaps. Indeed, the issue of logistics has been the bottleneck of e-commerce development. China and ASEAN countries need to pay more attention to the development of infrastructure-related services with both physical and cyber connectivity to support e-commerce. Efforts are needed to form a regional virtual network of e-commerce parcel collection points with data exchange through an interoperable platform to facilitate last-mile fulfillment across borders.

---

[32] Taglioni, D. and Winkler, D., Making global value chains work for development, World Bank. https://openknowledge.worldbank.org/handle/10986/24426.

Human skill development and digital capacities building

Considering the potential of ICTs to achieve the SDGs, everyone should have an equal opportunity to become empowered through ICT. Efforts should be intensified in digital literacy programs, capacity building, and promotion of digital skills to build workforce capacity in the digital age. Related measures should be implemented to help people acquire the necessary digital skills and competencies to adopt and adapt frontier technologies into their countries' existing production bases. And digital capacity building must be more needs-driven and tailored to individual and national circumstances, and better coordinated regionally. Measures should be encouraged to provide better inclusion of disadvantaged groups to leverage the Internet and digital economy to improve their living standards, which will ultimately contribute to inclusive human resource development in the region.

As a pacesetter in digital inclusion agenda in the healthcare sector, China can cooperate with other AMS on digital healthcare projects, considering the importance of digital healthcare in the post-pandemic world. It would be possible for China to beneficially share best practices and rich data in combating COVID-19 with other AMS through online platform. It is practical to establish a digitally integrated data information system for the region to collect and manage data showing the status of digitization of China and ASEAN in the long term.

Strategies for regionally advanced manufacturing value chain

China and ASEAN have established manufacturing bases as a part of global value chains. Services such as research, consulting, advertising and marketing throughout the supply chain are significantly contributing to creating value added in manufacturing. It is crucial to add a new dimension to the existing framework of China–ASEAN cooperation. Action plans should be made to increase collaborative manufacturing and to develop mutual trust in supply chains.

China–ASEAN Manufacturing Related Services Action Plan may be imperative to promote the role of services in enhancing regional value chains, either through their supportive role in RVCs or as service RVCs, and seeking to reduce barriers both at the border and behind the border. A key action agenda is to examine trade-related measures affecting manufacturing-related services, with a view to increasing the availability and accessibility of services through progressive liberalization and facilitation of manufacturing-related services,[33] and cooperation and capacity building by enhancing transparency and sharing experiences and best practices. It is more important to explore cooperation on industrial design and increase the value of industrial manufactured products with innovative design. Accordingly, we need to conduct targeted capacity building to help better understand and stimulate the development of services within GVCs.

Many leading digital platforms in manufacturing function as IT solutions to introduce smart factory into the manufacturing sites, but do not have an optimization model that encompasses the entire supply chains. Concerns should be paid to build leading digital platforms in manufacturing, with focus on connecting data and expanding the scope of their data use to the whole supply chains ranging from raw materials to intermediate procurement, manufacturing, distribution and sales, separately managed by business divisions or factories. In addition to digital platforms, the digital transformation of manufacturing sector, including utilization of AI, IoT, and 5G technologies enables non-face-to-face operation in manufacturing sites, development of unmanned store operation systems, use of medical surgery support robots, and digitalization of skilled workers' know-how.

Supply chain innovation policy: Digital technology capacities

China and ASEAN member countries should proceed to the next industrial development stage, firms need to create unique "product

---

[33] The types of manufacturing-related services covered by this Action Plan are: (i) pre-manufacturing stage, including sourcing and importation of raw materials; (ii) manufacturing stage; and (iii) post-manufacturing stage.

innovation" of goods and services, wherein existing industries can be transformed. This transition requires innovation capability to achieve technology-driven development. Advances in AI and new technologies may present opportunities for further supply chain innovation. Furthermore, supply chains innovation should consider to integrate environmental protection, product sustainability and inclusive economic growth into practices.[34]

To catch up and forge ahead, the governments need to strengthen their innovation systems and to address systemic failures and structural deficiencies. China and ASEAN should align science, technology and innovation (STI) policies with industrial policies and cooperate to adopt frontier technologies while continuing to diversify their production bases by mastering many existing technologies. To support investment in the new digital technologies, government should act as investor of first resort and increase the role of development banks.

Coordinated border management and developed border clearance procedures

To overcome the challenges in the coordination and harmonization of different practices toward e-commerce and digital trade, intergovernmental mechanism is desirable and needs to be explored to enable our businesses to trade and transact digitally and securely. China and ASEAN are encouraged to elaborate and promote measures and policies aimed at effective development of e-commerce including policy and regulatory management that are predictable, transparent and consistent. Two sides should continue to facilitate e-commerce, including paperless customs clearance, electronic transaction documents, digital authentication, and electronic and online payments. What is more, regional free trade agreement (RTA) is especially valuable in seeking greater harmonization and a higher level of interoperability among e-trade systems.

---

[34] Hedwall, M., *op. cit.*

Promotion of single window interoperability

After the entry into force of WTO Agreement on Trade Facilitation, international trade single window is now globally recognized for processing import, export and transit-related data and procedures. Measures should be taken to ensure harmonized and compatible implementation of the trade facilitation commitments so as to reduce transaction costs.

We propose the following work programs to accelerate the progress in constructing a paperless trading environment within the region. On the one hand, pilot projects are introduced to harmonize customs declaration items among interested countries. And we could launch a new Pathfinder on cross-border electronic transmission of customs clearance data for express consignment based on WCO customs data model. On the other hand, China and ASEAN should make action plan to promote international interoperability between Single Window systems and paperless trading, based on the existing digitalization of import and export procedures.

As to the activities for the implementation of the interoperability among single windows, list of Best Practice Technology Solutions for Single Window Interoperability can be developed at the very beginning. For the next stage, it is necessary to hold Supply Chain Integration workshop to discuss the pilot model, pain points in cross-border supply chain management, and the role of TradeTech in solving the pain points. Finally, the project is aimed at the terminology, technology and documents requirements for single window interoperability in East Asia.

Regional collaboration of data regulation framework

(1) To address legal and procedural uncertainties, China and ASEAN should promote mutual understanding and strengthen cooperation on data regulation. Regional support may also focus on a range of specific areas. First, China and ASEAN should collaborate to promote a regulatory approach that provides

appropriate legitimate and data protection, while respecting applicable domestic laws and regulations. Second, cooperation of countries is needed to formulate national strategies for dealing with data and cross-border data flows in ways that can help reap economic development gains, while at the same time respecting various security and rights concerns. Third, capacity-building activities may be needed to raise awareness of data-related issues and their development implications. For instance, in 2020, China indicated its willingness to permit cross-border data flows in Hainan Pilot Free Trade Zone. Considering the importance of international coordination on data security, a "one-size-fits-all" stipulation for local data storage is not suitable to ensure national security in a digitally driven global economic environment.

https://doi.org/10.1142/9789811257896_0002

Chapter

2

Advancing Regional Cooperation on Managing Digital Platforms: Implications and the Way Forward for ASEAN and China in the New Normal — A Case Study on Singapore[*]

Tai Wei Lim[†] and Bojian Liu[‡]

East Asian Institute, National University of Singapore, Singapore
†eailimt@nus.edu.sg
‡eailiub@nus.edu.sg

---

[*]Lim, Tai Wei, *Industrial Revolution 4.0, Tech Giants, and Digitized Societies*, London: Palgrave MacMillan, 2019.

Introduction

In recent years, Chinese online industries have experienced tremendous development in innovative technologies and business models centered on the digital economy. Southeast Asia, with its fast-growing Internet population, has become a foremost target arena for Chinese Internet service providers to invest and seek collaborations. As this chapter will discuss, there are various factors driving Chinese tech giants to seek cooperation with companies in Southeast Asia and make Southeast Asian countries welcome China's investments. Demonstrated in their mooted cooperation in constructing 5G and smart cities networks as well as the commercial popularity of Chinese smartphones, the nexus between Southeast Asian and Chinese technological exchanges in the digital era is potentially more connected.

In this writing, the authors organized the chapter structurally to first discuss exchanges and collaborations between China and Southeast Asia at a micro-level in the tech eco-system. It seems that entities like Chinese tech giants and private firms are exploring new markets, acquisitions, partnerships and investments in Southeast Asia. It is a study of mainly private-sector led initiatives. The analytical angle then widens to a macro perspective where the writing will examine larger structural collaborations such as smart cities network and policy responses to COVID-19. Such collaborations are mainly multilateral in nature and involve regional organizations as well as states in the planning stages. Together the micro and macro perspectives paint a broad outline of development in this matter.

Background: Micro Entities in the Tech Ecosystem

Southeast Asia as China's potential partner for digital collaboration

In particular, Singapore has demonstrated that it is an innovative and financial hub in the region, and thus it is unsurprisingly one of the major destinations for Chinese online companies (especially tech giants). For example, in addition to Alibaba's acquisition of Singapore's largest e-commerce platforms (Lazada), TikTok, one of the world's leading social network application developed by a Chinese company, has set up a data center in Singapore. Bitmain, a top China-based provider specialized for providing cryptocurrency mining equipment, has chosen Singapore as its regional headquarters.

In fact, in the recent two decades, in accordance with the major economic policy orientation known as "Going Out," the Chinese government has been encouraging China's leading companies to invest overseas and to become more competitive *vis-á-vis* multinational corporations (MNCs). More importantly, as opposed to state-owned enterprises (SOEs) that had taken lead in the first decade of implementing "Going Out," there are a growing number of Chinese private companies, particularly those in the Internet sector. They are emerging as prominent players running business outside China.

Indeed, Chinese top e-commerce companies have already found their niches in their respective business sectors within China but the fierce competition in domestic market of China has forced them to consider and offer their investments and services in overseas market. Moreover, as the demographic dividend ends, the growth of China's Internet population is approaching its bottleneck while the Internet online industries in most countries of Southeast Asia at large are still at a nascent stage compared to China and many developed countries. In other words, China's capital, technology and experience of business operations can help boost the development of Internet online industries in Southeast Asia.

In fact, the tensions between China and the United States have strengthened the importance of Southeast Asia for Chinese companies to seek business opportunities overseas. Another two major markets, European Union (EU) and Japan, that Chinese private companies had pursued, are somewhat overshadowed by Southeast Asia in many aspects, such as mutual political trust, labor costs, sizes of their younger populations as well as political-economic/socio-economic acceptance of Chinese high-tech goods. Moreover, in forging collaborations on digital platforms, taking e-commerce as example, its success of e-commerce largely depends on highly efficient logistics. Therefore, considering the geographical proximity and the associated logistical/transportation costs, many Southeast Asian countries hold potential advantages as top choices for Chinese companies to seek international collaborations in the e-commerce industry and select site of regional operational headquarters (OHQs).

In general, there are four major reasons explaining why Southeast Asia is regarded by the Chinese tech giants as a primary location for Chinese investments.

First, Southeast Asia is home to 600 million consumers. They are a large and comparatively younger[1] group, and it is particularly easier for them to accept innovative Internet-based applications and services. Southeast Asia, with over 600 million-strong population, has experienced rapidly growing demand for various Internet services that have already matured in China's domestic consumer market, and it is said that individuals in Southeast Asia spend 3.6 hours on Internet on an average every day, the highest in the world.[2] Taking the gaming industry for example, younger generations of online users and potential cultural resonance as fellow East Asian, gamers may more likely to successfully localize mobile games. Several Chinese games, such as "Honor of Kings" developed by Tencent, have achieved phenomenal success in Vietnam (where it is known as "Arena of Valor"), ranking top in iOS and Google Play application stores in 2017, according to the survey by Sensor Tower.[3]

Second, in recent years, under the backdrop of a generally sluggish global economy, Southeast Asia has maintained rapid economic growth[4] with greater potential in new services of digital platforms.

---

[1] Overman, Jeremiah, Vina Salazar and Gembong Nusantara, Passing the baton (accessed August 20, 2020). https://www.imf.org/external/pubs/ft/fandd/2018/09/southeast-asian-youth-on-the-future-overman.htm.

[2] Hollander, Rayna, Southeast Asia could be a leader in mobile Internet usage next year (accessed August 20, 2020). https://www.businessinsider.com/southeast-asia-could-be-a-leader-in-mobile-Internet-usage-next-year-2017-12.

[3] Ahmad, Daniel, Vietnam snapshot: Southeast Asia's fastest growing mobile games market (accessed August 26, 2020). https://nikopartners.com/vietnam-snapshot-southeast-asias-fastest-growing-mobile-games-market/.

[4] The Organization for Economic Cooperation and Development (OECD), Economic outlook for Southeast Asia, China and India 2020 (accessed August 20, 2020). https://www.oecd.org/dev/asia-pacific/SAEO2020_PRELIMINARY_VERSION_FOR_WEB.pdf.

According to IMF statistics and forecasts, among the major countries in Southeast Asia, India, Cambodia, Laos and Vietnam have maintained their GDP growth rates between 6.6% and 7.3%, surpassing China and ranking among the top economic growth rates in the world. Philippines, Indonesia and Thailand followed closely as the top runners in the rankings, while the GDP per capita of the more developed Singapore, Brunei and Malaysia far exceeds China.

Third, the popularity of smartphones has reached a high level in Southeast Asia, and Internet infrastructure has enormously improved in this region. In recent years, several leading Southeast Asian economies such as Thailand, Malaysia, and Singapore are accelerating the deployment of 4G or even 5G signals, aiming to increase the speed of domestic communication networks. Further, as some of the global manufacturing sectors are shifting from China to Southeast Asia, China's leading mobile phone manufacturers such as Huawei, Vivo and OPPO are also embracing Southeast Asia. So, the barriers to Internet have been greatly reduced. According to estimates, the overall popularity rate of smartphone in Southeast Asia in 2018 has reached 65–70%, and Chinese brands accounted for more than 60%.[5] Catering well to the emerging smartphone market in Southeast Asia, China's cost-effective smartphones actually helped Southeast Asia skip the stage of Personal Computer (PC)-based applications and hence directly latched onto the platform of mobile Internet, providing a promising ground for mobile Internet-based economy.

Fourth, many Chinese Internet companies actually formulated a feasible approach to incubating start-ups in Southeast Asian countries. Specialized venture-capital firms such as Sequoia Capital, Softbank and Morgan Stanley had largely shaped leading Chinese tech giants such as Alibaba, Baidu and Tencent, while many leading Southeast Asian Internet companies today were actually funded by capital infusions from Chinese companies. For example, Alibaba acquired Lazada in 2016 (and infused another US$1 billion in 2017),[6] Didi and

---

[5] Canalys, Chinese smartphone brands take 62% of Southeast Asia's 30.7 million shipments (accessed August 20, 2020). https://www.canalys.com/newsroom/southeast-asia-smartphone-marketshare-Q22019.

[6] Saheli Roy Choudhury, Alibaba invests additional $2 billion in Southeast Asian e-commerce firm Lazada (accessed March 19, 2018). https://www.cnbc.

Japan's Softbank deepened their partnership with Grab with US$2 billion investment,[7] Tencent supported Sea by establishing a long-term partnership, which underpins further collaborations between China and Southeast Asia in the future.

For Chinese tech giants, Singapore has the greatest potential in the region as a hub to facilitate their business activities in Southeast Asia (Singapore considers itself as a "pathfinder" role between China and Southeast Asia in this aspect). Singapore not only has several regionally prestigious universities providing highly skilled software engineers but also has globally renowned financial infrastructure and culture, which is crucial for the forthcoming generations of Internet users when digital platforms will be gradually integrated with financial services. In the case of the current tech giants such as Apple, Facebook and China's WeChat and Alipay, payment systems incorporating services traditionally provided by commercial banks have increasingly depended on digital platforms such as those utilized for online shopping and social networking services. Furthermore, blockchain applications such as Bitcoin and Ethereum have brought the integration of digital platforms and financial services to a higher level.[8] In fact, according to China's National Development and Reform Commission (NDRC), in China's national Blockchain Service Network (BSN), a grand blockchain-based infrastructure for global market, Singapore is listed as one of seven places outside China connected by the network nodes.[9] The next section of the chapter will examine the broader

---

com/2018/03/19/alibaba-invests-addition-2-billion-dollars-in-e-commerce-firm-lazada.html.

[7] Grab Press Centre, Grab announces Didi Chuxing and SoftBank as lead investors for current round of financing (accessed July 24, 2017). https://www.grab.com/sg/press/business/grab-announces-didi-chuxing-softbank-lead-investors-current-round-financing/.

[8] Liu, Bojian, "Impact of blockchain on China's cyber statecraft: Opportunities and risks," *East Asian Policy*, 2018, 4(2018), pp. 71–78.

[9] Cortese, A. J., China's public blockchain service network to increase accessibility for global SMEs (accessed August 20, 2020). https://kr-asia.com/chinas-public-blockchain-service-network-to-increase-accessibility-for-global-smes.

framework in which the e-commerce engines, blockchains and online services are embedded.

The Macro Perspective: Smart Cities as Flagship Megaproject

China's ultimate goal for smart cities is to build a modernized socialist economy so that it has been promoting applications of high tech, like Artificial Intelligence (AI), Internet of Things (IoT), big data and robotics. These plans were made known publicly in 2012 after the Chinese government gave their official approval. The accent was on studying implementation of such technologies in the living labs of selected pioneering smart cities. The Chinese development model is typically regarded as top-down so some believe that if the government puts resources into their plans, they will generally drive it to fruition and completion.

The same strategy is now applied to smart cities schemes. Intelligent systems will complement connectivity infrastructures in China. For example, they are applied in the Beijing megacity area (a hyper-connected conurbation) known as the Jing-Jin-Ji (Beijing–Tianjin–Hebei) stretching out over 82,000 square miles to manage the highways and bridges that link up this large area.[10] Another conurbation focusing on implementation of smart technologies is in Chongqing. Incidentally, this is where Singapore is working with China to construct the third government to government initiative known as Chongqing Connectivity Initiative (CCI). Unlike physical hubs in connectivity projects, digital platforms are needed to connect cities, individuals and businesses. Digital platforms function as a secure, open, institutionalized, pragmatic and reusable/growing online marketplace for aspiring entrepreneurs and companies to expand their business activities. As a transboundary commerce platform, it can enrich individuals/businesses and give consumers affordable, authenticated and quality goods from

---

[10]Tabbitt, Sue, Could China's cities outsmart the West (accessed January 1, 2018). https://newsroom.cisco.com/feature-content?type=webcontent&articleId=1735469.

global producers. It has the potential to convert new ideas and young business minds into tomorrow's digital entrepreneurs.

There is a private component in this initiative because the authorities hope to encourage companies to become solution providers and they can use Chinese designated smart cities to implement and experiment with their technologies. When these companies successfully provide their solutions and overcome challenges, their systems will become entrenched in the smart cities, so they only need to provide upgrades, patches and further modifications to the basic systemic features to ensure its relevance to the city's constantly evolving development. Local companies are preferred because one of the major challenges of constructing smart cities is the idiosyncrasies of local conditions. Therefore, companies that are originally located in the smart cities are most well-placed to recognize these local features and develop solutions for them.

There is a sense of embeddedness when local companies are heavily involved in the projects. In addition, when the local companies are successful in one Chinese city, they can effectively market their track record and past achievements to other Chinese cities, given that China is such a large market and represents the largest national network of smart cities in the world. With a strong relationship forged in a particular smart city and by joint efforts of its local companies to provide solutions to problems in the city's development, these companies may cooperate and export the same jointly developed solutions to other economies.

Because China's cities are divided unofficially into tiers based on level of economic development, importance to provincial and central governments, solutions developed for the first tier cities can be used in other leading global cities while those developed for third tier cities may be more cost-effective and suitable to meet developing economies' needs and balance state budgets. If Chinese technologies turn out to be successfully implemented in the first city, they can then be exported to other countries, including ASEAN or Association of Southeast Asian Nations which has Singapore-led aspirations to link up all smart cities in the region. The state is more likely to benefit from such investments after the private sector installs technologies that can help the authorities in terms of governance and urban management.

In conclusion, ASEAN economies are very important to China's Belt and Road Initiative (BRI) regional map because it acts as a forerunner to leap frog in competition with companies from other countries. China is already helping to build High Speed Railway (HSR) systems in Laos, Thailand, Indonesia and Cambodia so smart systems that work for China's domestic public transportation needs may be helpful in the Southeast Asian context as well. Such technologies may be related to public transportation systems like sensors to detect and direct traffic, electronic boards at bus stops, traffic obstruction management/resolution, and big data utilization with predictive and extrapolation capabilities (analytics), etc. Beijing, the capital city for example, is especially vulnerable to traffic jams. Sensors provide real time data to commuters. Data from sensors can also be fed into intelligent controls for managing city infrastructural needs.

Reflecting the sentiments of regional cooperation, unfettered ecommerce trade and work towards common prosperity to overcome COVID-19, on June 18, 2020, Yong Ying-I, Permanent Secretary (Perm Sec) of Singapore's Ministry of Communications and Information (MCI), pointed out that the potential of the Singapore–Shenzhen electronic platform will be tapped. It can be offered to "… like-minded partners like Shenzhen, to drive innovation and entre-preneurship in digital economies, and to enhance trade and connectivity to create exciting opportunities for businesses, communities and individuals."[11]

The Singapore Platform

The core idea behind Singapore, China and ASEAN's digital cooperation and exchange is being articulated openly to set a new benchmark

---

[11] *SmartCitiesWorld News Team*, Singapore and Shenzhen hold first Smart City initiative meeting (accessed June 18, 2020). https://www.smartcitiesworld.net/news/news/singapore-and-shenzhen-hold-first-smart-city-initiative-meeting-5379.

for global smart city cooperation through the private sectors, universities and governments. There is a strong underlying commercial purpose for this collaboration in working with first tier cities in China like Shenzhen to foster market forces and create jobs. The first Singapore-China (Shenzhen) Smart City Initiative (SCI) Joint Implementation Committee (JIC) meeting was led by Singapore's Ministry of Communications and Information's Permanent Secretary (Perm Sec) Yong Ying-I, and Shenzhen Mayor, Chen Rugui signing eight MOUs on June 18, 2020 to offer more business opportunities by widening access to Guangdong–Hong Kong Macao Greater Bay Area (GBA) and Southeast Asia (SEA).

The signing of these MOUs in the backdrop of a COVID-19 coronavirus pandemic indicated that digital connectivity has been accelerated by the disease outbreak. The Singapore China Smart City Initiative (SCI) is established on the foundations of digital connectivity, innovation, entrepreneurship and Tech talent exchange so as to facilitate the development of businesses and individuals in digital economies and change their digital services offerings and utilization. Singapore Permanent Secretary of MCI (Ministry of Communications and Information), Yong Ying-I said, "The Singapore–China (Shenzhen) Initiative has produced substantial positive outcomes just months after its launch last year, in spite of the COVID-19 situation. Indeed, COVID-19 has accelerated the pace of digitalization in our economies. Singapore will continue to work with like-minded partners like Shenzhen, to drive innovation and entrepreneurship in digital economies, and to enhance trade and connectivity to create exciting opportunities for businesses, communities and individuals."[12]

Three points are clear in this announcement. Both countries are fully aware of the impact of COVID-19 on the demand for digital services. Many physical supply chains were broken during the

---

[12] Sagar, Mohit, Singapore–China Smart City Initiative agrees to accelerate and further digitalisation (accessed June 18, 2020). https://www.opengovasia.com/singapore-china-smart-city-initiative-agree-to-accelerate-and-further-digitalisation/.

pandemic, brick and mortar shops were also closed for business, physical office space could not be occupied for normal office work, and face to face as well as analogue communications were not possible. On the other hand, e-commerce, online communications, drone deliveries and robotic logistics thrived. Therefore, both sides are now eyeing the establishment of a new Asian SME Hub to facilitate access to an ecosystem of buyers, sellers, logistics service providers, financing, and digital solution providers that can enhance trusted cross-boundary partnerships as the private sector move into new markets to innovate enterprises and work on economic growth.[13] Chen Rugui, mayor of Shenzhen Municipality reiterated that the platform will be operated according to market forces: "Shenzhen will follow the principles of 'cooperation for mutual benefits, government-guided, enterprise-led and a market-based approach.'"[14]

Eezee.sg (a B2B digital platform supported by Infocomm Media Development Authority IMDA and Enterprise Singapore ESG) under the Grow Digital initiative is a digital platform for Small and Medium Sized Enterprises (SMEs). Around 50 SMEs are already selling industrial products, chemicals, safety/medical/office items on this platform with its exposure to a consumer/distributor network of 4 million SMEs in the Chinese YiQiYe's SME Ecosystem and, when more SME ecosystems emerge in ASEAN, they will be able to work with SMEs in China through the new Asian SME Hub.[15] The Asian SME Hub would be constructed and run in Singapore for 3 years by OneConnect Financial Technology (a subsidiary of China's Ping An Group) to empower SMEs with an integrated eKYC (electronic Know-Your-Customer) toolkit for secured business transactions.[16]

---

[13] *Ibid.*
[14] SmartCitiesWorld News Team, Singapore and Shenzhen hold first Smart City Initiative meeting (accessed June 18, 2020). https://www.smartcitiesworld.net/news/news/singapore-and-shenzhen-hold-first-smart-city-initiative-meeting-5379.
[15] Sagar, Mohit, *op. cit.*
[16] Yu, Eileen, Singapore, Shenzhen push smart city partnership with SMB hub (accessed June 18, 2020). https://www.zdnet.com/article/singapore-shenzhen-push-smart-city-partnership-with-smb-hub/.

Digital trade connectivity, faster digitalized insurance and more efficient bank financing processes are advanced by efficient validation of data, fast speed documentation with mutual recognition function and seamless electronic transactions which are mediated through an efficient and effective cross-boundary "mediation–arbitration" dispute resolution set up by Singapore International Mediation Centre in collaboration with the Shenzhen Court of International Arbitration.[17] Singapore is the ideal partner to work with due to its wealth of experience. It has already held on to its number one world ranking in this aspect for half a decade. In 2015, more than 6% of all new ICC cases designated Singapore as the arbitration platform, making it top ranking in ICC Arbitration in Asia and retaining its position in the top five most chosen cities for the 10th consecutive year and ranked the 4th most preferred seat of arbitration in the globe.[18]

Boosting business confidence and enforcement of contract law, both cities can then move on to human talent exchanges, cooperation in digital identity platforms, digital trade, digital payment and cross-border data management. These activities and facilities will be in the second phase of the Singapore–Shenzhen collaboration.[19] It is useful to note that human talent exchanges had already been established. Infocomm talent and intellectual capital were previously forged in a 3-year partnership between the universities in Singapore and China organized by the Infocomm Development Authority of Singapore (IDA), the National University of Singapore (NUS) in cooperation with 10 highest-ranking universities in China. The objective was to grow intellectual capital and talent for the Infocomm industry as part of a strategic alliance for increasing competitiveness of the two countries' workforces.[20]

---

[17] Sagar, Mohit, *op. cit.*

[18] International Chamber of Commerce (ICC), ICC report confirms Singapore as a leading Asia arbitration hub (accessed January 1, 2020). https://iccwbo.org/media-wall/news-speeches/icc-report-confirms-singapore-as-a-leading-asia-arbitration-hub/.

[19] *Ibid.*

[20] Infocomm Media Development Authority (IMDA), Singapore–China Academic Partnership Accelerates Infocomm Talent Development (accessed January 1, 2020).

Chen Rugui, Mayor of Shenzhen Municipality hoped the Singapore–China (Shenzhen) Smart City Initiative can adhere to the "principles of cooperation for mutual benefits, government-guided, enterprise led and a market-based approach."[21] A market-based approach means private sector entities can also join in the process. Kinofy Singapore is a good example. Kinofy is Singapore's major private commerce cross-boundary retail platform, giving entrepreneurs smart, user-friendly, seamless methods to introduce their brand identity into the Chinese digital market with its ecosystem of marketing, logistics and warehousing, licensing, training partners.[22] Aimed at entrepreneurs, this also dovetails with conventional Industry 4.0-era which motivates and encourages more young people in the region to seek job opportunities and create value instead of solely depending on joining multinationals due to the ability of AI and other industry 4.0 technologies in replacing jobs.

---

https://www.imda.gov.sg/news-and-events/Media-Room/archived/ida/Media-Releases/2002/20061120113659.

[21] Sagar, Mohit, *op. cit.*

[22] Kinofy.com, About Kinofy (accessed July 1, 2020). https://kinofy.com/about-us/.

Chapter

3

Fostering Sustainable Tourism in ASEAN and China: A Case Study in the Philippines

Eylla Laire M. Gutierrez

Asian Institute of Management, Makati, Philippines

egutierrez@aim.edu

Introduction

Tourism has played a pivotal role in deepening Association of Southeast Asian Nations (ASEAN)–China relations for years now. In the context of globalization, tourism served as a springboard for strengthening cultural identity and enhancing cultural exchanges.[1] In recognizing this opportunity, tourism cooperation has therefore

---

[1] Honglei Rui, A probe about the new ways of deepening China–ASEAN tourism cooperation in the new era, *International Conference on Strategic Management*, 2019. https://webofproceedings.org/proceedings_series/ECOM/ICSM%20 2019/ICSM046.pdf.

become a priority in enhancing ASEAN–China cooperation as marked by the "ASEAN–China Tourism Cooperation Year" in 2017 which emphasized higher levels of tourism cooperation among parties through collaboration in promoting quality tourism, greater liberalization connectivity, among others.[2] Cementing this continued partnership is the creation of the "ASEAN–China Strategic Partnership Vision 2030" in 2018, which emphasized the value of tourism in furthering ASEAN–China relations.

Deepened relations through tourism have been largely influenced by the parties' significant roles as source markets and tourist destinations. Over the years, it serves as a significant component of ASEAN and China economies, specifically contributing to their respective gross domestic product (GDP) and employment as seen from Tables 1 and 2. As shown in the tables, tourism's contribution to GDP and employment is expected to grow exponentially.

Table 1: Travel and Tourism Direct Contribution as Percentage of GDP, 2015–2020

Country	2015	2016	2017	2018	2019	2020
Cambodia	14.23	13.74	14.03	14.46	14.44	14.38
Philippines	10.06	10.66	12.08	12.38	12.34	12.21
Thailand	8.76	9.10	9.47	9.62	9.72	9.89
Vietnam	5.66	5.83	5.92	6.02	5.93	5.84
Malaysia	5.84	6.00	5.89	5.77	5.8	5.81
Singapore	3.89	4.17	4.12	3.97	4.00	4.04
Laos	4.51	4.16	4.14	3.92	3.9	3.87
Myanmar	2.91	2.95	2.93	2.81	2.74	2.73
Indonesia	1.89	1.86	1.85	1.90	1.90	1.87
Brunei	1.11	1.17	1.25	1.26	1.26	1.28
China	2.51	2.66	2.77	2.79	2.79	2.82

Source: Knoema World Data Atlas.

---

[2] ASEAN Secretariat News, ASEAN, China to boost tourist traffic in the year of tourism cooperation, *ASEAN*, 2017. https://asean.org/asean-china-to-boost-tourist-traffic-in-the-year-of-tourism-cooperation/.

Table 2:   Travel and Tourism Direct Contribution as Percentage of Employment, 2015–2020

Country	2015	2016	2017	2018	2019	2020
Cambodia	12.80	12.75	13.54	14.63	15.32	16.00
Philippines	12.60	12.66	12.93	13.23	13.18	13.05
Thailand	5.93	6.06	6.26	6.46	6.54	6.70
Malaysia	5.54	5.72	5.64	5.55	5.60	5.64
Vietnam	4.41	4.55	4.63	4.71	4.70	3.67
Singapore	4.36	4.47	4.62	4.69	4.68	4.63
Indonesia	3.53	3.64	3.61	3.7	3.70	3.73
Laos	3.82	3.53	3.51	3.33	3.31	3.29
Myanmar	2.54	2.67	2.74	2.70	2.70	2.76
Brunei	2.25	2.33	2.42	2.44	2.44	2.44
China	3.62	3.63	3.64	3.69	3.73	3.78

Source: Knoema World Data Atlas.

For years now, a surge in tourism activities between ASEAN and China has been observed.[3] Both parties are considered to mutually benefit as major tourist markets to each other. China serves as the top regional source of visitors to ASEAN as seen from Table 3, whereas China's major tourist markets include seven ASEAN countries (Myanmar, Vietnam, Malaysia, The Philippines, Singapore, Thailand and Indonesia) in 2020.[4] In 2018, there were 50 million tourists between ASEAN and China, where the number of Chinese tourists to ASEAN countries reached 30 million, and the number of tourists from ASEAN countries to China reached 22 million.[5]

---

[3] Forging closer ASEAN–China economic relations in the twenty-first century, *ASEAN–China Expert Group on Economic Cooperation*, 2001. https://www.asean.org/storage/images/archive/newdata/asean_chi.pdf.
[4] 2018 Tourism Facts & Figures in China and between ASEAN & China, *ASEAN–China Centre*, 2020. http://www.asean-china-center.org/english/2020-02/4251.html.
[5] *Ibid.*

Table 3: Number of Tourist Arrivals in ASEAN by Origin (in person), 2015–2019

Origin Country	2015	2016	2017	2018	2019
Intra-ASEAN	45,991,764	46,570,159	48,492,849	49,598,981	51,570,903
China	18,596,288	20,339,261	25,285,205	29,116,894	32,280,135

Source: ASEANstats, 2018.

Without a doubt, tourism is a critical industry for both ASEAN and China, with arguably strong growth potential. However, accompanying its success is the challenge of committing to sustainability.[6] The prospects of pursuing sustainable tourism for both ASEAN and China have become increasingly apparent as a variety of issues surfaced including problems with conserving natural environment and biodiversity, managing resource consumption, reducing pollution, and more recently, the consequences of the COVID-19 pandemic to the future of travel. With these issues comes an unprecedented call for a more sustainable form of tourism.

Given the abovementioned background, this chapter primarily aims to answer: "What are the best practices in sustainable tourism in the Philippines?" In doing so, this chapter can contribute to answering: "what sustainable tourism practices can be shared between the ASEAN and China?" This chapter will employ a case study approach[7] to depict actual situations in a specific locality.[8] A plethora of secondary resources will be used. Findings of the study will provide policy recommendations and strategies on how sustainable tourism practices can be shared between the ASEAN and China.

[6] Chheang, Vannarith, Tourism and regional integration in Southeast Asia, Institute of Developing Economies, *VRF Series*, No. 481. 2013.
[7] Hollwec, Trista and Robert K. Yin, *Case Study Research Design and Methods*, Thousand Oaks, CA: Sage, 2014, p. 48.
[8] Flyvbjerg, Bent, "Five misunderstandings about case-study research," *Qualitative Inquiry*, 2006, 12(2), pp. 219–245.

Challenges to Tourism Sustainability

Sustainable tourism is generally accepted to pertain to "tourism that takes full account of its current and future economic, social and environmental impacts, addressing the needs of visitors, the industry, the environment and host communities."[9] Simply, it is understood in terms of the triple bottom line approach (TBL) or the people, planet, profit (3Ps) concept which translates to tourism that promotes not only financial growth (profit) but also environmental (planet) and social development (people).[10] Within the plethora of literature on the topic, sustainable tourism is primarily viewed as an ongoing process involving concerned stakeholders.[11] Underpinning this concept is the inability of tourism to balance its rapidly growing demand on natural resources.[12] Given this, sustainable tourism in the case of ASEAN–China relations has been focused on four points of intervention as suggested by the ASEAN Sustainable and Inclusive Tourism Development Committee (ASITDC)[13]:

- *Conservation of Natural Environment and Biodiversity*: Tourism is considered a critical factor affecting biodiversity loss and its conservation.[14] In most cases, tourism serves as a mechanism which supports biodiversity conservation and management, and to an

---

[9] Sustainable Development, UN World Tourism Organization (UNWTO). https://www.unwto.org/sustainable-development.

[10] Elkington, John, "The triple bottom line," *Environmental Management: Readings and Cases*, 1997, p. 2.

[11] Hardi, Peter and Juanita Ama DeSouza-Huletey, "Issues in analyzing data and indicators for sustainable development," *Ecological Modelling*, 2000, 130(1–3), pp. 59–65.

[12] Hall, Michael C., "Degrowing tourism: Décroissance, sustainable consumption and steady-state tourism," *Anatolia*, 2009, 20(1), pp. 46–61.

[13] Ocampo, Rosa, Philippines makes deeper push for sustainable tourism, *TTG Asia*, 2020. https://www.ttgasia.com/2020/02/17/philippines-makes-deeper-push-for-sustainable-tourism/.

[14] Hall, Michael C., "Tourism and biodiversity: More significant than climate change?" *Journal of Heritage Tourism*, 2010, 5(4), pp. 253–266.

extent as an economic justification for conservation.[15,16] However, biodiversity loss has been accelerated over the years as a result of human activities, climate change, and pollution which are often related to tourism activities.[17]

- *Consumption of Resources*: Managing the consumption of a variety of natural resources such energy, land, water, flora and fauna, among others has been proven to be a challenge in tourism. In this case, tourism activities must foster minimal consumption of these resources while accounting for the needs of the local communities in destinations.

- *Pollution Reduction*: This refers to forms of tourism activities that minimize pollution in water, land, and air ecosystems which are commonly contaminated by excess use of plastics and high coliform levels in bodies of water. Discharges into bodies of water, increased solid waste, sewage materials, among others have been largely observed in destinations where there is high concentration of tourist activities. In most destinations, issues of proper waste disposal are common,[18] where tourists are claimed to generate substantial amounts of solid and liquid waste.

- *COVID-19 Pandemic*: Tourism has been one of the hardest hit sectors by the coronavirus disease (COVID-19) pandemic, fuelled by extensive international travel restrictions and the fear of infections. In 2020, Asia is expected to have welcomed 75% fewer international tourists compared to 2019. The economic consequences

---

[15] Buckley, Ralf, Evaluating the net effects of ecotourism on the environment: "A framework, first assessment and future research," *Journal of Sustainable Tourism*, 2009, 17(6), pp. 643–672.

[16] Newsome, David, Susan A. Moore and Ross Kingston Dowling, *Natural Area Tourism: Ecology, Impacts and Management*, Bristol: Channel View Publications, 2012.

[17] Gössling, Stefan and C. Michael Hall, "Uncertainties in predicting tourist flows under scenarios of climate change," *Climatic Change*, 2006, 79(3), pp. 163–173.

[18] Ferronato, Navarro and Vincenzo Torretta, "Waste mismanagement in developing countries: A review of global issues," *International Journal of Environmental Research and Public Health*, 2019, 16(6), p. 1060.

for economies most dependent on tourism are severe.[19] The challenge of sustainability is therefore compounded by issues in relation to restoring confidence in travel and tourism.

With these identified points of intervention, several issues are found common in most nature-based destinations in ASEAN and China that are experiencing massive influx of tourists or overtourism. Justifying these points are numerous studies which suggest that environmental sustainability and tourism has a bidirectional relationship which means that environmental sustainability contributes to growth of tourism activities, and that tourism growth may accelerate environmental degradation.[20] Often unresolved, these issues are further exacerbated by the rapid growth in tourism activities in destinations.

Sustainable Tourism: The Case of the Philippines

Philippine tourism was one of the pillars to the country's economy in 2019, accounting for 12.7% of its GDP and employing approximately 6 million people.[21] For the past decade, the country was ranked 7th among countries that have witnessed the largest growth in tourism in terms of its GDP contribution.[22] However, despite its stellar performance, the country's tourism industry continues to lag in terms of reaching its full potential. Mirroring the experiences of other developing economies, the country faces issues that accompany its industry's rapid growth such as environmental degradation and depleting resources.

---

[19] Helble, Matthias and Anna Fink, *Reviving Tourism Amid the COVID-19 Pandemic*, Asian Development Bank, 2020.
[20] Hong Shi, Xia Li, Han Zhang, Xiaojuan Liu, Taohong Li, and Zhentao Zhong, "Global difference in the relationships between tourism, economic growth, CO_2 emissions, and primary energy consumption," *Current Issues in Tourism*, 2020, 23(9), pp. 1122–1137.
[21] Philippine Statistics Authority, Press Release No. 2020-013, January 23, 2020.
[22] Rocamora, Joyce Ann L., PH among world's top 15 travel, tourism powerhouses: WTTC, *Philippines News Agency*, 2018. https://www.pna.gov.ph/articles/1049359.

Tourism destinations in the country are facing a variety of challenges which are mostly a consequence of the rapid growth of tourism activities in destinations which put increased pressure at the local level. This includes issues in relation to environmental stress, exposure to natural disasters, weak capacity to handle crisis management and lack of local development planning in local destinations. These issues have become more apparent in the face of the outbreak of the COVID-19 pandemic where tourism activities were put into halt.[23] In ensuring that its tourism industry is developed in a sustainable, inclusive and competitive manner, the Philippine government, along with the Department of Tourism (DOT), crafted the National Tourism Development Plan (NTDP) 2017–2022 which serves as the blueprint of tourism development in the country. The NTDP emphasizes on the value of infrastructure development while ensuring the sustainable growth of micro, small, and medium enterprises as well as in enhancing capacity for crisis management.

Complementing and supporting this general framework, several initiatives have been developed and implemented by a range of stakeholders from governments (both national and local), tourism enterprises, local communities and non-government organizations (NGOs).

Cases on Sustainable Tourism in the Philippines

The chapter reviewed some of the initiatives spearheaded by a variety of stakeholders in the country, in support of tourism sustainability. Desk research, specifically using existing scholarly and industry-generated materials, was conducted to assist in the selection of cases. A total of eight cases were identified:

DOT's Anahaw Philippine Sustainable Tourism Certification

DOT launched its first national green certification program, "ANAHAW-Philippine Sustainable Tourism Certification," to

---

[23] Lesley Jeanne Yu Cordero, Madhu Raghunath, Philippe De Meneval, *Philippines — Sustainable Inclusive and Resilient Tourism Project*, The World Bank, 2020.

mainstream energy and resource-efficient efforts in promoting sustainable tourism in the country. The certification is provided to the members of the accommodation sector following a variety of levels (levels 1–5) and indicators as developed by the Center for Appropriate Technology (GrAT). Assessments include measuring water and energy consumption as well as the establishment's contribution in promoting environmental protection, cultural heritage, community involvement and compliance to government regulation.[24] As an ANAHAW-certified establishment it also entails operational savings which emphasize the value of resource conservation alongside business profitability. In doing so, the certification not only influences business operations but also educates tourists on the value of conservation.[25]

El Nido Resorts, Palawan

El Nido Resorts (ENR) is a multi-awarded and internationally recognized sustainable resort in the Philippines, owned and operated by the Ten Knots Development Corporation (TKDC). It operates in several island resorts: Lagen Island Resort, Miniloc Island Resort, and Pangulasian Island Resort, Apulit Island Resort and the Lio ecotourism estate development for 30 years now. ENR focuses on sustainability and resilience through the Quadruple Bottom Line Strategy shown in Table 4. The Quadruple Bottom Line Strategy is underpinned by (1) financial growth, (2) environmental stewardship, (3) community engagement and (4) organizational development. For ENR the strategy is implemented by integrating both the community and employees of El Nido to a series of training and learning opportunities that facilitate discussions on environmental management, conservation and preservation. ENR offers its best practice by

---

[24] ANAHAW certification awards environmentally sustainable hotels and resorts, Philippine Primer. https://primer.com.ph/blog/2019/07/07/anahaw-certification-sustainable-hotels-resorts/.

[25] Incentive to go green Anahaw certification program helps hotels, resorts become eco-warriors, *Manila Bulletin*, 2019. https://www.pressreader.com/philippines/manila-bulletin/20190516/281891594727188.

Table 4:   Summary of Case Studies and Practices

Case	Key player/s	Location	Practice/s
Anahaw Philippine Sustainable Tourism Certification	National Government	—	Acknowledgement of sustainable tourism practices.
El Nido Resorts	Private Organization	El Nido, Palawan	Quadruple Bottom Line of Sustainability: Financial growth, environmental stewardship, community engagement, and organizational development.
Daluyon Beach and Mountain Resort	Private Organization	Puerto Princesa, Palawan	3Rs of Sustainability: Replace inefficient appliances and equipment, reduce energy consumption, and redesign buildings into more self-sufficient, carbon-neutral structures.
Masungi Georeserve Foundation Inc.	Private Organization	Baras, Rizal	Georeserve model: Innovative tourism and engineering, supported by conservation, education and research, and engineering and design.
Transforming Tourism Value Chains Project	Government Agencies, INGOs, NGO	—	Monitoring of GHG emissions and introducing resource conservation practices.
Visita Project	Private Organization	—	Digitalization of registration process to enforce carrying capacity and manage tourist flow.
Marine Protected Areas (MPAs)	Government Agency, Local Government Unit	Maite, Bino-ongan, and Caticugan, Siquijor	Women participation in the management of protected areas.
Sugba Lagoon	Local Government Unit, NGO, Local Community	Sugba Lagoon, Siargao	Local community participation and capacity-building of LGUs.

combining sustainability efforts from the national government, NGOs, private sectors and the local communities to achieve genuine ecotourism. ENR management ensures that the local community is actively taking part in the planning of policies, implementation, up to the monitoring and evaluation.[26] ENR exemplifies a tourism management practice whereby private businesses incorporate local community participation in their tourism development strategy. In this example, the local community is seen as significant stakeholders whose opinions and views matter in the pursuit of development.

Daluyon Beach and Mountain Resort, Palawan

Daluyon Beach and Mountain Resort is dubbed as one of the leaders in the green movement taking place in the country's hospitality sector. Its efforts have been widely acknowledged in the field of sustainable tourism where it has received multiple prestigious awards including the ASEAN Green Hotel Award in 2012. Daluyon functions primarily by using green technologies, water-saving equipment and energy-saving measures.[27] Its movement toward sustainability is guided primarily by the principles of 3Rs by the Zero Carbon Resort Project (ZCR)[28]: replace inefficient appliances and equipment, reduce energy consumption, and redesign buildings into more self-sufficient, carbon-neutral structures. This includes the use of solar water supply system, installation of water meters, among others. Through these efforts, the resort was able to reduce its greenhouse gas emissions,

---

[26] Laririt, Mariglo, El Nido resorts: A study in sustainability and resilience, Presentation during the Global Network Week of the Global Network for Advanced Management, 2015.

[27] Johannes Chua, Sustainable resorts: Transforming the tourism landscape, *Manila Bulletin*, 2019. https://www.pressreader.com/philippines/manila-bulletin/20190202/page/65.

[28] Zero Carbon Resorts (ZCR) for Sustainable Tourism Project is a 4-year project, which ran from May 2014 to August 2018, is funded by the European Union-Switch Asia Program. It seeks to encourage the growing hospitality industry in Thailand and the Philippines to reduce their consumption of resources such as water and electricity and shrink their carbon footprint by investing in and applying appropriate technologies developed by experts from around the world.

water and electricity consumption which tantamount to a reduction of approximately 40% of the total running cost.[29] The experience of Daluyon proves that resource conservation can go hand in hand with business profitability, thereby resulting in a more sustainable way of doing tourism business.[30]

Masungi Georeserve Foundation Inc.

Masungi Georeserve is an internationally awarded privately managed conservation area known for its sustainable conservation effort, and innovative Geotourism practice.[31] Masungi follows the Georeserve model, a trademarked innovation, which highlights conservation efforts through innovative tourism and engineering, which is further supported by the three pillars of conservation, education and research, and engineering and design.[32] These models support Masungi's functions, which offers low-volume trail experiences that serves as the epitome of capacity management. Actively supporting its conservation efforts are more than 100 residents and volunteers.[33] Through their proactive approach, Masungi was able to thwart illegal mining, logging, quarrying and unregulated development in the area, as well as, in supporting local communities through trainings, environmental

---

[29] Tacio, Henrylito, A greener Philippines through zero carbon resorts, *Gaia Discovery*, 2011. https://www.gaiadiscovery.com/latest-places/a-greener-philippines-through-zero-carbon-resorts.html.

[30] Manalo, Jazztin, "Zero carbon resorts best practices: A case of Palawan, Philippines," *Ecoforum Journal*, 2019, 8(3).

[31] Aquino, Richard S. and John Paolo R. Rivera, "Public–Private partnership framework for sustainable geopark development," in *Handbook of Geotourism*, Cheltenham: Edward Elgar Publishing, 2018.

[32] Dumaliang, Billie, The Georeserve model: Mindful engineering as a means to build sustainable tourism value and income in conservation areas, *Panorama*, 2018. https://panorama.solutions/en/solution/georeserve-model-mindful-engineering-means-build-sustainable-tourism-value-and-income.

[33] Mayuga, Jonathan, Conservation innovation works wonders for Masungi Georeserve but threats remain, *Business Mirror*, 2019. https://businessmirror.com.ph/2019/10/07/conservation-innovation-works-wonders-for-masungi-georeserve-but-threats-remain/.

education, and enterprise training on food and crafts. Masungi has been chosen as one of the finalists for the United Nations World Tourism Organization Awards in 2019 and has received a special commendation from the UN Convention on Biological Diversity (UN-CBD) in 2018, among others.

Transforming tourism value chains

Pioneered by the Philippine Center for Environmental Protection and Sustainable Development, Inc., the Transforming Tourism Value Chains (TVC) project is primarily aimed to reduce greenhouse emissions and support resource efficiency in 45 hotels, food and beverage, and meetings, incentives, conferences, and exhibitions (MICE) groups. In doing so, the project aims to encourage more tourism stakeholders to be involved in monitoring their GHG emissions as well as in reducing other pollutants as a consequence of tourism activities. In doing so, sustainable business practices such a sustainable procurement, life cycle costing, resource efficiency tools are introduced to key players in the industry. In this approach, emphasis is given to stakeholder participation which includes private–public actors, as well as larger value chain players.[34]

Visita

Visita is a tech and education initiative which positions sustainable tourism as the springboard for environmental conservation. It provides a platform which professionalizes and digitizes in-destination registration process for better management. It primarily aims to address issues in enforcing carrying capacity, tourist flow management, and policy implementation. In doing so, it allows for carrying capacity implementation, data collection and management, and visitor education. Part of this initiative is a series of trainings which equip

---

[34] Philippine Center for Environmental Protection and Sustainable Development, INC (PCEPSDI), Transforming tourism value chains. https://pcepsdi.org.ph/projects/transforming-tourism-value-chains/?fbclid=IwAR3nFpOu2zVtyR-PxcJj9RKcpUuN5F9gDfkiKAQH2xupOfdm-W1vpb6Brn0.

destination managers the best practices in pursuing sustainable tourism, along with skills that will allow them to use technologies to foster conservation in destinations. Existing partners of the initiative include destinations managed by local government units across the country.[35] This is implemented by the Planning Network Inc. and supported by the Masungi Georeserve Foundation Inc.

Marine Protected Areas (Mpas) in Siquijor

The management of MPAs in the villages of Maite, Bino-ongan, and Caticugan, Siquijor, has been dubbed as an exemplar of how sustainable tourism and conservation can be achieved through gender mainstreaming. As an area known for its illegal poaching activities, an alternative source of income as presented by protecting its environmental area has been presented. By enabling and capacitating them to take responsibility of managing protected areas, women were empowered to conserve and protect the area in a non-consumptive manner. The community benefits from sustainable dive tourism activities, seaweed farming, among others.[36]

Sugba Lagoon Siargao

The Sugba eco-tourism project is managed by the local government of Del Carmen along with other government agencies, non-government organizations, and two people's organizations. As a world-renowned tourism destination, tourism activities served as an alternative source of income for families who were recently involved in illegal fishing and illegal mangrove cutting. The practice in the lagoon highlights the importance of local community participation and education, as well as,

---

[35] TTG Asia, Visitor management system Visita ready for pilot testing (accessed July 21, 2020). https://www.ttgasia.com/2020/07/21/visitor-management-system-visita-ready-for-pilot-testing/.
[36] Clabots, Barbara, Gender dimensions of community-based management of marine protected areas (MPAs) in Siquijor, Philippines, *Panorama*, 2017. https://panorama.solutions/en/solution/gender-dimensions-community-based-management-marine-protected-areas-mpas-siquijor.

increasing the capacity of LGUs to sustainably manage the destination. Positioned as a community-based social enterprise, tourism activities in the area have generated socio-economic benefits to its people which served as incentives to conserve resources and implement policies.[37]

As shown by the cases highlighted in this chapter, tourism stakeholders have an equally significant role to play — government, local communities, tourism enterprises and NGOs can actively participate in and contribute to the pursuit of sustainability, albeit in various ways. The key to the successful implementation of sustainability therefore lies in capacitating and empowering tourism stakeholders to take part in ways they can and know how.

Conclusion

While the pandemic has put tourism to a sudden halt, it has arguably given "opportunities" to re-think and re-assess the way tourism is developed as an industry. To an extent, this period is considered an "age of disruption" where innovative ideas of doing business are welcomed. This chapter was written with the goal of inspiring actions in making tourism a driver of sustainable development. The discussed case studies exemplify ways on how sustainable tourism can be a pillar for development. In reviewing the eight cases implemented by key stakeholders, a more holistic approach to promoting sustainable tourism was revealed as summarized in Table 4.

Following the cases explored, several strategies in incorporating sustainable tourism practices at the local and national levels are highlighted.

Stakeholder involvement in conservation of natural environment and biodiversity (value-chain approach)

At the core of all the cases explored in this chapter is the value of stakeholder involvement. Public–Private alliances are critical in

---

[37] Dugan, Cheryl, Balancing environment conservation and economic gain through community-based tourism, *Panorama*, 2018. https://panorama.solutions/en/solution/balancing-environment-conservation-and-economic-gain-through-community-based-tourism.

ensuring the checks and balances in conducting sustainable tourism projects, specifically in terms of financing, construction, and even in the management and maintenance of destinations.[38] More importantly, it is important to look at tourism development in value-chain approach where stakeholders from various lines of sectors interact and influence the delivery of tourism products and services.[39] Critical to ensuring proper management of destinations is the contribution of each stakeholder in the value chain.

Involvement of local community

This includes the involvement not only of the experts and policymakers in the industry but also those involved at the grassroot-level — the local community members.[40] Furthermore, local communities form part in the creation of a tourism development agenda as they play a role in bridging the gap between resource utilization and governance in destinations.[41] Among the range of tourism stakeholders, local communities are considered one of the most important given that their interests affect and are affected by the decisions of policymakers.[42] Tourism development is therefore meaningless if benefits are

---

[38] Albu, Ruxandra-Gabriela, The importance of the public–private partnerships for sustainable local development of tourism, in Faculty of Tourism and Hospitality Management in Opatija. Biennial International Congress. Tourism & Hospitality Industry, p. 60. University of Rijeka, Faculty of Tourism & Hospitality Management, 2012.

[39] Rivera, John Paolo R. and Eylla Laire M. Gutierrez, "A framework toward sustainable ecotourism value chain in the Philippines," *Journal of Quality Assurance in Hospitality & Tourism*, 2019, 20(2), pp. 123–142.

[40] Gutierrez, Eylla Laire M., "Participation in tourism: Cases on Community-Based Tourism (CBT) in the Philippines," *Ritsumeikan Journal of Asia Pacific Studies*, 2019, 37, pp. 23–36.

[41] Jamal, Tazim and Amanda Stronza, "Collaboration theory and tourism practice in protected areas: Stakeholders, structuring and sustainability," *Journal of Sustainable Tourism*, 2009, 17(2), pp. 169–189.

[42] McCool, Stephen F., "Constructing partnerships for protected area tourism planning in an era of change and messiness," *Journal of Sustainable Tourism*, 17(2), pp. 133–148.

not perceived by local communities in destinations. The key to community participation, therefore, is the participatory approach operating in destination — at what levels are communities allowed to influence decision-making.[43]

Incentive mechanism

The creation of an incentive mechanism emphasizes the critical role governments play in motivating tourism stakeholders to choose sustainable tourism. Incentives may come in the form of (e.g., financial and amenity) or intangible (e.g., environmental and status) forms with the over-all objective of promoting sustainability.[44] However, it is critical to note that incentives depend on the simultaneous adoption of sustainability efforts by other stakeholders including local governments and tourists. Other forms of incentives can therefore include the support of government to a wider green policy for tourism wherein the use of green technology and support of sustainable enterprises are given priority.[45]

Women participation

Tourism is considered a highly gendered industry where women are considered less involved and employed, mostly occupying low-paid and unskilled jobs.[46] The participation of women in tourism is largely influenced by the society and culture they belong in.[47] Thus, a

---

[43] Muganda, Michael, Agnes Sirima and Peter Marwa Ezra, "The role of local communities in tourism development: Grassroots perspectives from Tanzania," *Journal of Human Ecology*, 2013, 41(1), pp. 53–66.

[44] Line, Nathaniel D., Lydia Hanks and Li Miao, "Image matters: Incentivizing green tourism behavior," *Journal of Travel Research*, 57(3), pp. 296–309.

[45] Peng He, Yong He and Feifei Xu, "Evolutionary analysis of sustainable tourism," *Annals of Tourism Research*, 2018, 69, pp. 76–89.

[46] Kinnaird, Vivian and Derek Hall, "Understanding tourism processes: A gender-aware framework," *Tourism Management*, 1996, 17(2), pp. 95–102.

[47] Feldmann, Horst, "Protestantism, labor force participation, and employment across countries," *American Journal of Economics and Sociology*, 2007, 66(4), pp. 795–816.

persistent challenge for tourism is for women to have a higher level of participation and increased involvement in leadership roles.[48]

Education and training

Education and training are pillars to ensure that stakeholders have the capacity and skills to be actively involved in tourism development.[49] More than mere implementers, stakeholders should be empowered to take part in decision-making towards development.[50] With this in place, the level and degree of participation and involvement shift from mere subjects to active partners in fostering sustainable tourism may be observed.

Technology

Technology has played a critical role in changing the landscape of the tourism industry,[51] specifically in managing the demand and supply of tourism. Technology can help manage expectations and behavior. As explicated from the cases, the presence of technological infrastructure can assist managers in enforcing capacity management in destinations.[52] Similarly, it can serve as an alternative to tourism consumption, in the form of personalized, interactive real-time tours (PIRTs).[53]

---

[48] Tran, Linh and Pierre Walter, "Ecotourism, gender and development in northern Vietnam," *Annals of Tourism Research*, 2014, 44, pp. 116–130.

[49] Veron, Rene, Stuart Corbridge, Glyn Williams and Manoj Srivastava, "The everyday state and political society in Eastern India: structuring access to the employment assurance scheme," *The Journal of Development Studies*, 2003, 39(5), pp. 1–28.

[50] Gutierrez, Eylla Laire M., "Participation in tourism: Cases on Community-Based Tourism (CBT) in the Philippines," *Ritsumeikan Journal of Asia Pacific Studies*, 2019, 37, pp. 23–36.

[51] Neuhofer, Barbara, Dimitrios Buhalis and Adele Ladkin, "A typology of technology-enhanced tourism experiences," *International Journal of Tourism Research*, 2014, 16(4), pp. 340–350.

[52] Dumaliang, Billie, 2018, *op. cit.*

[53] Fennell, David A., "Technology and the sustainable tourist in the new age of disruption," *Journal of Sustainable Tourism*, 2020, pp. 1–7.

The use of technology can therefore be used as an approach to decreasing the ecological footprint of traveling.[54]

Focus on "small networks"

While managing tourist flows has been a challenge, sustainability is often synonymously understood in terms of enforcing carrying capacity. In doing so, a paradigm shift from mere quantity to quality of visitors must be made.[55] In the same logic, emphasis on targeting "small networks,"[56] rather than a large number of tourists must direct the operations in a destination. From a management perspective, this might entail expanding concepts of tourism development to include and focus on visitor spending over the number of visitors in a destination.

Following the deduced practices from the cases discussed, a bottom-up and top-down approach may be observed — where local communities including women can be empowered to participate in and manage tourism activities and where national governments put necessary institutional frameworks in place. To do so, it entails a multistakeholder approach: where private actors such as enterprises promote and operate tourism activities sustainably, where local government units support and empower their constituents, and where NGOs work to support the process of mainstreaming sustainability in tourism activities through technologies. Part and parcel of pursuing sustainability is learning from the experience of other neighboring countries — this is where continuous partnership and collaboration between ASEAN and China comes in. To facilitate this, several regional-level recommendations are thereby proposed.

---

[54] Hunter, Colin, "Sustainable tourism and the touristic ecological footprint," *Environment, Development and Sustainability*, 2002, 4(1), pp. 7–20.

[55] Gutierrez, Eylla Laire M., John Paolo R. Rivera, Fernando Martin Y. Roxas and Milette L. Zamora, "Rebooting Philippine tourism from the COVID-19 pandemic," *The World Financial Review*, 2020, pp. 35–39.

[56] Zamora, Milette L., "Space travel: Post-COVID-19 travel reboot [PowerPoint slides]," *Asian Institute of Management*, 2020.

- **Enhanced bilateral and multilateral cooperation:** With the goal of driving awareness and enhancing further discussions to stimulate initiatives and leadership, the agenda of pursuing sustainable tourism should be pushed at the regional level.
- **Strengthening stakeholder participation and engagement:** Increase the number of platforms and avenues to facilitate the discussion of sustainable tourism with locals in ASEAN and China. Local stakeholders such as businesses, enterprises, organizations, communities, youth, among others should be empowered to participate in and be involved in fostering sustainability. This can be done through platforms that encourage education and training that capacitate individuals and groups such as cultural exchanges, stakeholder forums, workshops and other initiatives.
- **Promoting shared experience and local knowledge:** In strengthening collaboration to foster sustainable tourism development, cross-border exchanges of practices and knowledge from ASEAN member states and China are encouraged. The facilitation of local knowledge from local stakeholders should be encouraged. This could come in the form of compiling practices and cases that will help increase knowledge and expertise exchange in the region.
- **Reducing barriers to cooperation:** Domestic regulations that impede regional cooperation in sustainable tourism must be mitigated. Regional interests and cooperation must be given priority in terms of facilitating sustainable tourism development.

Chapter

4

Achieving Sustainable Development Goals by 2030: Reducing the Gap of Inequality through ASEAN–China Trade Relations

Yulida Nuraini Santoso* and Tunggul Wicaksono[†]

ASEAN Studies Center, Universitas Gadjah Mada, Yogyakarta, The Republic of Indonesia
**yulidanurainisantoso@ugm.ac.id*
[†]wicaksono@ugm.ac.id

Background

As Indonesia and China mark their relationship of 70 years, we witness stronger economic ties and political engagement in various sectors of life.[1] However, along with this development, we also witness

---

[1] Mulyanto, Randy, After 70 years of ties, China and Indonesia have a fruitful, complicated relationship, *South China Morning Post* (accessed January 20, 2021).

the rise in criticism among many Indonesians highlighting govern-ment favoritism toward Chinese workforce, trade and goods. This includes the phenomenon of a mass of Chinese workers imported to complete the Joko Widodo's mega infrastructure projects, particularly visible during his first presidency period of 2014–2019. These migrant workers correspond to China's Belt and Road Initiative (BRI) implementation. Indonesia is one of its major destinations and has brought many to speculate more significant engagements between the two nations to come.

With United Nation's Sustainable Development Goals yet to be accomplished within the targeted timeframe of 2030, we highlight in particular goal number 10, namely *reduced inequalities within and among countries*,[2] which has the closest pertinence to the current situ-ation. With the global spread of the coronavirus in 2019, many, if not all, aspects of livelihood have been affected, including trade, ongoing bilateral and multilateral negotiations, as well as socio-economic affairs. The pandemic also affects vulnerable groups, including older persons, persons with disabilities, children, women, migrants and refugees. The phenomenon rings true not only for Indonesia but for the entire Southeast Asian region as well as China.

Indonesia–China Trade Relations

A depiction of Indonesia and China's relations is most clearly seen in the ACFTA (China–ASEAN Free Trade Area) agreement. The ACFTA is meant to open Indonesia's opportunities to benefit from non-tariff barriers on several products.[3] However, it has been argued

---

https://www.scmp.com/week-asia/politics/article/3079446/after-70-years-ties-china-and-indonesia-have-fruitful.

[2] UN, Reduce inequality within and among countries, 2021 (accessed January 20, 2021). https://unstats.un.org/sdgs/report/2020/goal-10/.

[3] APINDO-EU, Indonesia–China Trade in ACFTA: Mapping of competitiveness and specialization, *Asosiasi Pengusaha Indonesia* (*APINDO*), 2013 (accessed January 20, 2021). https://apindo.or.id/userfiles/publikasi/pdf/Paper_Indonesia-China_Trade_in_ACFTA.pdf.

that a notable deficit in Indonesia's trade balance has accumulated due to the provisions and lack of competitiveness against China's more draconian approach where its spurring economy is gained from investing heavily abroad. Compared to investments that enter China, the numbers are relatively lower and mainly focus on parts of investment that have strategic value to China's economic growth.[4] In 2013 alone, China's total foreign investment reached US$80.2 billion, exceeding the investment value in 2012, which reached US$77.2 billion. From that amount, more than 70% was aimed at ASEAN, the European Union, Australia, the United States of America, Russia and Japan.[5]

These phenomena can be seen as a double-edged sword as this remains a potential investment opportunity for recipient countries. Especially for ASEAN countries, it allows them to maintain a strategic partnership with their north Asian counterparts.[6] However, even with the liberalization of trade for both parties, China may still fare with better returns. In order to rebalance the nature of reciprocal cooperation, Indonesia must study the changing pattern of trade competitiveness and specialization between the two countries. A mapping by APINDO–EU Active shows products in which Indonesia is more specialized in bilateral trade with China. In addition, when a country has competitiveness in producing goods relative to the world's average ability, it does not necessarily mean it has specialization in bilateral trade. Therefore, country to country analysis should be considered in making trade policies for the successive international trade agreements. In doing so, Indonesia can individually set the tone for trade

[4] Jamilah, Bonar M. Sinaga, Mangara Tambunan and Dedi Budiman Hakim, The Impact of Indonesia–China Trade Agreement on Indonesia trade, *Longdom Publishing SL*, 2016 (accessed January 20, 2021). https://www.walshmedicalmedia. com/open-access/the-impact-of-indonesiachina-trade-agreement-on-indonesia-trade-performance.pdf.
[5] *Ibid.*
[6] APINDO-EU, *op. cit.*

entering its premises without compromising the ACFTA agreement's provisions in general.

Without careful mapping prior and throughout the trade, national governments can easily experience strained business, if not partially. This, in particular, is the case that this chapter wishes to argue. One of the most notable results of this is the rise in inequality, especially with the pandemic yet to come to an end. The 10th Sustainable Development Goals is prone to experience some degree of stagnancy.

Impacts of Partial Strained Trade Relations: The Rise of Inequality within and among Countries

This section studies the 10th Sustainable Development Goals, namely *reduced inequalities within and among countries.* Growing inequality undermines the fight against poverty, putting a brake on economic growth and threatening social cohesion.[7] The COVID-19 crisis is making inequality worse. It is hitting the most vulnerable people hardest, and those same groups are often experiencing increased discrimination.[8] As depicted in the Sustainable Development Goals Report 2020, several points within this particular goal are consistent with Indonesia's current battle against inequality.

Firstly, *while real incomes of the poorest within countries are rising, the rich still prosper disproportionately.* Since 2008, Indonesia's score on the UN's Human Development Index (HDI) has significantly increased. The proportion of people living in extreme poverty has fallen from 40% to 8%.[9] Alongside this, UN reports show that progress in shared prosperity has been most vital in Eastern and South-Eastern Asia, with the bottom 40% of the population growing

---

[7] Gibson, Luke, *Toward A More Equal Indonesia: How the Government Can Take Action to Close the Gap between the Richest and the Rest*, Briefing Paper, Oxford: Oxfam GB for Oxfam International, 2017.

[8] UN, *The Sustainable Development Goals Report 2020*, Report, New York: United Nations Publications, 2020.

[9] Gibson, Luke, 2017, *op. cit.*

annually by 4.9%, on average. However, Indonesia only sees 4–6% per capita in terms of the country's growth rate income of the poorest 40% between 2012 and 2017. Indonesia has the sixth-worst inequality of wealth in the world.[10] In the past two decades alone, the gap between the richest and the rest in Indonesia has grown faster than that in any other countries in Southeast Asia, with benefits of growth not being shared equally and leaving millions "behind."[11]

Secondly, *workers are receiving a smaller share of the output they helped produce.* This also rings true for Indonesia. To explain how this applies to this mega-sized nation of 273,523,615 people, we must understand the financial crisis which hit Asia in 1997. This crisis's remains are still felt to this day, leaving inequality as one of its largest homework yet. Gibson explains that the financial crisis of 1997 has produced an economy that enables those at the top to capture by far the greatest share of the benefits of growth which has resulted in an increase in political capture used to rig rules in their favor at the expense of the many.[12] Many countries implement taxation policies to safeguard those with the lowest incomes, redistribute wealth, and reduce the inequality gap to disrupt this cycle. However, in the case of Indonesia, this has resulted insignificantly. Indonesia's tax collection as a GDP percentage is the second-lowest in Southeast Asia.[13] The figure also applies for the (i) health sector where damaging insurance premiums are still reported across the country, (ii) education sector where the curriculum is not specially designed to support its citizens to enter the workforce and furthermore, is severely underfunded, therefore (iii) those in the highest paying positions often come from similar backgrounds which leads us to understand why families from low-paid jobs will generally remain this way for generations.

Third, *the global recession could constrict aid flows to developing countries.* With the pandemic yet to come to an end, economic

---

[10] *Ibid.*
[11] *Ibid.*
[12] *Ibid.*
[13] *Ibid.*

setbacks have been and will continue to be felt by many countries worldwide. This can be particularly alarming for developing nations as they struggle to tend to the weakest while keeping the outbreak at bay and reviving the national economy. According to UN Reports, the Organization for Economic Cooperation and Development (OECD) projects a decline in global GDP of up to 7.6% in 2020 if there is a second wave of COVID-19 infections, which could put pressure on the Development Assistance Committee members' ODA budgets. Development resource flows fell in the aftermath of the 2008 economic and financial crisis, and the global recession could again put pressure on development resources. This is undoubtedly unfavorable for Indonesia as it is one of the few countries to deviate and restart its economic activities earlier than most. While other nations remained under a lockdown or partial restriction, Indonesia had already loosened its social restrictions and jump-started its national economy. However, if a global recession were to take place, this would severely affect the government as it currently relies on international aid from neighboring countries and close partners to secure and rebalance its economy. In the situation where aid flows would be further restricted due to the pandemic, Indonesia may once again find itself coming face to face with the outbreak and having to make a difficult choice between health and socio-economic concerns, seeing that its reserves are far from ready to secure both at the time. In the regional context, ASEAN also has a role to play. It has yet to find a workable solution to (economically) all its member states and leaving no one behind. Thus far, its initiatives have come in medical supplies, sharing of best practices, and moral support. However, if the pandemic continues to develop at this rate, this will no longer be enough for a bustling region of 600 million people.

From these three points, we can see that Indonesia is progressing, although relatively slow, in areas of proportionately prospering the poor, securing a fair share for the working class, and securing enough national reserves to face greater challenges, including the ongoing pandemic.

To navigate through the situation and alleviate inequality alto-gether, Indonesia and China can each play crucial roles in addressing the fundamental causes of inequality through proportional and mutual cooperation. This mutually beneficial and symmetric coopera-tion should be designed to address the root causes of inequality in both countries while being mindful of the ASEAN Centrality norm.

China: Goal 10 in Focus

As a worldwide effort and action to end poverty, protect the planet, and ensure that all people enjoy peace and prosperity by 2030,[14] the Sustainable Development Goals should be shouldered by all nations who have adopted, including China and Indonesia. China has com-mitted that it will shoulder the responsibility of implementing the 2030 development agenda, seeking solidarity and cooperation to push the cause of global development constantly.[15] The Gini index is a statistical measure used to represent unequal distributions, e.g., income distribution which can take any value between 1 and 100 points (or 0 and 1). The closer the value is to 100, the greater is the inequality which 40 or 0.4 is the warning level set by the United Nations.[16] According to Textor, in 2019, China reached 46.5 (0.465) points.[17] He also argues that over the last 20 years, China has become one of the world's largest economies. As parts of society have become more and more affluent, its Gini coefficient has also grown sharply over the last decades. China's Gini coefficient ranged at a level higher

---

[14] UNDP, Sustainable development goals, 2021 (accessed January 20, 2021). https://www.un.org/ohrlls/sites/www.un.org.ohrlls/files/2030_agenda_for_sustainable_development_web.pdf.

[15] UNDP–China, Goal 12: Responsible consumption and production, 2021 (accessed January 20, 2021). https://www.undp.org/tag/goal-12-responsible-consumption-and-production?utm_source=EN&utm_medium=GSR&utm_content=US_UNDP_PaidSearch_Brand_English&utm_campaign=CENTRAL&c_src=CENTRAL&c_src2=GSR&gclid=CjwKCAjw3K2XBhAzEiwAmmgrArXM9fdFC3exxmR8USbP3bEUbFB-0YpoTRIAueYmTY7kmrFEPQuHdRoCEhEQAvD_BwE.

[16] Textor, C., Gini index: Inequality of income distribution in China from 2004 to 2019, January 11, 2021 (accessed January 20, 2021). https://www.statista.com/statistics/250400/inequality-of-income-distribution-in-china-based-on-the-gini-index/#statisticContainer.

[17] *Ibid.*

than the warning line for increasing social unrest risk over the last decade. With Textor's context at hand, it can be understood that inequality is not only an issue for Indonesia or ASEAN member states as a whole but China too, with its relatively straightforward division of economic growth between the coastal Eastern and Southern China to Central and Western China.

Textor explains the history of China's development, starting with the initiation of an opening-up policy four decades ago, which enabled the coastal areas to attract a significant number of foreign companies with their easy accessibility, cheap labor costs, political incentives, and market potential.[18] According to OECD 2012, the key sources of inequality in China, as in other emerging economies, include geographical factors, a large and persistent informal sector, gaps in access to education, and barriers to employment and career progression for specific groups, mainly rural migrants. Although in later years inland regions have also been opened up to foreign businesses, they had no real edge over their coastal counterparts.[19] On top of this, economic development was further fuelled by intensive migration of workers into coastal cities and led to the Pearl River Delta and Yangtze River Delta's formation to what has soon coined the world's factory.[20]

In the 1990s, with acknowledgment of the disparity, various political measures were taken to speed up development in the central and western regions of China.[21] Massive investments in the infrastructure, political incentives, and social programs helped improve the situation. A general shift to a growth model based on consumption also contributed to more balanced development. The economic prosperity in less progressed regions began to catch up, and the number of poor people in the countryside declined considerably. Many labor-intensive industries moved from coastal Eastern and Southern China to Central and Western China.

---

[18] *Ibid.*
[19] *Ibid.*
[20] *Ibid.*
[21] *Ibid.*

Nonetheless, the economic gap between different regions in China can still be seen today, with the global economy continuously influencing the distribution of the Chinese domestic economy.[22] Well-connected coastal cities are still favored by leading industries, and their economic development is too far ahead to be matched easily. In recent years, several western regions displayed higher growth rates than the East, but economic development is still on a far lower level. Regions in the northeast, the rust belt of China, are even falling back and have no real prospect of catching up with the economic centers.[23] However, there is scope for increasing productivity and employment by introducing more competition into the network, energy, and transport industries that are largely controlled by state-owned enterprises.[24] Introducing more competition into sectors where a few state-owned enterprises hold dominant market shares would help reduce inequalities and boosting long-term growth.[25]

ASEAN and China: Fighting Inequality for Sustainable Development

Within the ASEAN–China Strategic Partnership Vision 2030 under socio-cultural cooperation, ASEAN and China commit to addressing sustainable development as stated under paragraph 39, to "promote policy communication among governments and welcome China's efforts to provide assistance to the ASEAN Member States, where appropriate, in implementing objectives under the UN 2030 Agenda for Sustainable Development, including poverty eradication in all forms and dimensions, in accordance with respective Sustainable Development Goals."[26]

---

[22] *Ibid.*
[23] *Ibid.*
[24] OECD, *China in Focus: Lessons and Challenges*, Report, Paris: OECD, 2012.
[25] *Ibid.*
[26] ASEAN, *ASEAN–China Strategic Partnership Vision 2030*, Draft Resolution, Singapore: ASEAN, 2018.

In his remarks at the Opening Ceremony of ASEAN–China–UNDP Symposium on Innovation in Achieving the SDGs and Eradicating Poverty held in Hanoi, September 4, 2019, H. E. Huang Xilian, former Ambassador of the People's Republic of China for ASEAN, named four ways to realize this effort. Firstly, the need to foster greater synergy between the BRI and ASEAN development plans to realize the SDGs and advance poverty reduction. Secondly, the importance of stepping up exchanges in innovation, in particular new theories, policies, and actions, to propel sustainable development and poverty reduction. Thirdly, the need for the ASEAN Secretariat, like-minded international organizations such as the United Nations Development Programme (UNDP), and China to complement each other by leveraging respective strengths in research, practice, regional cooperation and the networking of people, so that the multilateral work is more than the sum of each party working separately. Lastly, the need to look for new models of practical cooperation. In his speech, he explained that the Chinese Mission to ASEAN, the ASEAN Secretariat, and UNDP had agreed to implement projects on sustainable development in countries along the Mekong River.

ASEAN and China have also established the ASEAN–China Forum on Social Development and Poverty Reduction, which is held annually to exchange views on common concerns, explore ways to narrow development gaps and share best practices to achieve harmonious development based on the mutual benefits in a win–win spirit.[27]

In 2020, the 2020 Extraordinary ASEAN–China Social Development and Poverty Reduction Forum was held online in light of the pandemic. The following are key highlights of the discussions according to reports of the RKSI 2020.[28] Firstly,

---

[27] RKSI, 13th ASEAN-China forum on social development and poverty reduction, 2019 (accessed January 20, 2021). https://rksi.adb.org/events/13th-asean-china-forum-on-social-development-and-poverty-reduction/.

[28] RKSI, The 2020 Extraordinary Association of Southeast Nations (ASEAN)–China Social Development and Poverty Reduction Forum, Event Highlights, RKSI, 2020.

according to the report, China has made substantial progress in eradicating poverty, but COVID-19 has brought new challenges. From 2012 to 2019 alone, people living in poverty fell from 98.99 to 5.51 million, according to LGOP Director Guoxia Su. Simultaneously, rural areas have been revitalized, lifting the poor's income and improving their working and living conditions. However, COVID-19 has reversed some of these gains due to reduced working hours and the poor's income in cities, slow resumption of work of poverty alleviation workshops and enterprises, and the difficulty the poor find in selling their products. To overcome these, the government has helped migrant workers return to work, more closely monitored and assisted vulnerable communities in the remaining poor counties and villages, and facilitated the purchase of products from poor areas.

Secondly, RKSI 2020 also noted that to prevent the poor from falling back to poverty. China has committed itself to working closely with ASEAN.[29] World Bank estimates that in 2020, 70–100 million people will fall into extreme poverty due to the pandemic. And by 2030, there will still be 6% extreme poverty in the world. Recognizing this, China will strengthen research on the COVID-19 impact on poverty reduction globally, further promote experience sharing, deepen cooperation, strengthen innovation and jointly develop more useful knowledge products with other countries. Thirdly, it was also discussed that ASEAN had displayed solidarity through collective actions in tackling the pandemic since the very beginning. Still, the pandemic has caused some setbacks in poverty reduction. ASEAN Deputy Secretary-General Kung Phoak mentioned that ASEAN's poverty rate fell from 47% in 1990 to 15% in 2015, but COVID-19 has jeopardized economic, social, and human development gains, especially for vulnerable groups. More investment in terms of financial allocation, human capital development, and knowledge building to empower vulnerable communities would be essential to tackle poverty.

---

[29] *Ibid.*

Fourthly, as neighbors and partners with a shared future, China and ASEAN should strengthen cooperation in anti-pandemic and anti-poverty efforts which can be done through creating synergy in development programs, deepening the BRI cooperation, cultivating innovation, and promoting the digital economy.[30] Lastly, ASEAN countries have responded to the pandemic by stimulating economic activities and employment, providing special funds for small and medium enterprises (SMEs), and helping vulnerable communities. For example, Malaysia, Singapore, and the Philippines introduced stimulus packages; Myanmar and Cambodia, cash for work programs; Myanmar and Malaysia, special relief funds for villagers and SMEs. In addition, Singapore has provided psychological support through hotlines for seniors and vulnerable people. Thailand has implemented the Backyard Vegetable Gardening program to ensure food security.[31]

Proposed Ways Forward

More attention needs to be shed on each goal with less than a decade to realize the Sustainable Development Goals by 2030, particularly in achieving reduced inequalities within and among countries. The following are short, medium and long-term proposed ways to address and converge inequality in both regions through collaboration.

Short term: With the battle against the pandemic still high on all nations' agenda, it is pertinent that a sound plan to protect the most vulnerable is put into place. This group includes older persons, persons with disabilities, children, women, migrants and refugees. This needs to be prioritized as they are being hit the hardest by the pandemic implications, particularly in sectors of healthcare and socio-economics.

According to Wanandi, in facing the pandemic in East Asia and the world, we can depend on the ASEAN–China cooperation designed during the special ASEAN–China Foreign Ministers'

---

[30] *Ibid.*
[31] *Ibid.*

Meeting on the Coronavirus Disease in Vientiane on February 20.[32] ASEAN and China, both of which have had ample cases of the coronavirus, were the first to help East Asia, including Japan, India, South Korea, Australia, Russia and New Zealand in the context of the East ASEAN Summit, and later assisted and supported efforts in the world. For that purpose, the EAS can become an institution to initiate efforts and the world's support.

To do so, Wanandi proposes the five following action lines.[33] Firstly, to step up cooperation in the region against COVID-19 by sharing information and best practices in a timely manner, including exchanging available epidemiological information, technical guidelines, and solutions for epidemic prevention and control, diagnosis, treatment, and surveillance with a view on enhancing capacity in emerging preparedness and response. Secondly, to strengthen cooperation within ASEAN-led mechanisms and with external partners to address COVID-19 in a comprehensive and effective manner, taking into account the different levels of development of health systems in the region. Thirdly, to strengthen cooperation in risk communication and community engagement readiness and response to ensure that people are rightly and thoroughly informed on COVID-19 and are not being misled by misinformation and fake news pertaining to COVID-19. Fourthly, to strengthen policy dialogue and exchanges on the latest developments of the COVID-19, including its control and treatment, and its related studies and research through existing mechanisms, such as the ASEAN–China Health Ministers' Meeting and the ASEAN–China Senior Officials' Meeting on Health Development to fully implement the ASEAN–China Memorandum of Understanding on Health Cooperation and support more mutually agreed cooperation projects. *Lastly*, to commit to reducing the impact of the epidemic on the economic and social development of all

---

[32] Wanandi, Jusuf, ASEAN–China cooperation in time of COVID-19 pandemic, *Centre for Strategic and International Studies*, March 22, 2020 (accessed January 20, 2021).https://www.csis.or.id/publications/asean-china-cooperation-in-time-of-covid-19-pandemic/.

[33] *Ibid.*

affected countries, jointly maintaining people-to-people exchanges, trade, and investment activities in the region, and, based on the progress of the prevention and control of the epidemic, resuming and enhancing exchange and cooperation.

As the pandemic will continue to influence national and even regional policy-making for an unknown length of time, only by addressing it appropriately, ASEAN and China can move onto forging meaningful steps toward reducing and altogether alleviating inequality in both regions.

Medium-term: To allow for meaningful changes in narrowing the inequality gap, some steps can also be taken, firstly, through the creation of fair work and wages. This can be achieved by developing national plans to show clearly how it will tackle inequality and reach its targets to reduce the Gini coefficient, including between urban and rural areas, and work closely with local governments to ensure that local governments commit to reducing inequality.[34] ASEAN and China can also regulate companies to ensure that more workers are on secure employment contracts while at the same time close the gender pay gap and remove barriers to women's equal participation in the labor force.[35] Many civil societies across the region have actively promoted positive social norms and attitudes around women's work.[36] This effort is something that ASEAN and China can collaborate further on with the guidance of the ASEAN Commission on the Promotion and Protection of the Rights of Women and Children (ACWC). Secondly, by operationalizing fair taxations and encouraging private sectors to play their role. Many attempts have been made to connect the field of business and human rights. To achieve this, ASEAN and China can avoid offering harmful tax incentives and work closely at the regional level on tax cooperation with other ASEAN

---

[34] Gibson, Luke, 2017, *op. cit.*
[35] *Ibid.*
[36] *Ibid.*

countries.[37] On the other hand, private sectors can publish data on their gender pay gaps, ensure access to decent and safe employment opportunities for women, employ workers on secure employment contracts, support government actions toward a national living wage, and institute policies to move toward a living wage within their operations, and invest more in the skills of employees to meet the need for higher-skilled workers.[38] It is time that the private and business sectors play an active and meaningful part in developing their host nation.

Long-term: In the long run, the goal is to see meaningful convergence and a narrower gap of inequality. In order to do so, it would be ideal for forging issue-focused and symmetrical cooperation, which guarantees a mutually beneficial partnership that can further lead to a trickle-down effect. ASEAN has long been criticized for its elitist approaches and conducts. With more cooperation targeting the vulnerable and in-needed needs through the trickle-down effect, the cooperation will reach out to far more.

---

[37] *Ibid.*
[38] *Ibid.*

https://doi.org/10.1142/9789811257896_0005

Chapter

5

ASEAN–China Partnership on Sustainable Development: Vietnam's Perspectives

Chu Minh Thao

Diplomatic Academy of Vietnam, Hanoi, Vietnam

thaocm@dav.edu.vn

Introduction

The issue of sustainable development has always been an important issue of cooperation between ASEAN and China. In the aftermath of the 2008 global economic crisis, in 2010, the leaders of ASEAN and China gathered in Hanoi for the 13th ASEAN–China Summit to sign the Joint Statement on Sustainable Development. This year again, the sustainable development emerges to be a top-priority policy issue given the pandemic COVID-19. In the 23rd ASEAN–China Summit in 2020, the leaders set 2021 as a year for sustainable development. Accordingly, they agreed that ASEAN and China will strengthen trade connectivity, ensure stability of regional supply chains, carry out the AFTA, promote trade liberalization, step up the application of digital technology, ensure cyber security, and develop a digital economy.[1] These are some basic guidelines for cooperation while it is necessary to work out further steps to realize the SDGs.

Changing Trajectory Transitioning to Sustainable Development due to the COVID-19

The COVID-19 has caused the largest global crisis since the end of the Second World War, and has increased uncertainty about the progress of the sustainable development. COVID-19 has transformed the people's mindset toward sustainable lifestyles, work and priorities, with major implications for sustainable development by accelerating innovative trends, strengthening sustainable trends, and reversing other trends. First, it has acted as a catalyzer for mainstreaming innovative development trends such as digital transformation, in line with individual behaviors shifting to virtual and remote working.[2] Second, the sustainable trends have gained stronger support from the people, especially for a green and low-carbon economy. This is due to the enhanced awareness of the people regarding sustainability, as COVID-19 reflects a disaster rooted in a crisis of unsustainable practices. Besides, the restraint on transportation has shown lower air pollution levels and GHG emissions.[3]

In addition, the COVID-19 has revealed a more complex picture of sustainable development with the interdependence and connection with non-traditional security issues such as health security, environmental security. Emerging challenges caused by the COVID-19 have

---

[1] *Viet Nam News*, ASEAN-China ties among most substantive partner relations of ASEAN: PM Phúc (accessed November 12, 2020). https://vietnamnews.vn/politics-laws/805348/asean-china-ties-among-most-substantive-partner-relations-of-asean-pm-phuc.html.

[2] Echegaray, Fabian, "What post-COVID-19 lifestyles may look like? Identifying scenarios and their implications for sustainability," *Sustainable Production and Consumption*, 2021, 27(7), pp. 567–574.

[3] Nakada, L. Y. K. and R. C. Urban, "COVID-19 pandemic: Impacts on the air quality during the partial lockdown in São Paulo state, Brazil," *Science of the Total Environment*, 2020, p. 730.

redefined the concept of national security to include not only traditional but also non-traditional security issues as the pandemic has directly impacted on the global economic development. Global challenges and risks like pandemic, natural resources, inequality, environmental pollution, poverty, digital gaps, food security, water security, climate change and cybersecurity have become increasingly unpredictable, complex and complicated.

On top of these challenges, some macro issues also hinder the sustainable development, that is, the lack of global cooperation due to the weakening of the international order and global governance system as a result of the lack of global consensus and major power rivalry, rising nationalism, especially regarding vaccine. It is also the lack of fund, weaker competitiveness and middle-income trap that hinder the progress of sustainable development.

Despite the improved understanding regarding the pollution, there exists the imbalance between environmental security and sustainable development. The issue of air pollution is now coming back to Hanoi (Vietnam) or Beijing (China). Besides, the COVID-19 has also caused rising challenges to other trends such as distrust of the circular economy (more regular use of plastic single-use goods) due to sanitation concerns,[4] or the sharing economy due to social distancing policy.[5]

This new context together has reshaped the trajectory transitioning to sustainable development. On one hand, the sustainable development is moving toward more innovative trends and thus preventing the negative consequences of global economic recession, such as the rise of extreme poverty. But on the other hand, it also becomes more unpredictable and complex, hindering the progress, as resources are diverted. Hence, stronger political, global and regional cooperation is required to quickly transform sustainable economic development model accordingly, and more comprehensive economic governance reforms to cope with unpredictable threats. As such, the question is how ASEAN and China devote their efforts to their joint sustainable

---

[4] *The Economist*, Sea of troubles. COVID-19 has led to a pandemic of plastic pollution, June 22, 2020.
[5] Hossain, M., "The effect of the COVID-19 on sharing economy activities," *Journal of Cleaner Production*, 2020.

development programs suitable for the changing risks, realizing the UN Sustainable Development Goals.

Complementarities Between China and ASEAN's Views of Sustainable Development

Both ASEAN countries and China share complementarities regarding commitments to implementation of the UN 2030 Agenda for Sustainable Development. The UN's subthemes of the SDGs, including people, planet, prosperity and peace, are integrated into the socio-economic development plans and strategies of relevant countries and ASEAN's master plan. ASEAN and China have shared objectives of people-centered, people-oriented sustainable development, "leaving no one behind" motto. In realizing this spirit, ASEAN and China have maintained a long-lasting development cooperation partnership with various strategies, including ASEAN–China Strategy on Environmental Cooperation (2016–2020) strengthening policy dialogues regarding environmental protection and regional sustainable development.

China has pursued a friendly neighborhood policy and hence become an important source of financial, technical and knowledge cooperation for ASEAN. China has restructured a new economic relationship with ASEAN by promising to import more goods from ASEAN and establishing the production networks[6] through important initiates such as BRI which is one of the main means of connecting with ASEAN.

ASEAN's main plan for sustainable development is covered in the Master Plan of ASEAN Connectivity (MPAC) 2025, including three community pillars, i.e., political-security, economic and social community. With the COVID-19, ASEAN's demands lack information, data and funding due to diversion of economic resources to cope with the COVID-19 and thus dependence on development partners.[7] One

---

[6] Yunling, Zhang and Yuzhu, Wang, ASEAN in China's Grand Strategy, Economic Research Institute for ASEAN and East Asia (ERIA), 2017. https://www.eria.org/ASEAN_at_50_4A.9_Zhang_and_Wang_final.pdf

[7] Anbumozhi, Venkatachalam, Ensuring ASEAN's Sustainable and Resilient Future, Economic Research Institute for ASEAN and East Asia (ERIA), 2017. https://www.eria.org/ASEAN_at_50_4B.7_Anbumozhi_final.pdf.

of the main methods for ASEAN's realization of SDGs is through, internally, intergovernmental mechanisms, and externally, cooperation with development partners such as China who is one of most important partners.

Thus, the two sides share interests in dealing with the COVID-19, adaptability to a new normal and sustainable economic recovery by promoting an inclusive and innovation-based economy to promote equity and sustainable development.

Policy Recommendations for ASEAN–China Sustainable Economic Development Cooperation

China and ASEAN countries have much room to realize the SDGs, to build an inclusive, resilient and sustainable future, by the application of a system-based approach:

- Firstly, ASEAN countries and China should continue to promote the implementation of UN's 2030 Agenda for Sustainable Development and the Sustainable Development Goals (SDGs) as one of the top priorities. Sustainability should become one of key criteria for socio-economic development plan and different models of economic development. Such commitment is especially important when the deadline of 2030 is reaching while the two are struggling with the COVID-19 and economic recovery in the middle of global economic recession.
- Secondly, the cooperation should be implemented both multilaterally in global systems which drive the progress of the implementation of the SDGs, and bilaterally through bilateral mechanisms. For a fruitful cooperation, trust and shared responsibilities, to foster inclusive and sustainable development, the goal of leaving no one behind, and win–win opportunities, are important, given the development gap and diversity between China and ASEAN countries. Trust is also one of key elements of ASEAN way.
- Thirdly, the two parties can focus on some key areas to narrow development gaps for regional inclusive growth and SDGs.

(1) Good health and well-being: As environmental security (climate change, water security, air security) linked with human security and health security serves as a basic foundation for sustainable development, ASEAN–China cooperation should focus on effectively handling the COVID-19 by increasing access to vaccine, by formulating a regional vaccine hub to attract the donation of vaccine from relevant countries and facilitate the distribution to the country in need.

(2) Sharing good practices, lesson and experience regarding application of innovation-driven sustainable development in various sectors (technology, infrastructure, agriculture and clean energy) for green recovery, sustainable consumption, reduced emissions and pollution. This can be done via program exchange, think tank dialogues and studies regarding sustainability, for sustainable production and consumption, green economy, digital economy and low-carbon economy.

(3) Establishing a joint regional platform to facilitate enterprises in their digital business, and increasing digital trade.

(4) Improving the regional connectivity and regional integration by increasing investment on infrastructure and green investments, and giving priority to high-quality, environmental-friendly investments with clear environmental protection standards.

(5) Facilitating trade through the implementation of signed FTAs including CPTPP, RCEP, and strengthening trade integration and connectivity through initiating digital FTAs.

(6) Strengthening inclusive and sustainable finance, in line with ASEAN Catalytic Green Finance Facility under the ASEAN Infrastructure Fund, and covering finance for women, small and medium enterprises (SMEs).

These are some recommendations to forge partnership between ASEAN and China at a more comprehensive and advanced level.

Chapter

6

ASEAN–China Partnership on Pursuing Sustainable Development: A View from Singapore

Yu Hong

National University of Singapore, Singapore

eaiyuh@nus.edu.sg

China–ASEAN Economic Ties: A Foundation for Partnership on Sustainable Development

China enjoys close and active trade links with its neighbors in Southeast Asia. As the world's largest trading nation, China is the largest trading partner of most of the Association of Southeast Asian Nations (ASEAN) members. The proportion of China's exports attributed to the ASEAN is on the rise. At the same time, the percentage of imports from ASEAN in China's total imports is also showing an upward trend. These signs are indicative of the close trading ties between ASEAN and China, the center of the global industrial chain.

In 2019, ASEAN's total foreign trade amounted to around $2.80 trillion, of which 18% was with China. This figure was much higher than those recorded by the European Union (10%) and Japan (8.1%).[1] Despite the impacts of the pandemic on global trade and economy, the bilateral trade volume between China and ASEAN reached over $500 billion in 2020. This reflects the resilience and the interdependency of economic ties between China and the ASEAN member states. Vibrant trade relations also present an opportunity for both China and the ASEAN member states to accelerate their economic recovery from the severe impacts of the COVID-19 pandemic.

Although China still has less investments in ASEAN than in the United States, European Union and Japan, Chinese companies' investments in Southeast Asia have grown considerably in recent years. In 2019, China's regional investments reached $15.5 billion, accounting for more than 13% of China's foreign investments.

Chinese enterprises are active in the Southeast Asian countries, and are involved in many large regional infrastructure projects, including the China–Laos Railway from Yunnan Province to Vientiane, hydropower projects in Lao PDR, power plants in Cambodia, coal-fired power plants and the Jakarta–Bandung High-Speed Rail in Indonesia, iron and steel plants in Malaysia, and mass rapid transit projects in Singapore. There is also significant domestic consumption of "Made in China" products in Southeast Asian countries, ranging from consumer goods, food and household appliances to high-end goods such as locomotive engines, smartphones and communications equipment.

In recent years, China and the ASEAN economic ties are stronger than ever. China and ASEAN members have established close economic ties and trade links through global supply chains. With a population of over 650 million, Southeast Asia is one of the fastest-growing regions in the world. In this region, the workforce is sizable and young, the middle class is expanding and the market has huge potential. With abundant natural resources and relatively low production

---

[1] Hong, Yu, Wake-up call for ASEAN countries: Curb over-reliance on China and seize opportunities of global supply chain restructuring, ThinkChina, March 26, 2020. https://www.thinkchina.sg/wake-call-asean-countries-curb-over-reliance-china-and-seize-opportunities-global-supply-chain.

costs, ASEAN has the prerequisites to become the next factory of the world and to play a more important role in the global industrial chain.

To further strengthen regional economic collaboration and to promote regional integration, the ASEAN countries and China have recently joined with other regional partners to sign the long-expected Regional Comprehensive Economic Partnership (RCEP) trade agreement. The implementation of the RCEP agreement will help ASEAN nations to better participate in regional industrial supply chains and strengthen their economic links with the world and the Asia-Pacific region in particular. Overall, through joining the RCEP, the ASEAN nations will benefit from an increase in exports, investment growth and more opportunities to engage in regional supply chains due to greater market access.

The agreement can help more ASEAN small and medium-sized enterprises (SMEs) to integrate with regional and global value chains and expand their businesses in the RCEP member nations and the global market. Due to the different levels of economic development and industrial structures among the ASEAN nations, the degree of benefits they derive from the RCEP varies.[2] However, Vietnam is an example of a member nation that has achieved noteworthy growth and is now becoming established in global value chains and as a destination for an increasing number of multinational corporations (MNCs) to set up production plants.

Being part of the RCEP is advantageous to China in the face of the triple threat of the China–US trade war, geopolitical change and global economic recession due to the pandemic. It also offers China more room to maneuver as its relations with several major trading partners such as the United States, the United Kingdom and Australia deteriorate. The implementation of the RCEP will help China's export enterprises expand their overseas market share and bring about expectations of stability. China will also have closer economic and trade ties with the Asia-Pacific, including ASEAN.

---

[2] Hong, Yu, RCEP: The benefits, the regret and the limitations. *ThinkChina*, December 29, 2020. https://www.thinkchina.sg/rcep-benefits-regret-and-limitations.

Partnership for Sustainable Development

Preventing and combating infectious diseases

In September 2015, heads of state gathered in the United States, in New York, to endorse *Transforming Our World: The 2030 Agenda for Sustainable Development*, which provides an aspirational roadmap for achievement of a sustainable future for the world. Sustainable development is a broad topic that requires a multifaceted and cross-sectoral approach.

These close bilateral economic and trade relations are valuable assets for China and ASEAN countries in pursuing sustainable development. Nevertheless, given the diversity of the countries in a region with a population of 650 million, the ASEAN faces challenges of significant scale in achieving its Sustainable Development Goals (SDGs), particularly in the case of the low-middle-income member countries.[3]

Hence, the ASEAN needs to facilitate collaboration on sustainable development with China and other development partners. Two priority areas could be identified for forging ASEAN–China partnership in pursuit of sustainable development, namely preventing infectious diseases (e.g., the novel coronavirus) and poverty alleviation.

Prevention of infectious diseases such as the novel coronavirus is an important area for sustainable development. The COVID-19 (novel coronavirus) pandemic was first reported in Wuhan, China in December 2019. It later spread to Southeast Asia and the rest of the world.

With the current COVID-19 coronavirus spreading across many countries and regions in the world, the open and highly connected Southeast Asia has been hard hit. Starting in January 2020, the ASEAN countries were among the first nations affected by the COVID-19 pandemic due to their geographical proximity with

---

[3] ASEAN low-middle-income countries include Cambodia, Indonesia, Laos, Myanmar, the Philippines and Vietnam.

China. Confirmed cases of COVID-19 have subsequently continued to increase within many ASEAN member states. The fight against the pandemic is grim as the situation in this region is fast deteriorating. Given the huge population size, total confirmed cases of COVID-19 in the region have now risen to over 3.77 million (accurate as of February 2021), with total deaths of 52,963. The number of people infected with the coronavirus is still rising day by day. Indonesia has been hardest hit by the pandemic in Southeast Asia, recording the highest numbers of both confirmed cases and deaths. Other member states, including the Philippines, Malaysia and Myanmar, have also been hard hit by the spread of COVID-19 (Table 1).

On the other hand, despite being a populous and developing country, Vietnam has emerged as the most successful country in Southeast Asia and the world so far in containing the spread of the pandemic, in terms of total number of confirmed cases and death toll.

Table 1:   Update on the Coronavirus Situation in the ASEAN

Country	Total confirmed cases	Total deaths	Total cases/one million population	Tests/one million population
Indonesia	1,334,634	36,166	4,846	39,209
Philippines	576,352	12,318	5,214	79,186
Malaysia	300,752	1,130	9,215	112,243
Myanmar	141,890	3,199	2,596	45,560
Singapore	59,936	29	10,192	1,239,784
Thailand	25,951	83	371	17,419
Vietnam	2,448	35	25	20,396
Cambodia	805	n.a.	48	28,739
Brunei	186	3	422	228,665
Laos	45	n.a.	6	15,269
Total	3,777,633	52,963	32,935	1,826,470

Note: The "n.a." stands for no public reporting of deaths from COVID-19.

Source: Worldometers on Coronavirus, https://www.worldometers.info/coronavirus/, updated on February 28, 2021.

Vietnam has[4] deployed a strategy which is centered on wide-scale testing, effective contact tracing and quarantine and has been relatively successful in containing the virus spread and bringing the pandemic under control.

Due to the vast differences in public health systems as well as medical facilities and resources among the ASEAN countries, their preparedness and resource deployment capabilities for large-scale infectious disease outbreaks are also different.[5] According to the Global Competitiveness Report 2019 covering 141 economies and published by the World Economic Forum, ASEAN countries' health capacities vary greatly. Singapore ranks first in the world on health and possesses a world-class medical system. However, Lao PDR (109th), Cambodia (105th) and the Philippines (102nd) lag far behind. If the COVID-19 outbreak worsens within the ASEAN, it will quickly overwhelm countries with weak public health systems and low medical standards, especially Lao PDR, Cambodia, the Philippines and Indonesia.

The member states' healthcare systems are under tremendous stress in struggling to deal with the pandemic outbreak and fast rising number of COVID-19 patients. Nevertheless, the real tests for the ASEAN countries still lie ahead as the long-term socio-economic impacts of the pandemic are just beginning to unfold.

Meanwhile, Southeast Asian countries such as Indonesia and the Philippines have already been ravaged by the coronavirus. Since the onset of COVID-19, the ASEAN countries have rolled out many containment measures to attempt to stem the pandemic's spread. These strictly enforced measures include quarantines, restrictions of movement and large gatherings, shop and school closures, and even economic shutdown. Revitalization of the ASEAN countries' economies in a post-COVID-19 world will depend on the spread of COVID-19 being rapidly brought under effective control.

China has also taken strict measures to date to contain the spread of COVID-19. Since the pandemic's outbreak in February 2020,

---

[4] https://www.worldometers.info/coronavirus/.
[5] Yu Hong, 2020, *op. cit.*

China has deployed a strategy based on wide-scale testing, effective contact tracing and quarantine, and targeted local lockdowns when deemed necessary. These measures have been relatively successful in containing the virus's spread and bringing the pandemic largely under control, although there are still occasional local infection flare-ups. China is taking a leading role in producing COVID-19 vaccines. Moreover, since the Chinese-made vaccines do not require refrigeration at extremely low temperatures, they are easier for developing countries to store and use.

In battling against the pandemic, ASEAN could cooperate with China to share information, exchange experience and best practices. China has already provided many needed supplies of testing equipment, personal protective equipment and other medical goods to the ASEAN countries. When China's Prime Minister, Li Keqiang, attended the online 23rd China–ASEAN Summit in November 2020, he stated, "To promote sustainable development and strengthen preparedness for risk, China stands ready to step up cooperation on ecological conservation, environmental promotion, disaster prevention and mitigation, climate change, and poverty reduction." He further declared China's preparedness "to defeat COVID-19 together and improve public health cooperation."

Availability of effective vaccines is the only way out of this crisis. Lockdown and other strict contingency measures are difficult to maintain for a long period in many of these countries, as people need to work to make a living due to lack of social protection and savings. According to the Asian Development Bank's estimation, disruption to regional supply chains, and the containment measures taken to control the virus, such as restrictions on the movement of people and goods and closure of non-essential businesses, could result in the loss of 11.6–18.4 million jobs across Southeast Asia.[6]

Additionally, several ASEAN countries, such as the Philippines and Vietnam, whose economies are dependent on remittances sent home by migrant workers, are being hard hit, given that many

---

[6] Chongvilaivan, Aekapol, Sustainable development is key in responding to COVID-19. East Asia Forum, July 6, 2020 (accessed January 7, 2021). https://www.eastasiaforum. org/2020/07/06/sustainable-development-is-key-in-responding-to-covid-19/.

migrant workers could have lost their jobs due to the pandemic out-break worldwide. Working poor in the region are vulnerable to falling back into poverty due to the pandemic and the strict virus-containment measures such as economic lockdowns. Many in the most vulnerable groups, including children, may fall below the poverty line and suffer from malnutrition. The virus-stricken member states have been forced to divert considerable resources to deal with the pandemic crisis, which will certainly have major effects on their fulfillment of other national goals and targets, including SDGs.

Leveraging its strong manufacturing capacity, China can demonstrate its goodwill by facilitating large-scale production of vaccines for provision to the virus-stricken Southeast Asian countries. China has already promised that Chinese-made vaccines will be used for the global public good, and priority has been given to the developing world. China has joined the COVAX[7] vaccine initiative, which was launched by the World Health Organization (WHO) and is aimed at distributing the vaccines equally among nations.

Poverty alleviation

The ASEAN countries have achieved reduction of absolute poverty incidence over the past decades. However, given their diversity and different stages of economic development, poverty alleviation[8] in Southeast Asia has varied in magnitude across member countries. In certain countries, such as Myanmar, Laos and the Philippines, the

---

[7] According to Gavi, The Vaccine Alliance worldwide, COVAX, is one of three pillars of the Access to COVID-19 Tools (ACT) Accelerator, which was launched in April by WHO, the European Commission and France in response to this pandemic. Bringing together governments, global health organizations, manufacturers, scientists, private sector, civil society and philanthropy, with the aim of providing innovative and equitable access to COVID-19 diagnostics, treatments and vaccines. For more information, please click https://www.gavi.org/vaccineswork/covax-explained.

[8] Living on below $1.9 per day was set by the World Bank in 2015 as an internationally recognized definition of extreme poverty.

Table 2: Proportions of Population below the International Poverty Line of $1.90 PPP in the ASEAN (2018)

Country	Below $1.90 PPP[a] (in %)	Below National Poverty Line[b] (in %)
Brunei Darussalam	n.a.	n.a.
Cambodia	2.2	13.5
Indonesia	3.6	9.8
Lao PDR	21.2	18.3
Malaysia	0.0	7.6
Myanmar	6.2	24.8
Philippines	6.1	16.7
Singapore	n.a.	n.a.
Thailand	0.0	9.9
Vietnam	1.9	6.8

Notes: [a]The latest available data for Cambodia and Lao PDR is 2012 while for Malaysia, Myanmar, and Philippines is 2015. [b]The latest available data for Cambodia and Malaysia is 2016 while for Myanmar is 2017. n.a. not applicable.
Source: ASEAN Statistical Yearbook, 2020.

proportions of people living below either $1.90 PPP or the respective national poverty lines are high compared to other member countries (Table 2).

The once-in-a-century COVID-19 pandemic could undo progress made in poverty reduction in the ASEAN. Based on the national poverty lines among the ASEAN countries,[9] an average of 13% of the total population was living below national poverty lines (Figure 1); meanwhile, the rural poverty rate was higher, with an average of 18% of rural population living below national poverty lines in 2018 (Figure 2). In the specific cases of two low-middle-income ASEAN countries, Laos and the Philippines, the proportions of population

---

[9] Poverty line levels are not comparable across the ASEAN member states.

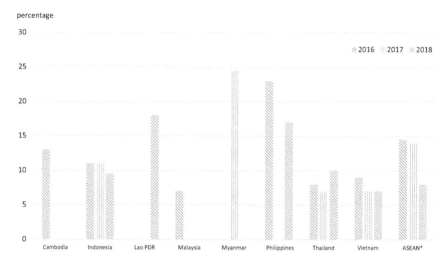

Figure 1:   Proportions of Population Living below National Poverty Lines in the ASEAN (2016–2018)

Note: *Malaysia's poverty rates refer to proportion of households living below the national poverty line while Vietnam's poverty rates refer to proportion of households living below the national multi-poverty index. Data were excluded in the ASEAN aggregate.

Source: The ASEAN Secretariat, 2020.

living below the national poverty line were even higher, at 18.3% and 16.7%, respectively, in 2018.[10] It is estimated that between 84.5 million and 117 million people in the Southeast Asian nations are still living in poverty. According to the Asian Development Bank's forecast, around 18 million more people who had been lifted out of absolute poverty would be at risk of falling back into poverty, and the poverty rate in Southeast Asia was considered likely to rise to 18% in 2020.[11] Southeast Asia's quest to eliminate poverty has suffered its worst setback in decades due to the

---

[10] The ASEAN Secretariat, ASEAN sustainable development goals indicators baseline report 2020. November 2020, pp. 1–244.

[11] Chongvilaivan, Aekapol, 2020, *op. cit.*

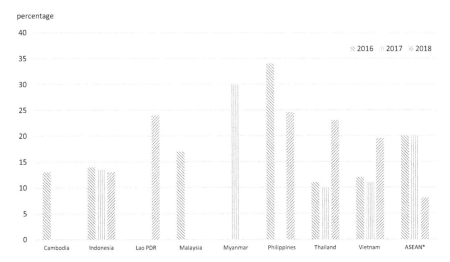

Figure 2:   Proportions of Population Living below National Poverty Lines in Rural Areas in the ASEAN (2016–2018)

Note: *Malaysia's poverty rates refer to proportion of households living below the national poverty line while Vietnam's poverty rates refer to proportion of households living below the national multi-poverty index. Data were excluded in the ASEAN aggregate.

Source: The ASEAN Secretariat, 2020.

pandemic. The United Nations warned that poverty reduction achievements in Southeast Asia could be reversed due to the severe impacts brought about by the pandemic. The pandemic crisis threatens to destroy the livelihoods of 218 million informal workers in Southeast Asia, potentially pushing their families into poverty as a consequence.[12]

Ending poverty was listed as the first among the 17 SDGs set up in *Transforming Our World: The 2030 Agenda for Sustainable Development*. As part of China's efforts to implement the 2030 Agenda, in October 2015, Xi Jinping, China's President, made a

---

[12] Allard, Tom, Southeast Asia poverty to surge in "socio-economic crisis"-UN, *Reuters*, July 31, 2020 (accessed January 9, 2021). https://www.reuters.com/article/uk-health-coronavirus-un-southeast-asia-idUKKCN24W06O.

commitment that China would lift all people (around 70 million) living under the national poverty line out of poverty by 2020.[13] China has recorded spectacular economic growth over the past four decades, with impressive poverty alleviation achievements and improvements in many other social indicators.

China has been implementing targeted poverty alleviation policies since 2013. Considering the varying conditions of different poverty-stricken areas and households, precise measures have been adopted to identify those who are impoverished and to provide needed assistance. The national poverty rate dropped to 0.6% in 2019 from 10.2% in 2012.[14] In February 2021, during a speech at a grand gathering to mark China's poverty alleviation accomplishments, Xi Jinping, China's President, declared that extreme poverty has been eliminated in the nation.

China spent around RMB1.6 trillion in poverty alleviation since 2013. China so far has accounted for over 70% of the world's success in wiping out extreme poverty since the 1980s.[15] Nevertheless, China will still need to revitalize the economy of rural areas and consolidate its poverty alleviation achievement by preventing the vulnerable groups of people falling back into poverty traps.

The year 2020 marked the comprehensive achievement of a Xiaokang society — a moderately prosperous society in all aspects — and eradication of absolute rural poverty. According to official data, all 832 impoverished counties and 128,000 rural villages had been

---

[13] Ministry of Foreign Affairs of the People's Republic of China, China's progress report on implementation of the 2030 agenda for sustainable development. August 2017, pp. 1–107.

[14] *China Today*, Poverty reduction ensures sustainable development, September 29, 2020 (accessed January 8, 2021). http://www.chinatoday.com.cn/ctenglish/2018/commentaries/202009/t20200929_800222404.html.

[15] Xi Jinping declares extreme poverty has been wiped out in China. *South China Morning Post*, February 25, 2021. https://www.scmp.com/news/china/politics/article/3123174/xi-jinping-declares-extreme-poverty-has-been-wiped-out-china.

removed from the nation's poverty list by 2020.[16] China achieved these goals, which were set out in the 2030 Agenda for Sustainable Development, 10 years ahead of schedule.

There is much the ASEAN could learn from China's success in fighting poverty and elevating living standards of the ordinary Chinese people. The ASEAN countries need to learn from the strategy of precise poverty alleviation and eradication implemented by the Chinese government. It would be desirable for China to share its own experience on how to lift the remaining poor people out of poverty, given the depth of their poverty and this group's weak capability for achieving self-development.

China could show further willingness to share poverty alleviation experience with the ASEAN and the rest of the world in areas such as developing rural industries and economies, improving rural governance, technological assistance, micro-credit policies for rural people, knowledge sharing and capacity building, vocational training and poverty alleviation management.

Millions of people in Southeast Asia are still living under extreme poverty. China has launched pilot projects in several ASEAN countries, including Cambodia, Laos and Myanmar, to disseminate its experience in village-by-village poverty reduction, developing local villages' organizational ability, encouraging local farmers to combine their efforts in agricultural activities.[17]

In addition, the ASEAN and China could deepen cooperation on achieving poverty reduction in Southeast Asia by using the established China–ASEAN Forum on Social Development and Poverty Reduction as an institutional mechanism to promote bilateral collaboration on poverty alleviation. Drawing on its own experience of poverty

---

[16] Xi declares complete victory in eradicating absolute poverty in China. *Xinhua*, February 26, 2021 (accessed February 26, 2021). http://www.xinhuanet.com/english/2021-02/26/c_139767705.htm.

[17] The State Council Information Office of the People's Republic of China, China's international development cooperation in the new era. January, 2021 (accessed January 10, 2021). http://www.xinhuanet.com/english/2021-01/10/c_139655400.htm.

alleviation, China has already helped to train local officials in poor villages in several ASEAN countries to promote development, infrastructure improvement and provision of basic public services to rural people.

Additionally, China can further promote the sustainable development agenda with the ASEAN countries under the "Belt and Road" Initiative (BRI) framework. In particular, intraregional and interregional infrastructure development could help to improve rural people's living standards and thus alleviate poverty. Lack of infrastructure is a barrier for the local people in the region to gaining better access to job and business opportunities, and limits their ability to improve their livelihoods. Many ASEAN member states face the challenge of large gaps in their infrastructure development, particularly in the cases of Myanmar and Cambodia. According to the International Monetary Fund's estimation, the ASEAN countries would need to invest an additional $35 billion in infrastructure development per year till 2030 to fulfill the 2030 Agenda on Sustainable Development Goals.[18]

The economic geography literature shows that infrastructure improvement could accelerate economic growth. Scaling up infrastructure investment forms an important part of many ASEAN countries' national development plans. Nevertheless, constrained by insufficient domestic investment and limited government fiscal ability, many ASEAN countries lack the requisite funds and technological capacity to develop large-scale infrastructure projects without external assistance.

External development financing is required for the infrastructure-underdeveloped but cashstrapped countries. It is perfectly normal for developing countries to seek to accelerate infrastructure construction by using borrowing-financing tools, given their huge investment needs and domestic financial restraints. The salient question is how to balance infrastructure development needs and domestic financial sustainability.

Connectivity based on infrastructure development is the key to China's BRI and the key selling point in encouraging the regional

---

[18] International Monetary Fund, ASEAN progress towards sustainable development goals and the role of the IMF. September 27, 2018, pp. 1–45.

countries' participation. The infrastructure connectivity centered BRI could be instrumental in boosting economic growth and improving people's living standards through infrastructure building, thus contributing to poverty reduction in the region and beyond. Many of the low-income and developing countries in the region have an urgent need to attract Chinese investments to fund infrastructure development and stimulate their domestic economic growth.

https://doi.org/10.1142/9789811257896_0007

Chapter

7

Coordinated Regulation on China– ASEAN Cross-Border E-Commerce on Medical Devices

Anyu Lee

Institute of Regulatory Science for Medical Device,
Sichuan University, Chengdu, China

javola@qq.com

Background and Significance

The global spread of the coronavirus pandemic (COVID-19) has caused major losses. During this global campaign against the common enemy, people around the world also realized that emergency medical devices such as *in-vitro* diagnostic reagents (IVD) and extracorporeal membrane oxygenation are desperately needed with difficulties in the cross-border transportation. China took the lead in putting the pandemic under control and resuming the production of anti-pandemic supplies. China could have become an important global supplier of these products but is constrained to play its role due to different rules and standards for medical products by the regulatory authorities in various countries as well as the difficulties regarding cross-border transactions and payments, leading to delays in the delivery of products and effective control at the early stage. The efficient flow of medical equipment for pandemic prevention is essential to protect the life and health of people in all countries, and is a major technical, management and ethical issue.

Despite the increasing globalization of medical devices, different standards and regulations for medical devices by various countries have not only increased non-tariff trade barriers in this industry, but also caused endogenous problems for traditional regulatory models when major public health crisis emerges. During the epidemic, cross-border e-commerce could have served as an efficient resource management and circulation platform but because of different policies in the management of the e-commerce market by various countries and the difficulties in cross-border payment, e-commerce failed to act as sufficiently as expected.

Great Potential for China–ASEAN E-commerce Development

China and ASEAN are important trading partners, and Chinese medical devices are well-recognized by institutions and people in ASEAN countries for its high-cost performance and advanced technology. However, since most of the regulatory systems for medical products in ASEAN countries adopt US or Japanese standards, Chinese medical products cannot enter the ASEAN market until they obtain FDA approval, which not only increases the cost but also delays the delivery of urgently needed devices. Therefore, China and 10 ASEAN countries (Indonesia, Malaysia, the Philippines, Singapore, Thailand, Brunei, Vietnam, Laos, Myanmar and Cambodia) need to establish regulatory coordination of medical devices that is in line with our trade volume and strengthen our collaboration in regional public health crises and increase our capacity for cross-border transportation of various medical devices. China–ASEAN regulatory coordination upon medical devices will promote the cooperation among China–ASEAN regulatory agencies in the approval and supervision on medical devices, and lay a solid foundation for the barrier-free trade of medical devices in China and ASEAN countries.

In the past decade, an integration of traditional trade and e-commerce has contributed to the rapid development of cross-border e-commerce between the two regions, making it an important part of international trade. Through online transaction and offline transportation, domestic manufacturers can directly sell retail consumer goods to foreign individual consumers or *vice versa*. As e-commerce has become an indispensable part of people's daily life, cross-border e-commerce would be the next growth point of China–ASEAN medical device trade and a defining trend for the future. China and ASEAN already have a good foundation for trade and investment cooperation. With the continuous development of Internet technology, e-commerce has become an important part of China–ASEAN trade. The 2019 China–ASEAN Foreign Ministers' Meeting designated 2020 as the Year of China–ASEAN Digital Economy Cooperation, and it was decided that the two parties would expand cooperation in e-commerce, technological innovation, 5G network and smart cities.

China is at the forefront of the development in e-commerce and does have the foundation for pragmatic cooperation with ASEAN. The development of China's e-commerce presents four characteristics: taking the lead in digital economy and strengthening development momentum; promoting full market open-up and seeking global collaboration; deepening the reforms and optimizing the regulatory environment; helping rural revitalization and reducing the urban–rural gap. In 2017, the online retail of tangible goods contributed 37.9% to the growth of total retail sales of consumer goods. In terms of innovation and development, digital technologies such as big data, cloud computing, artificial intelligence and virtual reality have created a wealth of application scenarios for e-commerce and given birth to new marketing models and business formats. When it comes to market regulation, new progress has been made in the legislation for the e-commerce industry after China published *The E-commerce Law* in 2018. The coordinated development of e-commerce and logistics express in China has yielded new experience and cities running pilot programs have achieved outstanding results in delivery vehicle management and end-user service innovation. Besides, significant progress has also been made in the commercial big data with full-fledged e-commerce platforms for statistical analysis and operation monitoring system. Therefore, we have so much experience to share with our ASEAN partners to build a regional coordinated e-commerce market.

Points of Weakness in Cross-Border E-Commerce during the Pandemic

As coronavirus impacted traditional trade models, cross-border e-commerce thus became an important trading method. During the epidemic prevention and control period, e-commerce guarantees the daily lives of residents and efficiently distributes emergency anti-epidemic products; medical devices merchants regard e-commerce platforms as an important channel to distribute personal hygiene protection products such as masks and hand sanitizers. Cross-border e-commerce should have served as an efficient regional and inter-country platform for emergency epidemic prevention and resource circulation which can distribute emergency protection products effectively based on the epidemic prevention methods of each country. However, due to the difference in e-commerce market supervision of various countries, cross-border payment and logistics standards hinder the normal flow of products. Moreover, scientific supervision is the basic guarantee for the safety and effectiveness of medical devices, and is the legal basis for maintaining the integrity of medical device transactions by e-commerce operators. But regulatory differences between countries have also reduced the efficiency of distribution which is particularly prominent during the epidemic. With the trend of globalization intensified, the differences in medical device standards and regulatory models in various countries have increased the non-tariff barriers to medical device trade, resulting in many endogenous problems in traditional medical device regulatory models when it comes to major public health safety incidents. Therefore, China and ASEAN countries should strengthen the coordination of e-commerce market supervision and medical device product supervision to lay a solid foundation for joint resolution of major public health incidents in the future.

Supervision and Coordination to Eliminate Barriers and Obstacles

Important prerequisites for promoting the development of China–ASEAN cross-border e-commerce for medical devices are: establishing product standards and protecting intellectual property rights; eliminating regulatory barriers to the circulation of medical devices; resolving disputes over cross-border e-commerce transactions; nurturing young talents and key enterprises in e-commerce; achieving logistics standardization; diversifying currencies for payment as well as the application of a clearing system. We suggest that China and ASEAN countries immediately carry out practical cooperation in the following areas:

- Establish a normalized communication mechanism for medical device regulators in China and ASEAN countries to promote mutual understanding in regulatory mechanisms, product standards and testing methods so as to better support each other in the collaborative efforts for regional supervision. Exchange experience in the policymaking of medical device supervision policies and the corresponding practices so that ASEAN countries can better understand China's regulatory standards in this industry and lower non-tariff trade barriers between the two sides.
- China can help ASEAN countries cultivate medical device supervisory talents with global perspectives and act with a spirit of cooperation, so as to prepare a talent pool for promoting regional and even global regulatory harmonization of medical devices. At the same time, China and ASEAN could jointly promote the

coordination of product standards and the collaboration of legislation on intellectual property protection; improve cross-border e-commerce laws and regulations so as to establish a *China–ASEAN regulatory harmonization for the e-commerce of medical devices*, through which businesses in this industry can develop in a healthy and orderly manner.

- Establish widely accepted standards for e-commerce logistics. Cross-border logistics covers a bigger area and involves more countries, which also means that more restrictions might be attached to this area, such as differentiated software/hardware development and logistics standards, thus putting more restrictions on the coordination of cross-border logistics. At the same time, differences in habits, technologies, concepts and languages will further increase the difficulty in the development of cross-border logistics. In addition, cross-border logistics will also be directly or indirectly affected by tariffs, costs and distance. Innovation on cross-border logistics is key to the development of this industry. In this regard, it is essential to strengthen the coordinated development between cross-border logistics, logistics network, cross-border e-commerce and multimodal transportation so as to lay a foundation for further development.

- Establish a dispute resolution mechanism for disputes over cross-border e-commerce transactions. At present, the Consumer Rights Protection Law is a temporary medium for handling cross-border e-commerce consumption disputes, but there is no specific mechanism yet to resolve these disputes. In contrast, dispute resolution mechanisms in Europe and the United States are relatively diversified. Establishing an online dispute resolution (ODR) system is a systematic project, involving basic standards, shared standards, application standards as well as management standards, etc., covering government management, platform operation, workflow, technical coordination, third-party agency services, dispute handling and many other aspects. At present, the number of complaints or reports from overseas consumers received by China's market supervision authorities is relatively small, but this does not mean that China's cross-border e-commerce platform services and products are flawless: perhaps this is because there are no accessible channels for complaints from overseas consumers. Therefore, it is essential to establish a China–ASEAN consumer dispute standard system and governance mechanism after the examination of theoretical analysis (legal status and content coverage, etc.), practical significance (implementation, management system and procedure setting, etc.) and market application (market supervision, identification, information sharing and information disclosure, etc.).

Conclusion

The China–ASEAN relation presents great vitality with multilevel, wide-area, and all-round development momentum. Specifically, there will be "clearer" development path, "greater" mutual-trust, "more stable" economic growth, "more frequent" people-to-people exchanges, and a "bigger say" on the international arena for both parties. China and ASEAN have established comprehensive dialogue mechanisms among national leaders, ministers of foreign affairs, officials at the ministerial level and other senior officials. The friendly relationship and people-to-people exchanges, as well as the cultures among ASEAN countries, have established the societal foundation for the bilateral development. At this new starting point, this relation will step into a new stage. In terms of economy and trade, ASEAN and China's economies are highly integrated, and bilateral trade volume has maintained steady upward momentum, reaching US$291.85 billion in the first half of 2019. ASEAN (including Indonesia, Malaysia, the Philippines, Singapore, Thailand, Brunei, Vietnam, Laos, Myanmar, Cambodia) has surpassed the United States to become China's second largest trading partner, and China–ASEAN economic and trade relations have made landmark progress.

China and ASEAN will launch multilateral collaboration among cross-border e-commerce companies on emergency medical devices, explore a working mechanism for the efficient and reasonable distribution of emergency medical devices when international public health crises occur; discuss important aspects of a *China–ASEAN regulatory harmonization for the e-commerce of medical devices* concerning the framework, standards, settlement and governance; promote regulatory harmonization and economic and trade cooperation; and bring benefits to the public and SMEs. Hopefully, in the near future, we can achieve the following goals with our joint efforts:

- Promoting regulatory harmonization for medical equipment between China and ASEAN member countries (Indonesia, Malaysia, the Philippines, Singapore, Thailand, Brunei, Vietnam, Laos, Myanmar and Cambodia), so as to enhance coordination in regional public health security and improve the supply capacity for the cross-border distribution of medical equipment. Such a mechanism may help realize the harmonization between regulators on the approval and supervision of medical equipment, and provide a solid foundation for further market access.
- Establishing a unified regional market for medical device e-commerce. Under the guidance of innovative international trade, all parties can take emergency medical device cross-border e-commerce as an opportunity to promote the regulatory harmonization of medical device supervision, encourage the interconnection of online transactions between China and ASEAN countries, improve the China–ASEAN online trade business environment, as well as promote China and ASEAN's international trade to further development.
- Supporting the construction of ASEAN's medical device logistics infrastructure and meeting the demand for extensive coverage of the mobile network by building a China–ASEAN Connectivity mechanism for the e-commerce of medical devices. Currently, Malaysia and Indonesia have chosen Chinese technology for 5G applications, and other ASEAN countries also have broad market prospects for 5G development.
- Improving public health response capabilities. All parties may explore a unified market of China–ASEAN cross-border e-commerce, use digital currency and other modern technologies

for cross-border payment, and give full play to the extensive coverage of mobile network to improve the regional distribution capacity of emergency anti-epidemic supplies, so that China and ASEAN countries can take joint action against the pandemic, work together to build a regional anti-pandemic community and contribute to the worldwide against this common enemy.

- Helping ASEAN countries to reduce the gap between urban and rural areas. E-commerce can promote the development of SMEs in poverty-stricken areas, and promote the entry of SMEs into large markets, thereby having an industry-driven effect on remote villages and benefiting people in the ASEAN region. In the post-pandemic world, cross-border e-commerce is the most important carrier and model to promote open economy with digital technologies. The goal of establishing a *China–ASEAN regulatory coordination for the e-commerce of medical devices* is to adapt to outside changes in the global landscape, promote open economic development and deepen China–ASEAN economic cooperation and, further, prepare for the establishment of a unified e-commerce market under the *Regional Comprehensive Economic Partnership Agreement* (RCEP). The project will pool together experts and scholars from ASEAN countries, government officials, industry professionals and world-class senior experts from other countries to conduct special meetings to systematically discuss the top-level design, basic frameworks, implementation methods, public policies and governance approaches in the *China–ASEAN regulatory harmonization for the e-commerce of medical devices*, and propose solutions that are acceptable, compatible and operable for multiple parties.

Chapter

8

ASEAN–China Partnership for Sustainable Development: Assessment of ASEAN–China Solutions toward Carbon Neutrality Goal

Bounphieng Pheuaphetlangsy

Institute of Foreign Affairs of Lao PDR, Vientiane, Laos

b.pheuaphetlangsy2020@gmail.com

Introduction

Climate change has become one of the most significant global challenges threatening socio-economic and human security. There has been overwhelming scientific evidence to prove that climate change is real, for instance, the raising global temperature, the melting polar ice, the rising sea level and devastating disasters.[1] According to a recent report by the National Aeronautics and Space (NASA 2021),

---

[1] https://www.undp.org/content/undp/en/home/sustainable-development-goals/goal-13-climate-action.html.

the average surface temperature has risen by about 2.12°F (1.18°C) since the late 19th century, with most of the rising took place in the past four decades. Greenhouse gases (CO_2) increasingly emitted by human activities, including burning of fossil fuel for electricity, heat and transportation are scientifically proven to be the major cause of such a rising global temperature.[2]

Therefore, to mitigate climate change, it is imperative that global emissions be reduced, and climate change action was put on the UN 2030 agenda (SDG 13).[3] More importantly, countries adopted Paris Agreement in 2015 during the 21st Conference of Parties when all parties including the 10 member states of the Association of Southeast Asian Nations (ASEAN) and China pledged their carbon emissions reduction targets to limit the global warming below 2 or even 1.5°C.[4] Since then, more and more countries and regions have announced the carbon neutrality (Net Zero CO_2) targets. China is one of those nations when President Xi Jinping declared China's climate pledge during the 75th session of the United Nations General Assembly (UNGA) that China will bring its emissions down to net zero by 2060.[5]

In fact, two decades ago before COP 21 took place, the United Nations Framework Convention for Climate Change (UNFCCC) had formulated various environmental policies and market-based instruments (MBIs), which include carbon tax and emissions trading schemes, aiming to achieve the global emissions targets. Specifically speaking, the purpose of the MBIs is to provide economic incentives for decarbonization by imposing carbon prices on carbon/energy-intensive producers so that they will find ways to pollute less by choosing to invest more in clean technologies. Also, it is believed that increased prices will encourage customers to consume more

---

[2] https://climate.nasa.gov/evidence/.
[3] Goal 13, UNDP.
[4] UNFCCC, *The Paris Agreement*. 2015.
[5] Normile, Dennis, China's bold climate pledge earns praise — But is it feasible, 2020, *Science*, 370(6512), pp. 17–18.

efficiently.[6] Accordingly, ASEAN and China have incorporated those tools in their strategies to achieve their climate targets.

This chapter will evaluate the solutions to achieving carbon neutrality recently implemented by ASEAN and China. It is argued that striving to completely decarbonize offers both opportunities and challenges for both ASEAN and China; and it is difficult for both ASEAN and especially China to turn their climate pledge into reality within the given time due to the fact that the economies of ASEAN and China are mainly driven by carbon-intensive-energy like fossil fuel and gas. However, before providing detailed justifications for such arguments, this chapter will review the current frameworks, mechanisms, policies, strategies and projects related to ASEAN–China cooperation in environmental field specially climate changes. Finally, conclusion will be made and recommendations offered for promoting sustainable development cooperation between ASEAN and China in order to achieve the SDGs in term of environmental protection.

Current Endeavors

ASEAN–China partnership has been developed and elevated to a high level rapidly within a short period of time. The year 2021 marks the 30th Anniversary of ASEAN–China Dialogue relations and the 18th Anniversary of ASEAN–China Strategic Partnership, respectively. During the past three decades, ASEAN–China cooperation has been expanded in various areas such as politics, economy, trade and investment. Specifically, under the socio-cultural cooperation, the environmental protection is prioritized by ASEAN and China.

In order to achieve the UN 2030 Agenda for Sustainable Development, particularly the environmental protection, ASEAN–China is one of the actors that actively promote sustainable development through regional cooperation via the strategies and action plans as follows:

---

[6] Romain, Pirard, "Market-based instruments for biodiversity and ecosystem services: A lexicon." *Environmental Science & Policy*, 2012, pp. 59–68.

The first ASEAN–China Strategy on Environmental Protection Cooperation 2009–2015 was adopted during the 11th ASEAN–China Summit in Singapore in 2007. The strategy was broken down into action plans such as Action Plan I (2011–2013) and Action Plan II (2014–2015). The implementation of action plans covered the ASEAN–China environmental cooperation forum held annually from 2011–2015 under various themes. ASEAN–China Green Envoys Program provided seminar and workshops on green development and environmental management, biodiversity and ecological conservation cooperation between the ASEAN–China environmental cooperation center (CAEC) and ASEAN center for biodiversity (ACB), cooperation on environmental industry and technologies, and made China–ASEAN environment outlook in line with joint research activities.

The second ASEAN–China Strategy on Environmental Protection Cooperation 2016–2020 (it is the Action Plan III afterward) was adopted after the achievement we have made in the first strategy. The implementation of the Action Plan III had focused on nine priority areas namely: Policy Dialogue and Exchange, Environmental Data and Information Management, Environmental Impact Assessment, Biodiversity and Ecological Conservation, Environmental Industry and Technology for Green Development, Environmentally Sustainable Cities, Environmental Education and Public Awareness, Institutional and Human Capability Building, and Joint Research.

Recently, during the 23rd ASEAN–China Summit[7] in 2020 in Vietnam, ASEAN and China have welcomed the designation of 2021 as the ASEAN–China Year of Sustainable Development Cooperation. In doing so, the two parties have agreed to place the importance on climate change and environmental protection, disaster prevention and mitigation, and poverty alleviation as a whole. It is well aware that the issues concerning sustainable development in all dimensions are crucial and ASEAN–China cooperation would contribute to the implementation of the *Paris Agreement* as well as the UN 2030

---

[7] ASEAN, Chairman's statement of the 23rd ASEAN-China Summit 2020 (accessed March 5, 2021). https://asean.org/wp-content/uploads/47-Final-Chairmans-Statement-of-the-23rd-ASEAN-China-Summit.pdf.

Agenda for Sustainable Development. In this regard, ASEAN–China would continue to implement the first and the second ASEAN–China Strategies on the Environmental Protection Cooperation in the form of the third strategy 2021–2025 (herein after referred to as the Action Plan IV).

Specifically, China has set its emissions target. That is to achieve its carbon neutrality by 2060 through three term goals[8] including: (1) Short-Term Goal: Electrification is the Core Task, China is aimed at weaning all sectors off fossil fuel and turn to electricity. (2) Mid-Term Goal: Large-Scale Commercial Application of Hydrogen. China is accelerating research on and application of technologies and reducing costs by applying hydrogen technology to achieve maturity and scale. According to the Development Plan for the New Energy Automobile Industry (2021–2035) issued by The General Office of the State Council in November 2020, China focuses on vigorously developing hydrogen fuel cells and hydrogen energy storage and transportation technologies. And (3) Long-Term Goal: Supplementary Role of Biomass Fuel and Carbon Capture. It is confirmed that biomass fuel could provide China's transportation sector with the energy equivalent of 30 million tons of standard coal, or 5% of the total energy needed by 2060. It is worth mentioning that power to fuel is also a possible future solution for carbon-free aviation and heavy transportation.

Likewise, ASEAN AMS has strongly implemented its commitment submitted to the UNFCCC in line with their ratification on the *Paris Agreement* and communicated their National Determined Contributions (NDCs) to enhancing global response to climate change. In order to turn "the sustainable climate" into practice, AMS, under the ASEAN Socio-Cultural Community (ASCC) Blueprint 2025, has set its emission target[9] to (1) achieve the energy transition

---

[8] Liu Qiyu and Zhe Wang, How China can achieve carbon-neutral transport by 2060 (accessed March 6, 2021). https://rmi.org/how-china-can-achieve-carbon-neutral-transport-by-2060/.

[9] ASEAN, ASEAN joint statement to the United Nations climate action summit 2019 (accessed March 8, 2021). https://asean.org/asean2020/wp-content/uploads/2021/01/AJSCC-to-UN-Climate-Action-Summit-2019-ADOPTED.pdf.

by reducing energy intensity by more than 21.9% compared to its 2005 levels, up to 30% by 2025 and to increase the proportion of renewable energy by 23% by 2025. (2) Achieving the land transport by reducing the average fuel consumption per 100 km of new light-duty vehicles sold in ASEAN by 26% between 2015 and 2025, and AMS is also (a) introducing and strengthening fiscal policy measures based on fuel economy or on CO_2 emissions at national level where applicable to incentivize consumers to purchase efficient vehicles; and (b) promoting the adoption of national fuel consumption standards for light-duty vehicles in all markets, striving toward a regional standard in the long term.

ASEAN–China Environmental Cooperation Achievements

ASEAN and China have made several achievements in environmental cooperation over the years. One of the most prominent successes of ASEAN–China environmental protection cooperation is the adoption of China–ASEAN Strategy on Environmental Protection Cooperation in 2009. Following that, ASEAN and China formulated ASEAN–China Environmental Cooperation Action Plans 2009–2015. Consequently, like mentioned previously numerous activities have been implemented under the framework of cooperation strategy, including the annual ASEAN–China Environmental Cooperation Forum from 2011 to 2015 under different themes; the China–ASEAN Green Envoys program; Cooperation on Biodiversity and Ecology Conservation; ASEAN–China Cooperation Framework for Environmentally Sound Technology and Industry; and joint research activities, in which ASEAN and China worked together to prepare the China–ASEAN Environment Outlook under the themed "Towards Green Development."[10] In addition, the China–ASEAN Environmental Cooperation Centre (CAEC) was officially established in Beijing, China in 2011. The center aims to further

---

[10] Ministry of Environmental Protection of China and Environmental Authorities of ASEAN, *ASEAN–China Strategy on Environmental Cooperation Action Plan (2016–2020)*, (n.p., n.d.), pp. 1–2.

strengthen the collaboration between China and ASEAN and contribute to environmental sustainability in the region.[11]

In order to ensure the continuity of cooperation and implementation of the Strategy, the ASEAN–China Environmental Cooperation Action Plan 2016–2020 have been developed, aiming to provide guidance to ASEAN and China to further collaborate in the areas of priority for the next 5 years to support the national environmental strategies of China and individual AMS. The Plan of Actions include some of the activities from the Action Plan 2009–2015 and proposed new activities including the Policy Dialogue and Exchange with the intention to provide various platforms for policymakers from China and ASEAN to discuss environmental issues in the region, share experiences of environmental management, promote collaboration through joint actions and put the consensus reached by leaders of ASEAN and China into effect; ASEAN–China Environment Ministerial Meeting, which serves as a high-level dialogue mechanism for ASEAN–China environmental cooperation; Cooperation on Environmental Data and Information Management and ASEAN–China Joint Platform on Environmental Information Sharing enhances the capacity of AMS and China to collect, process and use environmental data and information to support the progress of SDGs; Capacity Building Programme on Environmental Impact Assessment, which will be implemented for AMS and China's environmental officers, technicians and professionals in order to enhance their capacity to make strategic and environmental impact assessment through workshops, training courses, joint research and transfer of technology; Cooperation on Environmentally Sustainable Cities through knowledge and experience sharing boosts ecologically friendly urban development; and Environmental Education and Public Awareness which is conducted through the implementation of the ASEAN–China Green Envoys Programme

---

[11] ASEAN, ASEAN and China officially launch the establishment of the China–ASEAN environmental cooperation centre (accessed March 8, 2021). https://asean.org/asean-and-china-officially-launch-the-establishment-of-the-china-asean-environmental-cooperation-centre/.

with the objective to enhance public awareness on environmental protection.[12]

Although it is difficult to measure the tangible outcomes of these joint activities, they marked a critical step forward for ASEAN–China environmental protection cooperation. Furthermore, they indicate that ASEAN and China have commenced to place importance on the environmental protection in the region, and they play an essential role in mitigating climate change by setting climate targets and taking action toward such targets. This hopefully will influence other regional and sub-regional cooperation mechanisms to follow suit.

Opportunities

In making efforts to addressing climate change, it creates opportunities for AMS and China to accelerate industrial development on clean and renewable energy. Combined with ASEAN's growing demand for energy, there would have to be a major shift to the use of clean and renewables for electricity in particular, solar power, wind power and biomass to achieve such ambitious goals. If ASEAN accelerate decarbonization, it could seize business opportunities in clean and renewable energy sectors and reach its collective goal of achieving 23% renewable energy in the total primary energy supply by 2050.[13] The region is also rich in renewable energy sources and thus, have the potential to tap these areas. In fact, many countries in the region have already put policy instruments in place such as feed-in-tariff, tax incentives and capital subsidies to attract both domestic and foreign investment in the renewable energy sector. Although investment costs in this area are huge, the long-term benefits are well worth it. China, for instance, would need US$13.5–US$15 trillion to invest in renewable

---

[12] Ministry of Environmental Protection of China and Environmental Authorities of ASEAN, *ASEAN–China Strategy on Environmental Cooperation (2016–2020)* (China: 2016).

[13] ASEAN, ASEAN holds the key role in the energy transition in Asia, *ASEAN Climate Change and Energy Project* (accessed March 8, 2021). https://accept. aseanenergy.org/asean-holds-the-key-role-in-the-energy-transition-in-asia/.

energy projects in order to reach its emissions targets. In this connection, the International Renewable Energy Agency (IRENA) revealed that such investments will make a contribution to the GDP growth, creating employment opportunities.[14] Renewable energy technology could also bring revenues for the country. In fact, in the first quarter of 2019, China's solar component export value reached US$17.74 billion, according to Photovoltaic Industry Association.[15]

AMS may also benefit from technological development, in particular the Carbon Capture, Utilization and Storage (CCUS) technology, which is seen as vital to decarbonization goal. The ASEAN region is considered as a viable location for the development and deployment of CCUS technology as countries like Indonesia, Vietnam, the Philippines and Thailand have plenty of storage capacity to bury carbon dioxide.[16] This means that there is a room for fostering ASEAN–China cooperation on CCUS through the transfer of low-carbon energy technologies, which would have a significant impact on technological capacity development in developing nations of ASEAN. In addition, if AMS and China were able to reduce the output of CO_2, it would allow them to sell their extra allowances to larger polluters at a market price through the emissions trading schemes (ETS).[17]

To achieve the "Net Zero Carbon emissions," there must be a transition from gas and diesel engines to Electric Vehicles (EVs). The Southeast Asia region is well known for their roads jam-packed with

---

[14] Chen, Baiping, How China can achieve carbon neutrality by 2060, *Boston Consulting Group* (accessed March 9, 2021). https://www.bcg.com/publications/2020/how-china-can-achieve-carbon-neutrality-by-2060.

[15] Xu, Muyu and David Stanway, China solar exports hit 58 GW in the first three quarter of 2019, *Reuters* (accessed March 9, 2021). https://www.reuters.com/article/us-china-solarpower-idUSKBN1Y906Z.

[16] Rabintra, Nepal, Han Phoumin and Abiral Khatri, "Green technological development and deployment in the Association of Southeast Asia Economies (ASEAN) — At crossroads or roundabout," *Sustainability*, 2021, 13(758), p. 9.

[17] Ha, Tim, The time is ripe for carbon pricing in Southeast Asia, *Eco-Business* (accessed March 9, 2021). https://www.eco-business.com/news/the-time-is-ripe-for-carbon-pricing-in-southeast-asia/.

cars and motorcycles. Vehicle ownership in the region is also pro-jected to beat other regions in the world. Apart from the traffic con-gestion, another major concern is air pollution caused by these vehicles.[18] EVs, however, could come into play. ASEAN's abundant natural resources could be a key strength in attracting investment in EV sector. Indonesia, for instance, is rich in raw materials such as zinc and manganese, which are needed for EV batteries.[19] Thus, ASEAN could be a new assembly plant and market for China as the country is the world's largest producer and buyer of electric vehicles, which accounted for half of all electric vehicles made and sold in the world in 2018.[20] When more and more EVs are on the road, it is hoped that they will help displace large amounts of gas and diesel consumption, and thus reduce greenhouse gas emissions.

ASEAN and China's greenhouse gas emissions mitigation efforts could be potentially associated with its socio-economic prospects. As ASEAN member countries adopt more sustainable energy, they could satisfy national demands as well as potentially export excess electricity, which would generate income to the counties. Renewable industries could also provide green job opportunities. It is, for instance, esti-mated by the IRENA that the region's clean and renewable energy sectors would employ approximately 1.7–2.2 million workers by 2030.[21] Similarly, China's green sectors would create 4.4–7.8 million new jobs by 2030.[22] What's more, CO_2 reduction could literally

---

[18] The future of electric vehicles in ASEAN, *The ASEAN Post* (accessed March 9, 2021). https://theaseanpost.com/article/future-electric-vehicles-asean.

[19] Growing EV industry in ASEAN, *The ASEAN Post* (accessed March 9, 2021). https://theaseanpost.com/article/growing-ev-industry-asean.

[20] Thornton, Alex, China is winning the electric vehicle race, *World Economic Forum* (accessed March 9, 2021). https://www.weforum.org/agenda/2019/02/china-is-winning-the-electric-vehicle-race/.

[21] Renewable energy development to create jobs in Southeast Asia, *The ASEAN Post* (accessed March 9, 2021). https://theaseanpost.com/article/renewable-energy-development-create-jobs-southeast-asia.

[22] World Bank Group, Seizing the opportunity of green development in China (accessed June, 2012). https://www.greengrowthknowledge.org/sites/default/files/downloads/resource/Supporting_Report_3_WB.pdf.

mean better air quality for all, which help reduce health risks caused by air pollution. However, in spite of opportunities, there are numerous challenges associated with addressing the issue of climate change, specifically implementing the solutions to achieving net zero emissions target made by not only ASEAN and China but also the rest of the world.

Challenges

Although both ASEAN and China have set their emissions reduction targets and come up with their national environmental policies and strategies toward their goals,[23] implementing those policies is not straight-forward. This is because that there are myriad challenges and obstacles that need to be deliberately coped with.

The first (perhaps the biggest) challenge is the development gaps among the AMS and between ASEAN and China. Such gaps, could result in different expectations and needs between countries in the region, particularly between the more developed and least developed countries in terms of setting their national emissions reduction targets and taking action to reach those goals. For instance, Singapore, the wealthiest nation in ASEAN seems to place more importance on the quality of the air and the overall environmental condition, whereas the rest of AMS, specifically Cambodia, Laos, Myanmar and Vietnam, where poverty remains a pressing issue tend to focus more on economic aspect rather environmental well-being when making development policies. This is because there is an urgent need for the governments of these countries to uplift their citizens from the extreme poverty. Therefore, it is difficult for these countries to balance between economic growth and environmental protection. It is true that rapid growth has been witnessed in this region over past few decades, but the unwanted-by-product of such growth is a significant

---

[23] Wang, Pu, Lei Liu, Xianchun Tan, and Zhu Liu, "Key challenges for China's carbon emissions trading program," *Wiley Interdisciplinary Reviews: Climate Change*, 2019, 10(5), p. e599.

increase in CO_2 emissions.[24] Moreover, when it comes to making collective action at regional level to address the issue of climate change, countries are reluctant to do so due to the fact that they have different expectations and needs. However, over the recent years they have begun to take the environmental concerns into account, particularly when countries came to recognize that growth derived from exploitation of natural resources are unsustainable.

In fact, the situation in which countries had different expectations and needs occurred in the EU, where climate policies are learned by the rest of the world. For example, the old EU members including UK (former EU member), Belgium and Denmark seemed to be very enthusiastic about implementing the EU ETS and other environmental policies, whereas new members, such as Poland, Romania, Bulgaria and other Central Eastern European Countries/CEEC or "economies in transition" were reluctant to implement those policies, specifically to impose carbon taxes on their industries. This made it difficult to reach agreements among them regarding the implementation of their climate policies. Moreover, in some situations, this has resulted in strong opposition or conflicts among them. Evidence of such situations can be seen when the CEEC led by Poland opposed the revision of the EU ETS; these countries strongly opposed the plan to replace allocation with full auctioning because their fossil-fuel based economies (their industries) would be adversely affected by such ETS.[25] This could explain why the parties to the *Paris Agreement* set the principle of "common but differentiated responsibilities and respective capabilities."[26] However, this principle can hinder some countries in the world including ASEAN members from making progress toward its decarbonization target as countries with more

---

[24] Rifa'i, Achmad and Nurvita Retno Dewi, "Environmental quality and economic growth: Evidence from 10 ASEAN countries," *Sustinere: Journal of Environment and Sustainability*, 2018, 2(2), pp. 65–75.

[25] Hepburn, C., M. Grubb, K. Neuhoff, F. Matthes and M. Tse, "Auctioning of EU ETS phase II allowances: How and why," *Climate Policy*, 2006, 6(1), pp. 137–160.

[26] UNFCC, *The Paris Agreement* (accessed March 6, 2021). https://unfccc.int/files/meetings/paris_nov_2015/application/pdf/paris_agreement_english_.pdf.

capacities (developed nations) are reluctant to shoulder the burden, particularly climate finance.

Another challenge faced by the solutions to decarbonization is that both AMS and China are carbon-intensive-energy based-economies. Fossil fuel, for instance, accounts for more than 86% of the total energy consumption in ASEAN in the recent years, whereas renewable energy makes up only 14%.[27] Similarly, China the so-called "the world's factory" has been powered mainly by coal. Since 2011, coal has been consumed by China more than the rest of the world combined. In 2019, coal made up for almost 60%,[28] and fossil fuel combined with gas accounted for about 27% of the total China energy consumption while renewables were responsible for the rest.[29] These figures indicate that both ASEAN and China are mainly driven by carbon-intensive energy.

In addition, ASEAN and China are in the process of industrialization, modernization and urbanization aimed at boosting socio-economic development. This has resulted in rapid economic growth, especially in the East Asia including China, known as "economic miracle" over the past decades although countries in the region experience economic contraction due to the spread of COVID-19. In this connection, the combined population of ASEAN and China is more than 2.1 billion people (as of early 2021), making up of almost 30% of the world population.[30] It is also projected that the population of

[27] ASEAN Energy Center, ASEAN energy country profiles 2020 (accessed March 5, 2020). https://youtu.be/Ajlo4L0FmnI'.

[28] China Power, How is China's energy footprint changing (accessed December 9, 2021). https://chinapower.csis.org/energy-footprint/.

[29] Hart, Christina, Carbon-neutral China by 2060: Governance challenges of achieving China's net-zero emissions plan (accessed January 15, 2021). https://www.researchgate.net/publication/348522751_Carbon-Neutral_China_by_2060_Governance_Challenges_of_Achieving_China's_Net-Zero_Emissions_Plan/citation/download.

[30] The World Population Review, ASEAN Countries Association of Southeast Asian Nations 2021. https://worldpopulationreview.com/country-rankings/asean-countries.

ASEAN and China will continue to grow at an average rate of 0.85% and 0.16% per annum respectively over the next decade and a half.[31] Given the economic and population growth, it is inevitable that the demand for energy consumption is increasingly high over the past decades. For instance, a study by the Asian Development Bank (ADB) Institute (2020), reveals that:

> ASEAN is one of the most important participants in the global economy and energy portfolio and was considered the seventh largest economy and the fifth-largest investment destination in 2016. As one of the largest economic coalitions, ASEAN has a cumulative GDP of USD2.5+ trillion. This robust economic growth has resulted in an increase in energy demand by 70% compared to the energy demand in 2000 and the region currently accounts for 5% of the total global energy demand.[32]

Similarly, due to its economic reforms over the past four decades, China's economy has grown rapidly with the average GDP growth rate at 9.5% until 2018, making China one of the world's fastest growing economies and the world's second largest economy (with GDP of US$14.34 trillion as of 2019)[33] after the US. With such rapid growth, China is able to help more than 800 million people out of poverty. Remarkably, by the end of 2020, China has announced that its success in eliminating extreme poverty within the nation.[34] Moreover, China has become the world's largest economy in terms of purchasing power, manufacturer and merchandise trader. This, in

---

[31] ASEAN, ASEAN+6 population forecast: Global share, aging and dependency ratio (accessed 2013). https://www.miti.gov.my/miti/resources/fileupload/ASEAN_Population%20Forecast.pdf.

[32] Yang, Liu and Riasat Noor, Energy efficiency in ASEAN: Trends and financing schemes, Asian Development Bank Institute (accessed October, 2020). https://www.adb.org/sites/default/files/publication/648701/adbi-wp1196.pdf.

[33] The World Bank, GDP(Current-US$)–China, https://data.worldbank.org/indicator/NY.GDP.MKTP.CD?locations=CN.

[34] GCTN, Zero poverty: China eliminates absolute poverty one month before self-imposed deadline (accessed March 7, 2021). https://news.cgtn.com/news/2020-11-23/China-eliminates-absolute-poverty-one-month-before-schedule-VEp8VAJJS0/index.html.

turn, has made China a major trading partner of most countries around the world including ASEAN, the U.S. and Australia. Although growth has slowed from 2018 up to now (especially due to COVID-19 pandemic), it is estimated that China's economy will continue to grow at 5.5% by 2024. Furthermore, to avoid the "middle-income trap" or to further boost economic growth, China has made innovation a top priority in its socio-economic development, especially through the "Made in China 2025" initiative declared in 2015 to upgrade and modernize China's manufacturing in 10 key sectors in order to make China a major global player in these sectors.[35]

Inevitably, such strong socio-economic development is found to be in parallel with a sharp increase in demand for energy consumption and CO_2 emissions. For instance, a study by Peng *et al.* found that the demand for energy consumption in China had doubled from 0.4 billion tons of oil equivalent (toe) from 1979 to 1994, and after 1994 the demand for energy consumption in China continued to increase drastically. By 2014, energy consumption had reached nearly 7.5 toe. Unquestionably, along with the significant increase in energy demand and CO_2 emissions had experienced similar trend.[36] This is the reason why China has become the world's largest carbon emitter overtaking the U.S. since 2007. Recently, China's CO_2 emissions account for 28% of the total global emissions, and it is projected to peak by 2030.[37] This is because of the fact that China is the world's second largest economy and the world's factory making China the top importer and consumer of energy. Another major reason for the

---

[35] Morrison, Wayne M., "China's economic rise: History, trends, challenges, and implications for the United States," *Current Politics and Economics of Northern and Western Asia*, 2019, 28(2/3), pp. 189–242.
[36] Peng, Xiujian, Philip D. Adams, and Jin Liu, "China's new growth pattern and its effect on energy demand and greenhouse gas emissions," *Global Energy Interconnection*, 2018, 1(4), pp. 428–442.
[37] Science, Can China, the world's biggest coal consumer, become carbon neutral by 2060 (accessed March 7, 2021). https://www.sciencemag.org/news/2020/09/can-china-worlds-bigger-coal-consumer-become-carbon-neutral-2060.

significant increase in CO_2 emissions is that energy structure is dominated by coal.[38]

In addition, to accommodate the increasing demand for energy consumption, the Chinese government, which was lobbied by coal industry whose interests are to be affected by climate policies, is constructing new coal-fired plants with power generation capacity of 100 GW and increases its investment in oil and gas industry abroad.[39] Once the construction of these coal-fired plants and pipeline project is completed, carbon-intensive energy like coal and fossil fuel will even take a larger proportion of the total energy consumption in China. This can be implied that carbon emissions in China might peak after 2030. In case China's emissions peak after 2030, it means China will have a shorter period of time (30 years) to bring its emissions down to zero.

This could be the reason why some critics wonder if China's emissions target is achievable. Moreover, given the upward trend in the energy consumption, those critics, especially from Western countries assert that China's climate pledge at the 75th UNGA is probably aimed at improving its image at the global stage or to even taking the opportunity to gain its leadership in global issues like climate change, and replacing the U.S. (under Trump Administration) that withdrew from Paris Agreement.[40] This is, to some extent, reasonable because all global issues can be treated as a tool to increase diplomatic influence. Conversely, the proponents of China might rebut that China is ready to play a leadership role in such an issue because China today is different from what it used to be four decades ago. In a nutshell, whether China is able to turn its climate pledge into reality is questionable.

<hr/>

[38] Yan, Li, Yigang Wei and Zhang Dong, "Will China achieve its ambitious goal? — Forecasting the CO_2 emission intensity of China towards 2030," *Energies*, 2020, 13(11), p. 2924.

[39] Science, *op. cit.*

[40] The Conversation, China just stunned the world with its step up on climate action and implication for Australia maybe huge (accessed October 8, 2020). https://theconversation.com/china-just-stunned-the-world-with-its-step-up-on-climate-action-and-the-implications-for-australia-may-be-huge-147268.

Similarly, as discussed previously ASEAN is one of the fastest grow-ing regions of the world, accompanied by a significant increase in demand for energy consumption. This has already made ASEAN as a whole one of the world's top carbon emitters. Speaking of the indi-vidual AMS, for instance, a study by ADB (2016) estimates that most of the ASEAN countries such as Indonesia, the Philippines and Vietnam will see a significant increase in CO_2 emissions. This is because all ASEAN economies are driven by carbon-intensive energy. Therefore, it is a great challenge for ASEAN to meet its emissions targets submitted to the UNFCCC. It requires a colossal amount of money for AMS to invest in their clean energy development and apply such technologies as carbon capture and sequestration (CCS) and energy efficient technolo-gies. Investment in this area will enable ASEAN to reduce its emissions in the long run. Without energy transition, it can be argued that ASEAN's climate pledge will be too far from being realized or emis-sions might even be 60% higher in 2050 compared with the level in 2010.[41]

However, it does not necessarily mean that realizing ASEAN's and especially China's promise of achieving carbon neutrality by 2060 is undoable. It is achievable but significantly challenging.

Policy Recommendations

In order to address the identified challenges associated with turning climate pledge into reality, this chapter offers some policy recommen-dations as follows:

(1) First and foremost, it needs political commitment and concerted efforts. It is required that both ASEAN and China begin to take bold action with regards to restructuring not only their energy mix but also the entire economies. In doing so, it needs a gigan-tic amount of money to accelerate investment in green

---

[41] ADB, How will ASEAN members cope with their climate change challenges (accessed March 5, 2021). https://www.adb.org/news/op-ed/how-will-asean-members-cope-their-climate-change-challenge.

development including renewable energy industry. It is, as discussed above, estimated that China will need to invest about US$13.5–15 trillion in green economic development to help curb its emissions.[42]

(2) Advanced technologies need to be applied. These include CCS and energy efficient technologies which are found to be the most critical sources of carbon emissions reduction in the long run. Investment in these technologies might be expensive, but socio-economic and environmental benefits will outweigh the costs in the long term, not mentioning mitigating the economic consequences produced by fierce climate change and extreme weather events.

(3) To ensure both countries developed and developing are able to apply the needed technologies, it is essential that technologies and expertise are transferred from the more developed to the least developed nations, and financial assistance has to be provided to help the least developed countries to step up their investment in energy transition and other related green development projects.

(4) To accelerate investment in clean energy and energy efficient technologies in sectors ranging from energy to agricultural development, the governments of both AMS and China should offer incentives to firms to apply those technologies. Also, principle of "polluter pays" has to be strictly implemented. In addition, environmental legal frameworks need to be redesigned and strictly reinforced.

(5) In this connection, institutional capacities need to be enhanced in order to ensure environmental regulatory frameworks are effectively implemented.

(6) The rate of deforestation must be decreased significantly and we need to increase forest areas. This is because deforestation is one of the major sources of carbon emission, particularly in ASEAN.

---

[42] BBC, How China can achieve carbon neutrality by 2060 (accessed March 7, 2021). https://www.bcg.com/publications/2020/how-china-can-achieve-carbon-neutrality-by-2060.

Increasing forest areas can offer the cheapest solution to decarbonization.

(7) Due to the fact that climate change is one of the greatest challenges facing the world that no single nation or region can handle it alone, regional and international cooperation is also the most important when it comes to tackling the global challenges like climate change. Therefore, cooperation at local, national, regional and international levels is a must, particularly in the area of science, technological research and development as well capacity building in terms adaptation and mitigation.

(8) The EU cooperation can be a model to look at. Not only ASEAN and China but also the other dialogue partners should learn from the experience of the EU ETS that has proven successful in promoting low carbon technologies and technology transfer as well as designing and applying market-based instruments or regulatory frameworks and environmental standards. Also, China ETS pilot projects should not be neglected. They should be reviewed and assessed thoroughly in order to learn the lessons after launching for some years, aiming at improving the system so that it will be effectively and widely applied by both China and ASEAN.

(9) There is a wide range of instruments that are needed to achieve net zero emissions, be it government's policy, rules and regulations, financial and technological incentives, but perhaps something as basic as environmental education that could really change people's attitudes and behaviors to build a green and low carbon future. It is especially important to instill into children the importance of our environment and how future generations could be affected by our actions today. Thus, equipping children with necessary tools to behave in a responsible and informed manner toward the environment will be drastically impactful.

(10) Last but not least, it is vital to improve the quality of environmental governance. This can be done by making sure that all policy decisions are pragmatic, taking into account not only

economic aspect but also political, social and significantly environmental dimensions to ensure the well-being of both human beings and physical environment. Also, policy decisions shall be made based on scientific or research-based information to minimize unintended consequences of those decisions. In this regard, environmental transparency and accountability are imperative, especially when it comes to revealing the environmental impacts of development projects in the region and reporting the progress in emissions reduction.

Chapter

9

Offline and Online Perils of Digital Platforms with the Development of E-commerce in Laos

Bounphieng Pheuaphetlungsy

Institute of Foreign Affairs of Lao PDR, Vientiane, Laos
b.pheuaphetlangsy2020@gmail.com

Introduction

Digital platforms have offered new opportunities for companies regardless of their sizes to participate in economic activities, especially trade. They can promote effectiveness and efficiency gains through lower transaction costs and better access to information. In addition, other advantages include lower consumer prices with more choices to choose from around the world, increased market access regardless of location, more affordable marketing and advertisement, more competition, better use of underutilized resources and increased flexibility for service providers. These advantages can be

137

translated into higher sales volumes, thereby higher profits for firms or business owners.

In fact, there have been studies including by Cenamor, Parida and Wincent, who conducted research on "How entrepreneurial small and medium-sized enterprises (SMEs) compete through digital platforms: The roles of digital platform capability, network capability and ambidexterity," revealing that in a highly competitive environment, digital platforms have been utilized by numerous SMEs to effectively leverage their businesses. This is because digital platforms are technological tools that allow companies to edit, publicize and disseminate information/data swiftly and quite unlimitedly.[1] They enable new products to get known widely among consumers within a relatively short period of time both in the location where the products are made and overseas. This explains why digital platforms provide companies with more competitive advantages. Cenamor and his colleagues also found that there is a link between digital technologies and companies' improved performance.[2]

This study is consistent with a study by Okhrimenko *et al.*,[3] which[3] reveals similar results. That is, digital technologies assist firms to improve their overall resources management. It also accelerates innovation and enhances supply chain management. Significantly, digitalization fosters internationalization of industries and startups. That is the reason why European Union (EU) countries acknowledge that digitalization is one of the critical impetus for competitiveness, economic development and employment growth. Consequently, it has been included in various EU initiatives, for example, the Industrial Policy for the Globalization Era, Digital Agenda for Europe and the Innovation Union.

In recent years, digital platforms such as Google, Facebook, Amazon and Alibaba have been playing an increasingly important role

---

[1] Cenamor, J., V. Parida and J. Wincent, "How entrepreneurial SMEs compete through digital platforms: The roles of digital platform capability, network capability and ambidexterity," *Journal of Business Research*, 2019, 100, pp. 196–206.

[2] *Ibid.*

[3] Okhrimenko *et al.*, "Digital transformation of the socio-economic system: Prospects for digitalization in society," *Revista ESPACIOS*, 2019, 40(38), p. 26.

in the global economy. In 2017, the combined value of digital companies with a market capitalization of more than US$100 million was estimated at more than US$7 trillion, which is 67% higher than that in 2015. The global exports of ICT services and services that can be delivered digitally grew considerably faster than the overall services exports. For example, in 2018, the value of the export of digitally delivered services was US$2.9 trillion, accounting for 50% of the global exports of services. In the least developed countries that are striving to take advantage of digital technologies, such services also tripled from 2005 to 2018.[4] This shows that digitalization is rapidly increasing both in developed and developing countries.

In addition, another significant benefit of digital platforms is that they allow supply chain and people from across the world to stay connected[5] even in the time of crisis, though there is disruption. For instance, in the midst of the spread of COVID-19 when containment and mitigation measures such as travel restrictions and social distancing have been implemented, thanks to digital platforms and ICT, business operators are still able to continue to provide their services and regional and international cooperation can still be carried on.[6]

However, it must be conceded that the benefits of digital platforms are not straight-forward to gain. According to Okhrimenko *et al.*, having digital technologies in place alone will not improve performance of firms, meaning that firms' capacities to mobilize and utilize the digital platforms are the determining factors. Besides, there are increasing concerns over the rising market power of certain platforms and the related implications for competition, data protection and ownership, consumer protection and taxation, regulation, and employment policies.[7] Apart from these concerns, digital divide between developed countries and developing or least developed

---

[4] United Nations Conference on Trade and Development, Digital Economy Report 2019, https://unctad.org/en/PublicationsLibrary/der2019_en.pdf.

[5] Tiago, M. T. P. M. B. and J. M. C. Veríssimo, "Digital marketing and social media: Why bother?" *Business Horizons*, 2014, 57(6), pp. 703–708.

[6] United Nations, Making Digital Platforms Work for Development, 2019. https://unctad.org/en/PublicationsLibrary/presspb2019d2_en.pdf.

[7] *Ibid.*

countries as well as between urban and rural areas is widening. For instance, "the United States of America and China make up of more than 75% of all patents related to block chain technologies, and they account for over 90% of the market capitalization value of the world's 70% largest digital platforms, whereas Europe's share is 4% and Africa and Latin America's together is only 1%."[8]

Moreover, the lack of ICT-related infrastructure is also a huge challenge for numerous countries including Laos that are now trying to digitalizing their economies in the hope of boosting economic growth and societal change.[9]

This chapter identifies the challenges associated with the development of e-commerce in Laos. It also examines the experience of China in digitalizing its economy, from which lessons are drawn for other countries to learn so as to ensure the effective management of digital platforms.

Background of E-commerce in Laos

In recognizing the benefits of digital technologies, Laos, like other nations, is striving to apply science and technologies in its national development processes and public services delivery.[10] Particularly, to further facilitate trade and investment, aiming at enabling domestic producers and service providers to gain better access to both domestic and overseas markets, especially ASEAN market, the GoL is promoting the development of e-commerce, which is an integral component of the ASEAN Economic Community (AEC) Blueprint 2025. To achieve such goals, the Lao Ministry of Commerce and Industry together with the Lao National Chamber of Commerce and Industry with the support from the Asian Development Bank (ADB) in 2017 created an e-commerce platform, "http//www.plaosme.com." Among other digital platforms like Facebook and Instagram that are

---

[8] *Ibid.*
[9] Afonasova, M. A., E. E. Panfilova and M. A. Galichkina, Social and economic background of digital economy: Conditions for transition, 2018.
[10] MoPI, The 8th Five-Year-Socio-Economic Development Plan, 2016.

so popular in Laos, Plaosme is a platform for both online and offline businesses.[11]

Unprecedentedly, during the spread of COVID-19 from March to May 2020, when the GoL implemented containment and mitigation measures including lockdown and social distancing, service providers, particularly those in Vientiane, were forced to explore ways to survive economically. They turned to provide their services via digital platforms. For example, local residents in Vientiane became familiar with Go Teddy and Food Panda through which they can order food and drinks from home or office. It is estimated that online orders increased "roughly between 100 and 200 to around 1,200 and 2,000 orders per day. Moreover, the number of local restaurants and small shops registered on both platforms has also multiplied threefold from 50 in January to 150 in May."[12] This indicates that digital technologies could transform the way businesses are operated and could have implications for the overall development of Laos in the future.

Nevertheless, due to the fact that e-commerce is relatively new for Laos, there are challenges that need to be addressed and so much work to be done to pave the way for e-commerce in Laos to take off. For instance, the lack of complete e-commerce related regulatory frameworks, including the law on privacy and protection of online consumers. As a result, most consumers are not confident to participate in online trade, especially when it comes to conducting online financial transactions although the law on national payment system was passed in 2017. Sometimes, there are cases of scams on Facebook and Instagram when customers order products and advance payment is made, but the ordered products are not delivered and the scammers could manage to get away with the money transferred. Another concern is that tax revenues could be lost, mainly because traditional traders have turned to sell their products and services on digital

---

[11] Leebouapao, L., P. Sitthideth, K. Douangpaseuth and Y. Suhud, E-commerce development in the Lao PDR: Some policy concerns, 2020.

[12] UNDP, How COVID could accelerate digitalization in Laos, 2020. https://www.la.undp.org/content/lao_pdr/en/home/blog/2020/how-covid19-could-accelerate-digitalization-in-laos.html.

platforms such as Facebook and Instagram, which is conducted informally and the Lao government has no specific regulatory framework in place. This literally means that whoever with or without business registration or patents are able to sell things online, while paying no tax to the government.[13]

In addition, the lack of ICT-related infrastructure including smartphones and limited Internet access with relatively high costs while slow speed, especially in rural and remote areas, are found to hinder the general public from participating in online trading. According to the ASEAN (2020), Laos' fixed broadband speed is at 13.11 Mbps slightly faster than that of Cambodia, whereas that of Singapore is at 181.47 Mbps which is the fastest in the world and Thailand at 47.35 Mbps. Within ASEAN, Singapore has the lowest Internet cost, at US$0.05 per Mbit per month, followed by Thailand (US$0.42),[14] while in Laos the average cost is at US$4.25 per Mbit per month.[15] When compared with other ASEAN member states (AMS), the Internet cost in Laos is among the highest. Also, inadequate transport infrastructure and ineffective postal systems, at times, have resulted in delayed shipping[16] although these days the number of private companies engaged in providing logistical services increases and delivery can be punctual in major cities.

In terms of online payment, it is still difficult as some of the customers, specifically those in rural and remote areas, do not have a bank account, and even they do, not all of them own a smartphone and are familiar with Internet of things (IoT) such as online banking applications. What is more, the lack of skills and abilities among domestic companies, entrepreneurs and individuals to mobilize the ICT resources to improve their performance is also obvious. This barricades the development of e-commerce in Laos.

---

[13] *Ibid.*

[14] The ASEAN Post, Singapore wins the internet speed race, 2020. https://theaseanpost.com/article/singapore-wins-internet-speed-race#:~:text=If%20Internet%20speed%20was%20an,to%20Ookla's%20Speedtest%20Global%20Index.

[15] The Ministry of Post and Telecommunications, Lao PDR.

[16] Leebouapao, L., 2020, *op. cit.*

In short, constraints in the e-commerce environment, such as incomplete regulatory infrastructure, the lack of ICT-related infrastructure including limited internet access with relatively high costs while slow speed, inadequate transport infrastructure, poor delivery systems, technological divide between urban and rural areas as well as the lack of technological knowledge hinder e-commerce from thriving in Laos. These challenges need to be tackled in order to boost the development of e-commerce so that the nation will be able to grab the opportunities that it offers.

What has GoL done so far?

Having acknowledged the challenges associated with the development of e-commerce in Laos, the GoL in recent years has made continued efforts. As discussed earlier, one of the efforts is the initiative to establish an online trading platform, "Plaosme," aiming at promoting commercial activities through opening up market opportunities for domestic firms and entrepreneurs.[17] However, this platform is still in its infant stage since this trading platform was created in 2017, and having this trade platform in place alone will not allow e-commerce to thrive, meaning there are other ingredients to be added.[18]

In addition, regulatory frameworks, for example, the Law on Prevention and Combating of Cyber Crime which was passed in 2016 with the aim of protecting personal information and database in order to maintain national peace and stability, and the law on payment system in 2017, have been put in place to maintain monetary stability and financial systems and to reduce the use of cash on trading in Laos. Yet, there are no specific laws such as the law on privacy and protection of online consumers that need be formulated and implemented to boost confidence of both service providers and online consumers.

---

[17] *Ibid.*

[18] Sengpunya, P., "ASEAN E-commerce legal framework and alignment of Lao PDR: A review," *Lentera Hukum*, 2019, 6(3), pp. 371–392.

That is to ensure that both service providers and customers can enjoy the benefits of participating in online trading.[19]

Moreover, as e-commerce is an integral part of AEC Blueprint 2025, the GoL is committing to implementing the ASEAN Work Program on E-commerce 2017–2025. Efforts have been directed to, among others, ICT-related infrastructure development, education and technology competency, consumer protection, enhancing regulatory framework, security of electronic transaction and logistics.[20]

Recently, building on the first ASEAN ICT Master Plan/AIM (2010–2015), the AIM 2020 was formulated. It aims at:

> Enabling the transformation to the digital economy and developing the human capacity necessary for this transition, facilitating the emergence of a single integrated market that is attractive to investment, talent and participation, and building a digital environment that is safe and trusted.[21]

The AIM emphasized on eight interconnected strategies as follows:

(1) *Economic development and transformation: Strengthen digital trade via establishing appropriate policy innovation and creating more options for payment and transaction particularly for SME in ASEAN.*

(2) *People integration and empowerment through ICT: Emphasize on connectivity and develop broadband and digital services to be made available and accessible for ASEAN citizens.*

(3) *Innovation: Promote and enhance smart city development in ASEAN by developing the best practice guides, policy guides, infrastructure and monitoring new technological innovation.*

---

[19] Leebouapao, L., 2020, *op. cit.*

[20] *Ibid.*

[21] Secretariat, ASEAN, The ASEAN ICT master plan 2020, Jakarta: Association of Southeast Asian Nations, 2015.

(4) *ICT infrastructure development: Strengthen Internet access by identifying new technologies and new digital divides.*

(5) *Human capacity development: Balancing demand and supply in ICT human resources by providing training programs in ASEAN and giving necessary basic skillset.*

(6) *ICT in the single market: Enlarge ASEAN market by promoting and encouraging foreign investment.*

(7) *New Media and content: Support new conduction and creation of media in ASEAN.*

(8) *Information security and assurance: Emphasize on regional data protection and develop security principal in ASEAN.*[22]

The aim is compatible with the vision and strategies of Laos for developing its e-commerce. Therefore, the GoL will continue to cooperate with the AMS to equip its people and businesses so that they can reap the benefits of digitalization. However, having plans in hand is not sufficient to guarantee that Laos together with other ASEAN countries will equally thrive in terms of fostering e-commerce. This means that it is important to learn from the successful models of e-commerce development. The following section examines the case of China's e-commerce development.

Case Study of China's E-commerce

The experience of China with regard to e-commerce can serve as a reliable reference for developing economies in the region and the world. In recent years, China has become one of the frontrunners in e-commerce in the Asia-Pacific region for a number of reasons. One of the reasons is that China is among the largest economies in East Asia with one of the largest population engaged online. According to the China Internet Network Information Center (CNNIC), up to March 2020, the Internet users in China hit 900 million. It is also important to note that among those figures, the size of rural Internet users was 255 million, accounting for 28.2%

---

[22] *Ibid.*

of the total number of the Chinese Internet users. These figures show that China is an already well-developed market for e-commerce. The CNNIC's report also cited that as of March 2020, there were around 710 million Chinese individuals shopping online and the number of mobile shoppers had climbed up to 707 million from 116 million in 2018.[23] The Chinese National Bureau of Statistics revealed that the online retail sales in China reached 7,032.6 billion yuan (approximately $1,038 billion) from January to August 2020, which accounted for approximately 24% of the total retail sales of consumer goods.[24] This is largely due to its highly advanced ICT (particularly the Internet and smartphones) in China combined with the readiness of the Internet users who have developed the needed skills that allow them to grab the opportunities that the Internet provides.

In terms of legal frameworks, there are a number of favorable e-commerce policies tailored for both sellers and consumers because the Chinese government has placed great importance to the development of e-commerce, which it regards as a crucial instrument for economic transition and opening up. For instance, one of the policy focuses is lowering the access threshold for e-retailers. The government supports the construction of e-commerce platforms by simplifying capital registration procedures, reducing entry barriers, as well as supporting the establishment of logistical infrastructure to facilitate express delivery services. Furthermore, e-commerce platform providers are prohibited from imposing unreasonable restrictions, conditions or fees on merchants so as to encourage more local merchants to take part in e-commerce activities. As a result of this, the C2C e-commerce has become a dominant in China's online retail market over the years. Another example is the revised Consumer's Interest

---

[23] CNNIC, Statistical report on internet development in China, CNNIC, 2020 (accessed August 22, 2020). https://cnnic.com.cn/IDR/ReportDownloads/202008/P020200827549953874912.pdf.

[24] National Bureau of Statistics of China, Total retail sales of consumer goods achieve positive growth in August 2020, 2020 (accessed October 14, 2020). http://www.stats.gov.cn/english/PressRelease/202009/t20200916_1789791.html.

Protection Law, which fosters consumer protection, requiring e-retailers to disclose accurate information of their products and services, establish a system to allow consumers to post comments and introduce other methods to ensure truthful information including prohibitions of misleading promotions and fake reviews. To further minimize risks, there is a risk monitoring body who could conduct online spot checks aiming at cracking down fake and poor-quality products, identifying theft and other illegal online transactions.[25]

By reducing these risks, consumers will have greater trust in the e-commerce system. Manufacturers and designers will also be encouraged to participate in Chinese online environment, due to the recognition that they will be protected against the copying of their designs and theft of intellectual property. This also means more foreign participation which creates more choices for Chinese consumers and serves to address complaints that the Chinese government has been too soft on intellectual property protection.[26]

Moreover, domestic e-commerce companies have contributed to the boom of e-commerce industry in China. Alibaba group, one of the most outstanding representatives of e-commerce providers in China, has established "Taobao village," which allows grassroots entrepreneurs to participate in the digital economy. Across China, the number of Taobao villages has exceeded 4,000 as of June 2019.[27] With the use of Taobao marketplace, groups of local firms work together as online merchants to trade their local specialties, enabling them to reach a wider range of consumers. Although local entrepreneurs have become a significant force behind the success of Taobao

---

[25] Hongfei, Yue, National report on e-commerce development in China, United Nations Industrial Development Organisation (UNIDO), 2017 (accessed August 22, 2020). https://www.unido.org/sites/default/files/2017-10/WP_17_2017.pdf.

[26] Clark, Eugene, China's new e-commerce law: A step in the right direction, 2019 (accessed August 22, 2020). http://www.china.org.cn/opinion/2019-01/09/content_74355741.htm.

[27] Jing, Wang, Taobao Villages Driving "Inclusive Growth" in Rural China, *Alizila*, November 25, 2019. https://www.alizila.com/taobao-villages-driving-inclusive-growth-rural-china/.

villages, Alibaba has provided numerous support, which is essential for the survival of new businesses. The support includes the development of express delivery routes and provision of a large amount of bank loans for the local businesses.

On top of that, favorable government programs include training, infrastructure, public services, and a business-friendly environment to support rural e-retailers in establishing online stores.[28] In addition, to make online shopping easier for consumers, Alibaba has introduced Alipay, a mobile payment application, which is safe, convenient and useful in daily life activities including online shopping.

Discussions

Having examined the case of China's e-commerce, it can be seen that China's relentless efforts on advancing its ICT infrastructure have led the country to be one of the largest nations having the highest population of Internet users. Consequently, the exponential rise in the number of Internet users has potentiated the growth of e-commerce in China. Online trading has become more convenient in China due to the improvement of physical infrastructure including roads and express delivery routes enabling distribution services in rural areas and ensuring reliable and fast delivery. In addition to hard infrastructure, soft infrastructure including a reliable Internet network, Internet coverage and the emergence of fintech, which makes banking accessible even in remote villages, makes the online transactions more convenient than ever before. These are factors that boost the number of consumers engaging in electronic transactions, while Laos has limited ICT infrastructure such as lack of access to smartphones, high-speed and low-cost Internet and online banking, limited digital knowledge in rural areas and ineffective logistical systems mainly attributed to the inadequate transport infrastructure. These factors hinder Lao population to fully enjoy e-commerce.

---

[28] Lulu, Fan, Taobao villages: Rural e-commerce and low-end manufacturing in China, East-West Wire, 2019 (accessed September 14, 2020). https://www.east-westcenter.org/news-center/east-west-wire/taobao-villages-rural-e-commerce-and-low-end-manufacturing-in-china.

What's more, China's e-commerce policy frameworks are also behind the success of its e-commerce industry. The Chinese government pays attention to designing e-commerce policies that fit the needs of stakeholders involved in the electronic transactions. E-commerce platform providers are highly encouraged by favorable policies regarding business set-up. Meanwhile these providers are prohibited to impose unreasonable restrictions or entry fees which can discourage e-merchants to join their platforms. This in turn would encourage more local traders to take part in online trade. In customers' point of view, more e-retailers also mean more options to choose from. The Chinese government also places importance on protecting the online consumers. China's consumer protection policy, for example, also further increases the confidence of consumers with regard to online purchase, giving them a sense of security. Meanwhile in Laos, such a policy has not yet been formulated, which also means consumers are not confident in online shopping.

The case of e-commerce in China shows that having an improved ICT infrastructure combined with favorable policies in hand does not translate the country into an advanced digital economy. Capacity of domestic e-commerce firms, local entrepreneurs and residents are also an important driving force for growth. The central government and local authorities also work hand in hand with private sectors to accelerate the growth of the digital economy by providing necessary skill training, financial and infrastructural supports for grassroots entrepreneurs to participate in e-commerce activities. For these reasons, China is able to accelerate its socio-economic development at such a fast pace. Most significantly, e-commerce industry has played an essential role as it has generated employment and income. This suggests that developing nations provided that they have appropriate policies, better developed infrastructure and other instruments with the participation of private firms, could use e-commerce to thrive in a way that benefits all aspects of society.

Policy Recommendations

Multiple efforts are needed in order to support e-commerce development in Laos, reduce digital divide and digitalize its economy so as to boost the economic growth in the country. Some key policy recommendations are drawn from examining e-commerce industry in China, which could be adapted and applied to the processes of Lao e-commerce development.

Invest in digital (soft) and hard infrastructure development

First and foremost, as Laos still lags behind in ICT infrastructure development among ASEAN member states, more efforts should be put in this field in order for the country to keep up with regional peers. Due to the fact that Laos has limited capacity and resources (capital and technology) to advance its digital infrastructure, the GoL should enhance regional and international cooperation on ICT improvement. The government should work closely with Internet-advanced countries like Singapore, China and Japan among others to build a more affordable, more widespread and higher-speed Internet access for consumers in Laos. It is recommended that Laos should also seek cooperation with other countries in order to effectively upgrade its telecommunications infrastructure to international standards.

With regard to logistics systems, although there are numerous road construction projects supported by international donors, there seems to be insufficient. Some remote villages remain inaccessible. Therefore, such cooperated projects need to be concentrated in rural areas as well as major cities. Also, cooperating with other partners including private sectors to upgrade postal systems, combined with improved roads, could facilitate delivery of goods and services. In fact, apart from China's lesson, the experience of Japan that was ranked fourth in the world and first in Asia in 2012 indicates that its modern and efficient digital infrastructure and shipping systems are the key factors underlying the success of Japanese e-commerce. In Japan, the number of private firms that provide logistics or postal services keeps increasing, promoting competition while lowering prices and improving the quality of services. That is, goods digitally ordered are delivered on time, encouraging more consumers to shop online.[29]

---

[29] Leebouapao, L., 2020, *op. cit.*

Create regulatory framework and strengthen regulatory capacity and expertise

As demonstrated by the China's case study, legal instruments are another factor behind the growth of its e-commerce. Although the GoL has passed some laws on cybersecurity in recent years, there is the absence of specific e-commerce related laws, such as Consumer's Privacy Protection law as well as favorable policies tailored for private online trading platforms and e-retailers. Therefore, it is required to speed up the e-commerce policy improvement and development in order to formalize the e-commerce industry in Laos. Having effective and enforceable e-commerce laws/policies in place would boost the consumers' confidence in online shopping and encourage more private sectors to establish online trading businesses. In addition, it is essential to build and strengthen regulatory capacity and expertise to ensure the effective implementation of digital-related laws, rules and regulations. In this connection, e-commerce tax policies should be another area to focus on in order to prevent undertaxation of digital platforms. Otherwise, the government could lose its tax revenues when more traditional merchants shift to trading online.

Mobilize private sectors to participate in e-commerce development

The success of Alibaba has shown that the private sector is key to the development of the digital economy. It is, therefore, important that the GoL mobilizes support from the private sector, who may be better-equipped in terms of technological capacity and financial resources, to build e-commerce platforms. Lessons drawn from Alibaba case also indicate that local or rural merchants are possible to participate in the online marketplace provided that they are properly trained with necessary technological skills and equipped with financial support by the online trading platform providers with the help of local authorities. More stakeholders involved in the e-commerce industry could accelerate the transformation of Lao digital economy.

Invest in digital education

Literature shows that capacities of people and firms are the factors determining how great the benefits that firms can grab. However, digital literacy in Laos is still relatively low compared with that in other countries in the region. Therefore, it is imperative to invest in digital education so as to ensure all groups in society and firms regardless of size will be able to participate in digitalization. Otherwise, digital divide will be widened.

https://doi.org/10.1142/9789811257896_0010

Chapter

10

APPGM-SDG: Malaysia's Effort to Localize SDGS in Collaboration with Members of Parliament*

Anthony Tan

All-Party Parliamentary Group Malaysia on SDG (APPGM-SDG), Secretariat, Kuala Lumpur, Malaysia
akhtan@gmail.com

IF YOU WANT TO GO FAST, GO ALONE.
IF YOU WANT TO GO FAR,
GO TOGETHER.
(Ancient African Proverb — Source Unknown)

The fundamental question that I wish to pose in this chapter is, "What is THE main challenge in bringing the SDGs down to the local level?"

Relationships

In a multidimensional world that is obsessed with Gross Domestic Product and instant gratification, one of the most daunting challenges

---

*The All-Party Parliamentary Group Malaysia on Sustainable Development Goals was established by the Parliament of Malaysia in October 2019.

153

Table 1:   Matrix of APPGM-SDG Solutions Projects Compared to the 5P Categories

People Prosperity	State	Location	Code	Categories Planet 1,2,3,4,5	Peace 7,8,9,10,11	Partnership 6,12,13,14,15	16	17	
1.1	Kedah	Pendang	SP31	1	1	0	1	1	SDG Action Plan
1.2	Kedah	Pendang	SP32	1	1	1	1	1	Eco-Tourism
2.1	Selangor	Petaling Jaya	SP14	1	1	1	1	1	Women Empowerment
2.2	Selangor	Petaling Jaya	SP15	1	1	1	1	1	Education
2.3	Selangor	Petaling Jaya	SP16	1	1	1	1	1	Inter-Agency
2.4	Selangor	Petaling Jaya	SP17	1	1	1	1	1	Crisis Management
3.1	Selangor	Selayang	SP18	1	1	1	1	1	Improvement of Flats
3.2	Selangor	Selayang	SP19	1	1	1	1	1	Skills Training-café & baking
3.3	Selangor	Selayang	SP20	1	1	1	1	1	Micro Entrepreneurship
3.4	Selangor	Selayang	SP21	1	1	1	1	1	Air-Con training
3.5	Selangor	Selayang	SP22	1	1	1	1	1	Skills Fair
3.6	Selangor	Selayang	SP23	1	1	1	1	1	Digital Marketing
3.7	Selangor	Selayang	SP24	1	1	1	1	1	Basic Malay for Refugees
3.8	Selangor	Selayang	SP25	1	1	1	1	1	Housing Census

4.1	Johor	Tanjung Piai	SP03	1	1	1	1	Waste Management & Buyback
4.2	Johor	Tanjung Piai	SP13	1	1	1	1	Eco-Tourism
5.1	Kelantan	Jeli	SP27	1	1	1	1	Fish Project
5.2	Kelantan	Jeli	SP28	1	1	1	1	Mushroom Project
5.3	Kelantan	Jeli	SP29	1	1	1	1	Eco-Tourism
5.4	Kelantan	Jeli	SP30	1	1	0	1	Social Enterprise
6.1	Pahang	Bentong	SP01	1	1	1	1	Organic Farming
6.2	Pahang	Bentong	SP02	1	1	0	1	Unity-Film
6.3	Pahang	Bentong	SP33	1	1	1	1	Organic Farming
7.1	Sabah	Papar	SP10	1	1	1	1	Fish Project
7.2	Sabah	Papar	SP11	1	1	1	1	Unity Film
8.1	Sabah	Pensiangan	SP08	1	1	0	1	Health & Well-being
8.2	Sabah	Pensiangan	SP09	1	1	1	1	Waste Management
8.3	Sabah	Pensiangan	SP12	1	1	0	1	Women Empowerment
9.1	Sarawak	Bandar Kuching	SP06	1	1	1	1	TVET

(Continued)

Table 1: (*Continued*)

People				Categories						
Prosperity				Planet	Peace	Partnership				
State	Location	Code		1,2,3,4,5	7,8,9,10,11	6,12,13,14,15	16	17		
9.2	Sarawak	Bandar Kuching	SP07	1	1	1	1	1	Socio-Economy
9.3	Sarawak	Bandar Kuching	SP34	1	1	1	1	1	Socio-Economy
10.1	Sarawak	Batang Sadong	SP04	1	1	0	1	1	Marketing for Small Farmers
10.2	Sarawak	Batang Sadong	SP05	1	1	0	1	1	English Language
10.3	Sarawak	Batang Sadong	SP26	1	1	0	1	1	Women Income & Health
		Total		34	34	26	34	34	

is forming a meaningful and lasting relationship. I am referring to those forms of relationships that bond communities together, the kind of relationships that foster trust and build on that trust to achieve something that is greater than the sum of its components. Another word for Relationship that is probably more SDG related is of course "Partnership."

By the end of this chapter, I hope that you shall be convinced that SDG17 (partnerships toward achieving the goals) is the Key Factor in achieving the motto of "Leaving No One Behind," at any level. The purpose of this chapter is to support the notion that SDG17 should be given a higher priority over the other SDGs, especially in the introduction of SDGs at the local level.

It is one thing to talk about the SDG2030 Agenda to an international audience of willing and agreeable listeners in the comfort of an air-conditioned dining hall in a 5-star hotel, but it is totally different when one is talking about specific development issues while being faced by a group comprising single parents, unemployed youth, farmers and/or fishermen in a hot, fan-conditioned, town hall meeting conducted in a hut within a village.

Thirty-four Solution Projects were initiated as part of the APPGM-SDG pilot project in 2020 (see Table 1). This national undertaking involved 10 Parliamentary Constituencies with 6 in Peninsular Malaysia and 2 each in the Borneo states of Sabah and Sarawak.

The Role of a Member of Parliament in Malaysia

In Malaysia, the Member of Parliament (see Table 2) is given the honorific YB or Yang Berhormat (translated as the Honorable) as a pre-fix to their name. One can easily imagine a well-dressed official who is used to being driven around in a huge luxury car, with a trail of hangers-on waiting to serve his beck and call. Truth be told, this is not totally wrong. One needs to only walk around the Parliament building to see the wheeling and dealing going on in the cafes and rest areas and through the "Corridors of Power" that connect the Dewan Rakyat[1] with numerous meeting rooms.

---

[1] House of Commons.

Table 2: Parliamentary Constituencies and Member of Parliament

State	No.	Constituency	Member of Parliament	Party	Date of field visit
Kedah	1.	P011 — Pendang	YB Tuan Hj. Awang Hashim	PAS	July 18–20, 2020
Kelantan	2.	P030 — Jeli	YB Dato' Sri Mustapa Mohamed	BERSATU	August 07–09, 2020
Selangor	3.	P097 — Selayang	YB Tuan William Leong Jee Keen	PKR	January 18–20, 2020
	4.	P105 — Petaling Jaya	YB Puan Maria Chin Abdullah	PKR	Feb 19, 23 & Jun 5 2020
Pahang	5.	P089 — Bentong	YB Tuan Wong Tack	DAP	Jan 14–16, 2020
Johor	6.	P165 — Tanjung Piai	YB Datuk Seri Dr. Wee Jeck Seng	MCA	Jan 18–20, 2020
Sabah	7.	P175 — Papar	YB Tuan Hj. Ahmad Bin Hassan	WARISAN	Feb 21–23, 2020
	8.	P182 — Pensiangan	YB Tuan Arthur Joseph Kurup	Parti Bersatu Rakyat Sabah	Feb 25–27, 2020
Sarawak	9.	P195 — Bandar Kuching	YB Dr. Kelvin Yii Lee Wuen	DAP	Feb 02–04, 2020
	10.	P200 — Batang Sadong	YB Dato' Sri Hajjah Nancy Hj. Shukri	GPS-PBB	Feb 24–26, 2020

But all of that is stripped away when that same official goes home to their Parliamentary Constituency, going down to the ground to meet their electorate. Gone are the coat and tie. In the villages, some Members of Parliament can be found dressed in T-shirt and trousers or sarong, sitting comfortably on the floor of the Village Headman's home, as they discuss the problems and challenges faced by these village folk. This personal approach of SDG17 has an extremely important role to play in getting the whole Sustainable Development Agenda off the ground.

A Different Path for SDGs

Members of Parliament, politicians, academics and researchers, civil servants, civil society groups, businessmen, and even the *makcik*[2] and *pakcik*[3] on the ground have some form of understanding of sustainability. Not many of them may be able to articulate what exactly are these 17 individual goals, but it is clear to this author at least, that there is a rudimentary understanding that there is a need to come together to overcome these issues in a cohesive and, perhaps, communal manner.

The notion that "One Size Fits All" no longer applies in this 21st century. The top-down approach to development has to be relegated to the days gone by. The classic top-down approach is akin to building a bridge in every district, even in those districts without a river running through it.

In most countries, dare I say, the norm in almost all countries, is to delegate the localizing of SDGs to the Local Authority, be they be the District, Municipal or City Council. This model makes sense if, and only if, the Office of the District Officer or President of the Municipality or Mayor of the City has the decision-making power and regulatory oversight over critical services such as education, health, sanitation, water, energy, environment, and even the power to establish and enact new laws.

Malaysia is unique in that as it has three levels or layering of Government. We have the Federal Government, the State Governments of the 13 States of the Federation, and the Local Authorities whereby the District Officer, Municipal Council Presidents and City Mayors

---

[2] Aunty.
[3] Uncle.

are political appointees of the Federal Civil Service. I shall return to this conversation at a later point of this chapter.

It is our contention that the Member of Parliament can and has played an important role in getting the many Stakeholders involved in localizing SDGs to work together toward achieving the goals.

Partnerships within the Sphere of APPGM-SDG

All-Party Parliamentary Group Malaysia on Sustainable Development Goals (APPGM-SDG) pilot project were carried out in 2020, despite the onset of the COVID-19 pandemic. This national undertaking involves 10 Parliamentary Constituencies with 6 in Peninsular Malaysia and 2 each in the Borneo states of Sabah and Sarawak.

These 10 Members of Parliament have been promoted as the Local Champion of SDG, as they are the ones who really know what is happening on the ground. They know the pulse of the people. We also recognize that they require the support by a whole network of individuals and organizations to make localizing SDGs work effectively.

Members of Dewan Rakyat[4] *and Dewan Negara*[5]

The Pilot Project is dealing with the 10 Members of Parliament.

They are representing both sides of the political divide — on one side we have 5 MPs who are the Government-backed coalition Perikatan National members Bersatu, PAS, and PN friendly MCA, PBRS and PBB, while on the other hand we have 5 MPs who are Pakatan Harapan coalition members from PKR, DAP and PH friendly Warisan.

Speaking with the individual MPs, we have come to appreciate that they are truly concerned with the well-being of their constituents. Most, if not all of these individual MPs and Senators, have the

---

[4] House of Representatives.
[5] House of Senate.

Rakyat's best interest at heart. MPs and Senators have more items of agreement when they leave politics at the door.

Development is a bi-partisan issue. Once politicians can go beyond their political rhetoric, much progress can be gained. The rhetoric and ensuing arguments become a curtain that hinders the possibility of politicians with opposite views from engaging in fruitful and adult debate.

During the August 2020 Parliamentary Session, an APPGM-SDG Committee Meeting was convened during the lunch break at Parliament House itself. Two Ministers, one Government back-bencher and four Opposition MPs were present together with a Senator to discuss the 8 proposals for Selayang. All were passed with no objections whatsoever. In contrast, before and after lunch, name calling was the order of the day in the Dewan Rakyat, and no actual beneficial business was conducted in Parliament.

The Research Department of Parliament has a team of 14 researchers who are attached to the Research Department of Parliament. Their role is to provide Parliamentarians with support services whenever new bills are being introduced, and amendments to existing ones are being discussed. The APPGM-SDG initiated a meeting with researchers from the Research Department to forge better cooperation between the two parties, as well as pursue networking with the pool of researchers currently supporting the APPGM-SDG pilot project.

From the viewpoint of Sustainable Development, the APPGM-SDG Secretariat and its CSO-SDG Alliance partners would be a valuable and in-depth resource base for this Research Department as the NGO members cover almost every aspect and issue that is covered by the Parliament.

Government Agencies

As stated earlier, the Malaysian Government structure exists at three levels — Federal, State and Local. The nature of the Federation of Malaysia is a legacy left behind by its British Colonial past. It has left Malaysia with three distinct levels of Government.

The Federal Government or Executive is operating out of Putrajaya, governed by the laws passed by the Malaysian Parliament. Income tax goes to the Federal Government. It comprises the 13 State Governments, of which Sabah and Sarawak have autonomy on matters of immigration, and forestry just to name two. Exploitation of Natural Resources namely land and forestry are the main revenue generator for most States. The Local Authorities (City, Town and District Councils) which are the actual ones issuing the business licenses are required for productive activity and tax revenue purposes.

In Malaysia, we have what is called the Federal List, the State List and the Joint List of areas of responsibility between the Federal Government and the State Governments. Water, land, minerals and forestry are State matters. Health and education services, and the police force are under the purview of the Federal Government. Energy (electricity) generation and sewerage processing is regulated by the Federal Government. Solid waste management is under the responsibility of the Local Council. As you can see, this is already like a pot of boiling stew, with the potential of conflicts arising at so many levels.

"Silo mentality" exists between agencies within each level of Government. The cordiality of interaction between agencies at different levels depends on the amount of overlap of authority on certain issues between Federal Ministries. The more the overlap or ambiguity, the more contentious the relationship. Meanwhile, between States, it depends on the natural resources that are being pursued, especially if rivers are involved, and finally, between Local Authorities, it depends on which City or Town is given recognition and awards by the Federal and State Authorities.

The three levels of Government often work independently from each other. There are inconsistencies between the Federal, State and Local Agencies that eventually affect the smooth delivery of services to the Rakyat.[6] An example is about disrepair at a school in Batang Sadong, where the allocation was already made at the Federal

---

[6] Citizens.

Education Ministry Level, but the State and District Education Departments seemed oblivious to the danger posed by the rotten floorboards of some classrooms, and the rusted metal rail bars along the corridors.

Tanjung Piai in the state of Johor is another classic case of "silo" approach to problem solving. Garbage on the ground is under the jurisdiction of the Local Council. Once it gets into the river system, it is under the purview of the Irrigation Department. When the litter hits the sea, it becomes nobody's responsibility, not even the Marine Department! And for the people living in homes built on stilts in the Kampung Terapung,[7] the Local Council claims that garbage collection is not its problem because the occupants do not pay assessment fees since their houses are in the ocean. But, alas, the litter is still there!

Non-Governmental Organizations

The Malaysian CSO-SDG Alliance[8] is an informal umbrella group that brings together nearly 50 Civil Society Organizations from across the country. These CSOs represent a wide array of issues such as Human Rights (PROHAM), Environment (WWF Malaysia, CETDEM,[9] EPSM[10]), Indigenous Peoples Matters (Yayasan Kajian Pembangunan Masyarakat), Gender (National Council of Women's Organizations), Legal (Bar Council), Governance (C4) and Health (National Cancer Society Malaysia).

Through the Pilot Project, more NGOs are now our Partner/ Service Providers. These include non-Peninsular based Tulid Youth Club, Sarawak Dayak Iban Association (SADIA), Rise of Social Efforts (ROSE), Sabah Women's Action — Resource Group (SAWO) and Organization for Research Movement and Development of Singai, Sarawak.

---

[7] Floating Village.
[8] Civil Society Organizations for Sustainable Development Goals.
[9] Centre for Environment, Technology & Development, Malaysia.
[10] Environmental Protection Society Malaysia.

We discovered new partners based in the Klang Valley. These now include Petaling Jaya People's Movement Association (PPR-PJ), Organization for Community Building and Continuous Education, Organisation for Social Service and Community Building of Gobak District (PSPK), Children of Malaysia's Literary Association, Glorious Generation Foundation (YGG), Management of Selayang Makmur Garden, and, Association for Green Movement of Bentong, Pahang.

A new category of NGO partner is Social Enterprise. Social Enterprises are playing an important role in empowering people to create new job categories that never existed even 10 years ago. Our partner in the Tanjung Piai clean-up project is Impact Revolution Enterprise. It is involved in solid waste management. It does public good (cleaning up the garbage) and creates jobs for those involved in the process.

A unique feature of this NGO partnership is university-based participation. These include Sejahtera Centre for Sustainability and Humanity (IIUM[11]), Undergraduates Association for Faculty of Cognitive Science and Human Development (UNIMAS[12]), Faulty of Psychology and Education (UMS[13]), Association for Social Sciences Malaysia (PSSM), and, University College Sabah Foundation.

The communities

Community Leadership is a matter of great importance when viewing development from the bottom-up approach. Rural Communities are usually held together by leaders who grew up with their neighbors. There is a sense of familiarity, of family even. The Jawatankuasa Keselamatan Kampung[14] looks into the welfare of the people living in the village. These leaders know the members of their Community at more than just head level.

---

[11] International Islamic University Malaysia.
[12] Universiti Malaysia Sarawak.
[13] Universiti Malaysia Sabah.
[14] Village Security Council.

Meanwhile, Urban Communities are brought together by leaders who are trying to resolve common issues faced by the Community, such as security. These relationships are more of acquaintances than actual friends.

We have examples of Rural, Urban and a Mixed Leadership in different localities of the country.

Papar, Pensiangan, Pendang, and Jeli, are Rural examples where the local leaders seem to have a grasp of the heartbeat of the older folks who remain in the villagers, who are now dependent on the "remittance economy." According to Jeli's Member of Parliament YB Dato' Sri Mustapa Mohamad (Minister is responsible for Economic Planning), the younger folk have left the Felda[15] and Risda[16] schemes for jobs in Penang, and Kuala Lumpur. Young Kelantanese are remitting cash to the older generation to help make ends meet. The older settlers (1st generation is almost gone, and 2nd generation are in their 60s) are too old to tap rubber or harvest oil palm fruit branches. There are barely any 3rd or 4th generation settlers left in these settlements, so they depend on casual workers coming from across the Thai border to do the manual work. A similar situation was found in Pendang, and confirmed by the MP. Sadly, development does not seem to have reached these locations.

Petaling Jaya, Selayang (both in the State of Selangor), and Bandar Kuching (in Sarawak), are the Urban setting, whereby these are the people who are the providers of the "remittance economy." This means their living conditions are cramp, squalid and unhygienic. According to YB Dr. Kelvin Yii of Bandar Kuching, he grew up in Kuching, but he did not know of the existence of one particular squatter area until after he was elected as MP. Leaders here are faced with issues of urban migrants (Petaling Jaya), squatters (Bandar Kuching), illegal immigrants, UNHCR registered and unregistered refugees (Selayang).

Bentong (Pahang), and Tanjung Piai (Johor) are categorized as Semi-rural/Semiurban. These localities seem to be caught in a

---

[15] Federal Land Development Authority.
[16] Rubber Industry Smallholders Development Authority.

"Development Trap." On the one hand, the leaders here wish to see the continuous development in the area. Mono-culture of durians has plagued the fertile slopes of Bentong and the areas around it. In Tanjung Piai, the fishermen are lamenting the fact that they are the last generation of a long line of fishermen from their villages due to industrial pollution and illegal trawlers that have over harvested their traditional fish catching areas in the seas off Johor.

Researchers and research institutions

During the course of the Initial Site Visits,[17] it was a revelation of the expertise that already exists among local Researchers and Research Institutions in Malaysia. A few researchers and the research institutions have come into our purview, such as Mr. Alizan Mahadi, Director, Technology, Innovation, Environment and Sustainability, TIES (ISIS Malaysia), Associate Professor Dr. Zainal Abidin Sanusi, Director, Sejahtera Centre for Sustainability and Humanity (IIUM), Associate Professor Dr. Zaimuariffudin Shukri Othman, Faculty of Cognitive Sciences and Human Development (UNIMAS), Associate Professor Dr. Zaheruddin bin Othman, School of Government (UUM[18]), and, Associate Professor Dr. Wan Ahmad Zal bin Wan Ismail, Director, Institute for Poverty Research and Management, InsPek (UMK[19]).

Malaysia and its Government has been overly relied on foreign expertise and consultants when it comes to long-term planning, be it for Energy or Water resources management. During a number of meetings with the Economic Planning Unit of the Prime Minister's Department, Datuk Professor Dr. Denison Jayasooria[20] has called for the creation of a National Sustainability Institute. This would be a

---

[17] Three-day visits to each location to establish rapport with the Member of Parliament, Government representatives and the local people.

[18] Universiti Utara Malaysia.

[19] Universiti Malaysia Kelantan.

[20] Co-Chair of Malaysian CSO-SDG Alliance and Head of Secretariat, APPGM-SDG.

virtual institution, one that does not require any investment in new physical buildings or infrastructure, but connects all Research and Development Institutes which are related to the Sustainable Development Goals Agenda 2030. The National Sustainability Institute could be placed under the purview of the Economic Planning Unit, with a small secretariat to coordinate the communications of the Institute.

NGOs, members of Dewan Rakyat and Dewan Negara, government agencies and the communities they serve

Many MPs generally trust academicians and researchers more than NGOs. However, the COVID-19 pandemic has shown the Government that partnerships with NGOs can be utilized to mobilize Civil Society to deliver essential services and food packages to those in dire need.

State Governments that are in opposition to the Federal Government are cautious in their interaction with Federal Government approved initiatives like the APPGM-SDG. Even the very mention of United Nations still brings up thoughts of ICERT and other United Nations treaties into the minds of some PN[21] MPs.

Some communities are jaded by the experience of empty promises given by previous engagements with other groups conducting fact-finding research. Their request is simple, to have a feedback mechanism so that they know things are being looked into, and this will go a long way to allay their fears.

Private–Public Partnerships

There is an urgent need to nurture Private–Public Partnerships to achieve the goals. The private sector has been often left out of the discussions on local development. Instead of contributing to the planning phase, they are invited to bid for projects that have been planned

---

[21] Perikatan Nasional, the Coalition of Parties that have led the Malaysian Government since March, 2020.

by parties that may have no interest in seeing the actual success of these said projects.

Solution Projects and SDGs

Mapping the issues to SDGs was presumably straight forward. However, as the Solution Projects (SP01–SP34) have all been approved in progress and with some already completed, it was deemed timely to reconcile and identify the SDGs addressed by each Solution Project. It was during this exercise that the cross-cutting nature of SDGs became very apparent. A Solution Project may have started off to address the issue of a single SDG, but the solution itself could relate between 4 and 10 SDGs.

Example 1

In the case of the Projek Perumahan Rakyat[22] in Desa Mentari, located in the City of Petaling Jaya, the issue of Poverty (SDG1) came out strongly from the issue identification (mapping) exercise. Among of the Solution Projects proposed and approved with the purpose of addressing this issue was the "Setting up Soup Kitchen in PPR Desa Mentari," with the internal code SP14 (Solution Project 14). However, it has become apparent that the solution is related to the issues of education (SDG4), gender (SDG5), jobs (SDG8), infrastructure (SDG9), inequalities (SDG10), cities (SDG12), governance (SDG16) and partnerships (SDG17).

Example 2

In the case of Kampung Sinaron (Sinoran Village) in the Town of Papar, Sabah where the issue of rubbish which is an environmental issue, was translated to Life on Land (SDG15). The direct solution was "Waste Management & Economic Empowerment," with the internal code SP09. This has now been mapped to poverty (SDG1),

---

[22] People's Housing Project.

hunger (SDG2), health (SDG3), inequalities (SDG10), responsible consumption and production (SDG11), cities (SDG12), governance (SDG16) and partnerships (SDG17).

Example 3

This involves SP07 in the City of Kuching, which is to "Conduct 4 Series of Social Economic Related Training for the Community of Kampung Chawan (Chawan Village) to Enhance Their Self-Value & Overall Well-Being." Once again, this may have been borne from the need to address poverty (SDG1) and inequalities (SDG10), but this solution has been mapped to include education (SDG4), clean water (SDG6), energy (SDG7), jobs (SDG8), inequalities (SDG10), responsible consumption and production (SDG11), cities (SDG12), governance (SDG16) and partnerships (SDG17).

Cross-cutting nature of projects

The above are just three examples of the cross-cutting nature of SDGs in relation to a Solution Project. It suffices to say that the 34 Solution Projects in the pilot phase provide a window into the complexity of addressing SDG issues in a holistic manner.

With due respect to the research team, once the background study for a particular Parliamentary Constituency has been extensively researched, picking up on a particular SDG as an issue would be comparatively easy. For example, one would be correct to assume that poverty (SDG1) is the most pressing among the urban and rural poor. Through further research, and as the Solution Projects progressed, more underlying issues would become apparent.

Stating that all SDGs are interrelated is a given reality. However, it may also cause us to lose sight of the trees from the forest. There are nuances that need to be explored. Many would question as to why the 3 issues of inequalities (SDG10), governance (SDG16) and partnerships (SDG17) appear in ALL Solution Projects. Truth be told, inequalities is the major contributor to all SDG issues. And inequalities are more often than not linked to the issue of Governance, and

Governance itself is threatened by the sad state of partnerships that exist. In other words, Good Partnerships generally lead to Good Governance, and Good Governance leads to less inequality. On the other hand, it would be right to say that Bad Partnerships lead to Bad Governance and that leads to worse inequalities.

This leads us to the pressing need for a serious discussion to address these three SDGs on a local and national stage. One would argue that partnership (SDG17) is key to the successful implementation of solutions on the ground. The active role of the Member of Parliament in mobilizing his ground support staff, the local, State and Federal Authorities, Non-Governmental Organizations, Private Sector and especially the participation of the affected Community is NECESSARY for the successful implementation of the Solutions Project identified after the issue mapping exercise.[23]

Conversely, the lack of partnerships, or, difficulties to having strong cooperation between different stakeholders, is one of the biggest challenges to achieving the Sustainable Development Goals. One hypothetical situation would be a community leader who is unwilling to collaborate with an NGO from outside the community. Another would be a solution provider not fully understanding the "culture" of a community, and how it responds to invitations from people whom they consider outsiders.

On the other hand, good partnerships lead to positive outcomes. Perhaps there is a Government Department who goes the extra mile by being innovative in the service provided to a squatter community. Or, a Member of Parliament who takes the time to attend activities related to the Solution Project, to be seen to be giving their active support. Maybe a researcher who arranges for refurbished computers to be donated to a school that is in dire need for them.

Conclusions

No two constituencies have the same challenges, and no two solutions are exactly the same. Each issue and solution is unique.

---

[23] Done at the end of the 3-day site visit. This is followed by prioritization with the MP to identify possible solutions projects.

Having stated this, each project would have a particular SDG (or perhaps 2) which have a greater weightage compared to others. We hope to have all 34 Solution Projects show a level of success, leaving no one behind, through the implementation of SDGs on the ground. This is an ongoing Pilot Project. However, certain key topics are recurring throughout the 10 initial Site Visits, numerous meetings with Stakeholders including Members of Parliament. All these point to SDG17 being pivotal to the overall success of the SDGs.

Building trust

Additional time should be spent on the ground for fact-finding work. Three days are insufficient to draw adequate conclusions of the root causes of the most pressing issues in a Parliamentary Constituency. Interaction with the communities, and local NGOs and Government Agencies involved require additional Site Visits to inculcate a more mature partnership, instead of a superficial one. Trust deficit with Government Agencies is something that plagues many Civil Society Organizations in Malaysia.

Capacity building and training

Further research should be focused on the Capacity Building of front-line or program delivery staff at Local Authority and District Office levels to have a good grasp on development based on SDG principles. Possible collaboration is necessary among public and private colleges and universities in setting up certificate and diploma courses to upgrade these front-line civil servants to better understand SDGs.

Government servants should be trained as front-line service delivery providers no matter what position they hold, be it a junior clerk or the Chief Secretary to the Government. Their duty to the Rakyat is much more than to carry out the government policies to the letter, but to be seen delivering the services according to the spirit of the policies.

More empowerment for social workers

Malaysia has a social service network which is overstretched and understaffed. The social workers are focused on the immediate needs of their clients, for cash and material hand-outs. However, there seems to be a disconnect from the duties of the social worker, and bridging the needs of the community that they serve. For instance, a social worker may be the only point of reference for their client in accessing the government services. A sick spouse, coupled with a child not going to school, could be put in touch with the Health and Education Departments, respectively. Unfortunately, there is no such mechanism in place at this time.

Private sector participation and the Penta-Helix

There is a dire need to include private sector participation in the SDG implementation process. Real CSR should be viewed in terms of being proactive and finding out the development needs of the community, and it would be better if it was in cooperation with the local authorities and community leadership.

A successful Public-Private-Academia-Civil Society partnership should give birth to a new breed of innovative Social Entrepreneurs. This five party relationship is also known as the Penta-Helix.

Source: Vasconcelos, C. and Nguyen, M. H., Initial conditions for penta helix collaboration in social innovation — A case study of ReTuren, Malmö universitet/ Kultur och samhälle, 2018. http://urn.kb.se/resolve?urn=urn:nbn:se:mau:d iva-21056.

IN CLOSING

And finally, we return to that Ancient African Proverb …

IF YOU WANT TO GO FAST, GO ALONE.
IF YOU WANT TO GO FAR, GO TOGETHER.

Very often, all too often perhaps, we find ourselves in a situation where going alone will help us accomplish or implement a particular task/solution. And on hindsight, the efficacy of that action is diminished because the reasoning behind it was not fully understood or appreciated by those who are supposed to benefit from it. A group moving forward will move only as fast as its slowest member. But, it is moving forward nevertheless. A group running helter-skelter will remain stationary at best, and regress at worst.

It is the task of a good leader to build strong and lasting partnerships, to ensure that SDGs are transformed from grand plans to actualization. We have shown through this chapter, time and again, the Member of Parliament has the ability to play its important role. Therefore, it is our contention that SDG17 is necessary to achieve the other 16 SDGs. Drawing from Phase 1 of the APPGM-SDG Pilot Project, there are concrete examples that show the importance of "getting SDG17 right the first time" so that the right Sustainable Development projects actually needed by the people on the ground gets implemented and delivered.

And finally, it is our hope that the process and methodology that Malaysia has established through the APPGM-SDG shall be reviewed for adoption by our friends in ASEAN and China.

Chapter

11

Offline and Online Perils of Digital Platforms: A Case Study on Malaysia

Farlina Md Said

*Institute of Strategic & International Studies,
Kuala Lumpur, Malaysia*

fmdsaid@gmail.com

The movement control order (MCO) effective on March 18 shifted Malaysia's population — or those with access and are able to afford it — online. This figure translates to 90.1% of households in 2019[1] and around 133.6% mobiles in the population in 2020.[2] As a majority of the nation was made to stay indoors for the first four phases of the MCO (between March 18 and May 3), cyber became a means of livelihood. Digital services became a source of income where Shopee, the most visited e-commerce website according to Statista, introduced support programs that transformed 70,000 Malaysian small

---

[1] DOSM, ICT use and access by individuals and households survey report 2019.
[2] MCMC, MCMC 1Q 2020 facts and figures communication and multimedia, 2020 (accessed August 20, 2020). https://www.mcmc.gov.my/skmmgovmy/media/General/pdf/1Q-2020-C-M-Facts-and-Figures.PDF.

and medium enterprises (SMEs),[3] 1,500 local farmers, 100 Agribusiness Industry entrepreneurs and up to 56,000 fishermen to retain their income. The use of digital platforms and services was not the only marked growth in Malaysia's utilization of cyber. Pandemic-specific digital activities included the use of applications for contact tracing and to monitor the movement of people, digitization in healthcare and growth of cyber for business productivity. With adherence to the early phases of the MCO binding the Malaysian population indoors, Internet traffic in the first week of the MCO increased by 23.5% and a further increase of 8.6% was recorded in the second week.[4]

However, the silver lining offered by digital spaces to cope with stay-at-home orders saw unfortunate dark clouds. Cyber incidents peaked in April, the height of Malaysia's MCO where fraud figures registered above 1,000 incidents when figures commonly ranged around the 700s.[5] Approximately 266 investigation papers were open to dissemination of "fake news" as of July 6, 2020.[6] In addition, the National Cyber Security Agency of Malaysia had issued warnings on viruses delivered through websites or corrupted links related to coronavirus. According to cybersecurity research firm Sophos Labs, at the end of 2019, only one website was registered with "COVID" in its URL. Fast-forward three months later and more than 42,000 websites have bloomed with domains containing "COVID" and

---

[3] Muller, J., Top 10 e-commerce sites in Malaysia Q1 2020, *Statista*, 2020 (accessed August 20, 2020). https://www.statista.com/statistics/869640/malaysia-top-10-e-commerce-sites/.

[4] MCMC, Media statement: Changing usage patterns influence internet speed in Malaysia, 2020 (accessed August 10, 2020). https://www.mcmc.gov.my/en/media/press-releases/media-statement-changing-usage-patterns-influence.

[5] MyCERT, Reported incidents based on general incident classification statistics 2020, 2020 (accessed August 20, 2020). www.mycert.org.my/portal/statistics-content?menu=b75e037d-6ee3-4d11-8169-66677d694932&id=f88181d6-9839-4828-a612-1d27c820e1af.

[6] Bernama, COVID-19: 266 investigation papers on fake news opened, Astro Awani, 2020 (accessed August 23, 2020). https://www.astroawani.com/berita-malaysia/covid19-266-investigation-papers-on-fake-news-opened-250100.

"corona."[7] While good hygiene needed to address the pandemic, digital hygiene too came to the forefront as companies, small business owners, individuals and the government are forced to rely on digital spaces to facilitate the new normal.

Malaysia, Cyber and a Pandemic

Malaysia's MCO can be categorized in a few phases, namely the MCO, between March 18 and May 3 that consists of four phases, the conditional MCO (CMCO) between May 4 and June 8 and the recovery MCO (RMCO) from June 9 until August 31. Distinctions between the MCOs and phases are based on the regulations gazetted for each specific period. During the first few phases of the MCO, all business premises are ordered to close save for supermarkets and grocery stores selling daily essentials while government and private premises would be closed with the exception of essential services such as utilities, telecommunications, transport, banking, health, pharmacies, ports, airports, cleaning and food supplies.[8] These restrictions were eased during the CMCO and RMCO where business gradually returned to a semblance of normalcy with standard operating procedures applied. Among the standard operating procedures is for business operators to record details of patrons and to conduct temperature checks on visitors to the premises.

The MCO was legitimized by the Prevention and Control of Infectious Diseases (Declared of Infected Local Areas) Order 2020 based on Section 11 of the Prevention and Control of Infectious Diseases 1988 (Diseases Act).[9] The Diseases Act is supported in

---

[7] Gallagher, Sean and Andrew Brandt, Facing down the myriad threats tied to COVID-19, *Sophos*, 2020 (accessed August 23, 2020). https://news.sophos.com/en-us/2020/04/14/covidmalware/.

[8] Bunyan, John, PM: Malaysia under movement control order from Wed until March 31, all shops closed except for essential services, *Malaymail*, 2020 (accessed August 5, 2020). https://www.malaymail.com/news/malaysia/2020/03/16/pm-malaysia-in-lockdown-from-wed-until-march-31-all-shops-closed-except-for/1847204.

[9] RLSE, Legality of the movement control order, 2020 (accessed August 20, 2020). https://rlse.law/legality-of-the-movement-control-order/.

enforcement by the Police Act that should ensure adherence to specific regulations made to curb the spread of the pandemic. Malaysia's strategy toward mitigating the pandemic focused on flattening the curve and was followed by contact tracing efforts. As such, Malaysia's cyber environment was full of energy as trends of technological use ranged from monitoring and the identification of targeted groups to technology aimed at controlling the movement of people.

The following are categories of technological use to mitigate the spread of coronavirus in Malaysia.

Technology to monitor and identify targeted groups

In the same vein as the launch of other contact tracing applications such as Singapore's TraceTogether and Australia's COVIDSafe, the Malaysian government and the private sector launched various applications to monitor and identify targeted groups in the midst of the outbreak. The MySejahtera application was announced early April as a strategic collaboration among the National Security Council (NSC), the Health Ministry (MoH), the Malaysian Administrative Modernisation and Management Planning Unit (MAMPU), the Malaysian Communications and Multimedia Commission (MCMC).[10] Later, the application also credits the Ministry of Science, Technology and Innovation (MOSTI) in the strategic collaboration.[11] MySejahtera began as an application intended for individuals to assess the health of users while delivering information on the nearest health facilities though the application adapted to various market requirements — such as adopting web-based QR scanning functions — to maintain relevance.[12] Other applications launched by the federal government was

---

[10] Sagar, Mohit, Malaysian government next to launch app to monitor COVID-19 outbreak, OpenGov, 2020 (accessed August 20, 2020). https://opengovasia.com/malaysia-government-next-to-launch-app-to-monitor-covid-19-outbreak/.

[11] The FAQ adds MOSTI as a collaborator of MySejahtera aside from previous coverage. MySejahtera, FAQ MySejahtera App, n.d. (accessed August 20, 2020). https://mysejahtera.malaysia.gov.my/FAQ_en/.

[12] *Ibid.*

MyTrace, a Ministry of Science, Technology and Innovation endeavor and was developed with the Malaysian Institute of Microelectronic Systems (MIMOS), the Malaysian Global Innovation and Creativity Centre (MaGIC) with the International Islamic University Malaysia (IIUM), Google and strategic cooperation with the team behind MySejahtera.[13] MyTrace uses bluetooth and proximity functions to detect other devices with the same application installed. The information is stored in the smartphone thus offering a decentralized form of data storage in comparison to MySejahtera's centralized approach. Both applications allow access by the Ministry of Health (MOH) and can only be processed by MOH officers.

Malaysia's contact-tracing marketplace also featured homegrown entries founded and led by the States. Selangor's SELangkah, Sarawak's COVIDtrace and Qmunity, Sabah's SabahTrace, Terengganu's Masuk.la and Johor's Jejak Johor were among the efforts to ease the step of tracing contacts from infected individuals. The applications may utilize different methods for contact tracing. Applications such as SELangkah, SabahTrace, Masuk.la and Qmunity use locations as the anchor of tracking, as the GEO-QR code tagging method would trace possible encounters of infected individuals using venues that were visited by positive individuals. Sarawak's COVIDtrace uses the same method but also includes bluetooth to register those in proximity. As the MCO phases gradually eased the population to a pace of the new normal and to ease the centralization of data collection, MySejahtera was made mandatory for all businesses since August 3, 2020.[14]

The private sector too developed and innovated ways to adhere to shifting standard operating procedures (SOP). Among these is an Early Warning, Alert and Response system (EWAR), a thermal and

---

[13] MyTrace, a preventive counter measure and contact tracing application for COVID-19, MOSTI, n.d. (accessed September 1, 2020). https://www.mosti.gov.my/web/en/mytrace/#1588521061720-1739856b-c49b.

[14] Yusof, Teh Athira, MySejahtera app now mandatory for all businesses, *New Straits Times*, 2020 (accessed September 2, 2020). https://www.nst.com.my/news/nation/2020/08/613619/mysejahtera-app-now-mandatory-all-businesses.

optical camera backed by artificial intelligence capable of detecting individuals in a crowd with a higher body temperature by telecommunications powerhouse, TMnet. The product was slated to be deployed[15] in selected schools in Klang Valley, Perak and Pahang.[16]

Technology to control movement

The control of movement is imperative to curb rising numbers of infections. The situation is particularly illustrative in China's swift lockdown in central Hubei in late January and Italy's March 8 quarantine that saw the rush of movement to hometowns or to areas without movement restrictions thus seeding outbreaks at other parts of the nations.[17] Malaysia's MCO implemented on March 18 — currently extended December 31 — would restrict festivities whose yearly rituals include travel to hometowns and visits to relatives. Bearing in mind the impending need to fulfill such practices and to accommodate those stranded due to the swift announcement and extensions of the MCO, applications were introduced to control the movement of people across state borders. The Gerak Malaysia application was launched by the Malaysia Commission on Multimedia and Communications (MCMC) and the Royal Malaysia Police (RMP) to facilitate interstate travel. The application gave the police a measure of control over the movement of people as permissions to travel were

---

[15] TM assists schools to reopen safely with innovative smart digital health screening solutions, TM, 2020 (accessed August 20, 2020). https://www.tm.com.my/Newsroom/Pages/TM-ASSISTS-SCHOOLS-TO-REOPEN-SAFELY-WITH-INNOVATIVE-SMART-DIGITAL-HEALTH-SCREENING-SOLUTIONS.aspx.
[16] Telekom Malaysia rolls out digital health screening to selected schools with inhouse developed system, *Digital News Asia*, 2020 (accessed September 15, 2020). https://www.digitalnewsasia.com/business/telekom-malaysia-rolls-out-digital-health-screening-selected-schools-inhouse-developed.
[17] Travel chaos in world erupts as Italy quarantines north to halt virus, *The Star*, 2020 (accessed September 5, 2020). https://www.thestar.com.my/news/regional/2020/03/08/travel-chaos-in-world-erupts-as-italy-quarantines-north-to-halt-virus.

allowed under strict conditions.[18] However, as the MCOs gradually opened interstate borders, the utility of the application reduced and by July 31, the application ceased operations.[19]

Technology for communication

An MCO that kept people indoors, along with shifting standard operating procedure requirements, migrated many to the realms of cyber, with the intention of seeking or receiving information. Daily press updates along with communication channels ranging from traditional television channels to social networking sites such as Twitter, Facebook and applications like Telegram were used to deliver information to the widest extent as possible. The communication strategy utilized two official spokespeople delivering two aspects of Malaysia's battle against COVID-19 — those that are health related and those not health related.[20] The session featured interactions with journalists and updates on necessary figures of the day such as the COVID-19 cases, which were later reiterated through channels such as Twitter, Facebook and Telegram. Local media outlets assisted with the information dissemination through coverage as well as by hosting the information on their respective websites, as well as on platforms such as Youtube. Reminders via short message services (SMS) were also delivered containing the dos and don'ts in the current MCO SOPs and for safety reminders.[21]

---

[18] Loheswar, R., Senior Minister: Gerak Malaysia app no longer in use since interstate travel not allowed, 2020 (accessed August 25, 2020). https://www.malaymail.com/news/malaysia/2020/06/01/senior-minister-gerak-malaysia-app-no-longer-in-use-since-interstate-travel/1871357.

[19] *Ibid.*

[20] Good communication plan in place during pandemic, *New Straits Times*, 2020 (accessed August 20, 2020). https://www.nst.com.my/news/nation/2020/06/601597/good-communication-plan-place-during-pandemic.

[21] Malaysia shares key digital efforts in combating COVID-19 with ASEAN, China, AstroAwani, 2020 (accessed August 28, 2020). https://www.astroawani.com/berita-malaysia/malaysia-shares-key-digital-efforts-in-combating-covid19-with-asean-china-246864.

As the Internet was used as a source of information, disinformation and misinformation cases rose with 268 investigation papers reported on May 19.[22] In preparation, a response team was also formed under the Communications and Multimedia Ministry to counter fake news and verify news.[23] The Quick Response Team is headed by the Ministry's Strategic Communications Divisions and comprises staff from MCMC as well as NSC.[24] The government's fact-checking portal, Sebenarnya.my, was used as a repository for verified or debunked articles.

Technology and clinical assistance for the diagnosis of COVID-19

Local collaboration was not the only means of seeking solutions to mitigate the pandemic. Partnerships with the private sectors such as Microsoft and Huawei sought to bring technological solutions to healthcare. Microsoft introduced artificial intelligence, machine learning and data management facilities at the 5G-equipped Malaysia Agro Exposition Park (MAEPS) quarantine center.[25] Meanwhile, Huawei had provided core cloud services that utilize big data analysis and artificial intelligence to assist with diagnosis where hundreds of CT

---

[22] Daim, Nuradzimmah, COVID-19 fake news cases, *New Straits Times*, 2020 (accessed August 21, 2020). https://www.nst.com.my/news/nation/2020/05/593879/268-investigation-papers-opened-covid-19-fake-news-case.

[23] Ministry of Communications and Multimedia Malaysia "Bernama: 15 April 2020: KKMM quick response team takes 30 mins to 3 hours to verify viral news — Suriani," 2020 (accessed September 1, 2020). https://www.kkmm.gov.my/index.php/en/privacy-policy/233-kpkk-news/16862-bernama-15-april-2020-kkmm-quick-response-team-takes-30-mins-to-3-hours-to-verify-viral-news-suriani.

[24] Communications Ministry sec-gen says doing utmost to combat fake news amid COVID-19 pandemic, *Malay Mail*, 2020 (accessed August 30, 2020). https://www.malaymail.com/news/malaysia/2020/04/16/communications-ministry-doing-utmost-to-combat-fake-news-amid-covid-19-pand/1857162.

[25] Raman, K., Looking beyond COVID-19: The importance of public–private partnerships, 2020 (accessed August 20, 2020). https://news.microsoft.com/en-my/2020/08/18/looking-beyond-covid-19-the-importance-of-public-private-partnerships/.

images can be analyzed for diagnosis results produced within a minute.[26] The technology is deployed at Sungai Buloh Hospital, the main facility for treating COVID-19 in Selangor.[27] Technology also links clinical researchers across the globe as Skymind Holdings and Skymind Laboratory of Neurobionix Research in Shanghai,[28] China are linked for an on-premise artificial intelligence solution that utilizes patients' history and relevant data to conduct early intervention.[29]

Work-from-home for the private sector and home users

According to the Department of Statistics Malaysia's 2019 ICT Use and Access by Individuals and Households Survey Report, Malaysia's Internet penetration statistics is at 90.1%.[30] Amid the growth of business activities online, the work from home arrangements could be underprepared for cyber incidents. The first five phases of the MCO saw cyber incidents averaging 1,200 with the months of March, April and May recording 1,091, 1,488 and 1,045 incidents, respectively.[31] The

---

[26] Huawei contributes its technologies to join Malaysia's fight against COVID-19, Huawei, 2020 (accessed September 15, 2020). https://www.huawei.com/my/news/my/2020/huawei-contributes-its-technologies-to-join-malaysia-fight-against-covid-19.
[27] Henderson, James, Huawei strikes COVID-19 cloud pact with Ministry of Health in Malaysia, Huawei, 2020 (accessed September 15, 2020). https://sg.channelasia.tech/article/674883/huawei-strikes-covid-19-cloud-pact-ministry-health-malaysia/.
[28] Assistive diagnostic AI tool to tackle COVID-19 in Malaysia, *Biospectrum Asia*, 2020 (accessed September 15, 2020). https://www.biospectrumasia.com/news/46/15811/assistive-diagnostic-ai-tool-to-tackle-covid-19-in-malaysia.html.
[29] AI tech for COVID-19 research at Tunku Azizah Hospital, *New Straits Times*, 2020 (accessed September 15, 2020). https://www.nst.com.my/lifestyle/bots/2020/04/584607/tech-ai-tech-covid-19-research-tunku-azizah-hospital.
[30] Mahidin, Mohd Uzir, ICT use and access by individuals and households survey report, Malaysia, 2019, Department of Statistics Malaysia, 2020 (accessed September 2, 2020). https://www.dosm.gov.my/v1/index.php?r=column/cthemeByCat&cat=395&bul_id=SFRacTRUMEVRUFo1Ulc4Y1JlLzBqUT09&menu_id=amVoWU54UTl0a21NWmdhMjFMMWcyZz09.
[31] Incident Statistics, MyCERT, 2020 (accessed September 12, 2020). https://www.mycert.org.my/portal/statistics-content?menu=b75e037d-6ee3-4d11-8169-66677d694932&id=ff59a8c9-62af-4799-b14b-eeef3a275b80.

numbers tapered in the months of June, July and August, recording 871,642 and 611 incidents. The highest incidences are fraud cases with April recording 1,180 incidents. Fraud on e-commerce platforms between March 18 and June 30 recorded 2,020 cases amounting to losses worth RM12.6 million where the *modus operandi* centered on consumer demand such as selling counterfeit face masks.[32] Other instances included the misuse of personal data, online scams and soft loan scams.[33]

Online incidents were not the only result of cyber activities during the MCO. A demand for bandwidth to accommodate an increase in the Internet traffic was ignited due to dropping download speeds. Speeds averaging 13.4 Mbps in early February dropped to 8.8 Mbps in the last week of March.[34] Malaysians staying home increased Internet use by 23.5% in the first week of the MCO, followed by a further increase of 8.6% in the second week.[35] It was also reported that the lagging Internet could be due to damages of the Asia-Pacific Cable Network 2 (APCN2).[36] As education as well as commerce

---

[32] *The Malaysian Reserve*, MCO fraud losses over RM100m, 2020 (accessed September 10, 2020). https://themalaysianreserve.com/2020/08/18/mco-fraud-losses-over-rm100m/.

[33] *The Star*, More than 90% jump in cyber-crime complaints during MCO, 2020 (accessed July 3, 2020). https://www.thestar.com.my/tech/tech-news/2020/07/03/zahidi-cybercrime-complaints-spiked-more-than-90-during-mco.

[34] Media statement: Changing usage patterns influence internet speed in Malaysia, MCMC, 2020 (accessed September 12, 2020). https://www.mcmc.gov.my/en/media/press-releases/media-statement-changing-usage-patterns-influence#:~:text=Media%20Statement%3A%20Changing%20Usage%20Patterns%20Influence%20Internet%20Speed%20In%20Malaysia,-09%20Apr%202020&text=Adherence%20to%20the%20MCO%20by,a%20further%20increase%20of%208.6%25.

[35] Slow internet speed as more Malaysians go online during MCO, *New Straits Times*, 2020 (accessed September 15, 2020). https://www.nst.com.my/lifestyle/bots/2020/04/582739/tech-slow-internet-speed-more-malaysians-go-online-during-mco.

[36] Tariq, Qishin, Internet slowdown caused by submarine cable fault, says TM, *The Star*, 2020 (accessed September 12, 2020). https://www.thestar.com.my/tech/tech-news/2020/04/10/internet-slowdown-caused-by-submarine-cable-fault-says-tm.

moves online, the pressing need to address connectivity allocated RM400 million to increase network coverage and maintenance in the Prihatin Economic Stimulus Package.[37]

Work-from-home for the government

The private sector and general population were not the only parties embracing digitization. Government ministries and agencies adapted to the MCO by offering services online. However, the government as a user of cyber differs from consideration of government officials as operators and regulators in this space. The various jurisdictions in operating popular platforms can raise national security concerns as information on how government operations utilize applications parked in servers across different jurisdictions. An example is the video-conferencing application Zoom that rose to prominence in the midst of global lockdowns and travel bans. In a memo by Malaysia's National Cybersecurity Agency (NACSA), government bodies raised concerns over the application on the grounds of security vulnerabilities.[38] The memo came following incidents of Zoom bombing and Citizenlab's expose of Zoom's custom encryption that was not industrial standard of end-to-end encryption. NACSA and Cybersecurity Malaysia placed efforts to increase awareness of cyber threats through notifications and compiling the list of exploits on NACSA's website for the reference of the community as well as government bodies.

---

[37] Media statement: The people-centric economic stimulus package (PRIHATIN) no one will be left behind, MCMC, 2020 (accessed September 14, 2020). https://www.mcmc.gov.my/en/media/press-releases/media-statement-the-people-centric-economic-stimul.

[38] Dzulkifly, Danial, Bukit Aman confirms receiving memo about cyber threats, prohibiting use of Zoom, *Malay Mail*, 2020 (accessed September 12, 2020). https://www.malaymail.com/news/malaysia/2020/04/08/bukit-aman-confirms-receiving-memo-about-cyber-threats-prohibiting-use-of-z/1854768.

Perils of Cyber

If Malaysia's definition of cyberspace follows UN conventions as well as those in domestic legal documents, cyber can be defined as a complex environment, resulted from interactions between human, software and Internet services through technological devices and space of transmission of electronic messages whatsoever between computers through data communication pathways. Cyber is a domain encompassing social, logic and physical network layers (quote Solemn and Chung), which means threats can impact systems as well as the users offline. In Malaysia's approach to mitigate the virus, there were significant perils. Trends specifically on data retention and cybersecurity practices, misinformation and disinformation as well as digital literacy concern levels of digital hygiene needed for a secure cyberspace.

Data retention and management

The diversity of applications with unwritten specific national guidelines indicated different practices for data retention and management. Procedures under the Diseases Act would determine that data can be requested by Malaysian MOH. MyTrace and MySejahtera are administered by the MOH. However, different platforms may have different data retention practices. Some of the mobile phone applications declare a limit to the retention of individual's data. For MyTrace, the data obtained are retained for a total of 21 days. As an added security feature to the limit on data retention, applications such as MyTrace anonymizes data, as data are either encrypted or do not contain any personal information that may lead to the identification of individuals. Gerak Malaysia has already announced to users to delete the application with the record of the movement of users.[39] The different practices do not necessarily translate to high user protection.

---

[39] MCMC, Aplikasi Mudah Alih Gerak Malaysia akan ditamatkan perkhidmatan pada 31 Julai 2020 (accessed September 15, 2020). https://www.mcmc.gov.my/en/media/press-releases/aplikasi-mudah-alih-gerak-malaysia-akan-ditamatkan.

The dependence of the government on technology and digital applications also raises concerns over data management during the active use of the applications and post-pandemic application considerations. While the information for contact tracing would be under the jurisdiction of the Diseases Act that is the foundation of the Prevention and Control of Infectious Diseases (Measures within the Infected Local Areas) Regulations 2020, geo-location information would not be immediately accessible to ministries and agencies. Applications such as MySejahtera would bring such information to the fingertips of the seven people (from the national Crisis Preparedness Response Centre and disease control division under MOH and NACSA).[40] However, transparency in management of data could be clearly conveyed to build trust in the application, particularly as the application has experienced hacking attempts by malicious parties.[41]

Data use and management is under the Personal Data Protection Act 2010. However, the legislation makes exceptions for government ministries and agencies. This, coupled with weak enforcement from the PDPA and the PDPA's weakness in mandating compulsory declarations of data breaches, means that if MySejahtera or an application by the public or private sectors is compromised, repercussions may not be swiftly carried. Just in February 2020, a public consultation paper on an update to the PDPA had made its rounds with articulations of its implementation and clarity on the consent of the data subject. The data policy should be a well-rounded document with avenues for legal redress. While the pandemic is expected to cease only in 2021 or upon the development of the vaccine, surveillance would be a legitimate tool used by the state. However, greater discourse can be held to ensure that consumers are well-informed of the risks.

---

[40] *Ibid.*
[41] Nazari, Tasneem, More than 200 COVID-19 positive individuals successfully identified by MySejahtera app, *The Rakyat Post*, 2020 (accessed September 15, 2020). https://www.therakyatpost.com/2020/06/25/more-than-200-covid-19-positive-individuals-successfully-identified-by-mysejahtera-app/.

Misinformation

Misinformation and disinformation can be particularly harmful to the nation if viral texts circulate and are capable of jeopardizing the core of nation. As the MCO and mitigating the public require compliance with regulations out of the ordinary, misinformation and disinformation campaigns could endanger processes and progress toward mitigating the spread of the virus. In an ISIS Malaysia paper on the different types of false claims made in the pandemic climate, the classification was led by claims on authoritative action, followed by community spread and public preparedness.[42] The paper, classifying fact checks corrected by Sebenarnya.my using the CORONAVIRUS (COVID-19) tab on the website, saw 377 entries between January and June 15, 2020. Around 84% of the entries were debunked while 16% received clarifications. The paper had also found that WhatsApp was the medium most popular for false information, followed by Facebook, News and Twitter. However, the misinformation and disinformation paradigm can be impacted by the classification of "Fake News," journalistic practices and digital literacy levels in Malaysia. In regards to the first, with the repeal of the Anti-Fake News Act, the term "Fake News" has become a catch-all phrase to indicate purposeful sharing of information that could have specific intentions to mislead the public. The cases whose viral information was charged in court were not divulged, thus while Sebenarnya.my would record above 300 misinformation or disinformation entries, the exact details of the entries were not revealed to the public. This would impact the approach nations take to address viral information or coverage in the midst of the MCO, as even seeking clarification could be classified as misinformation or disinformation. The swift implementation of the MCO and fears over a community cluster could explain the high amounts of authoritative actions that required clarification, particularly given the shifting standard operating procedures and guidelines in the different phases of the MCO. Secondly, newsroom practices that do not include robust fact-checking preparedness can exacerbate

---

[42] *Ibid.*

the delivery of misinformation and disinformation. Lastly, the inability of the general public to verify information before sharing could be an issue.

Whole of society cybersecurity

Malaysia's experience during the MCO raised the necessity of addressing whole of society cybersecurity approaches. Vulnerabilities in cyber stem from various sources. Among them is related to human-induced factors. For instance, access to computer systems can be socially engineered through phishing e-mails or outdated programs which can open pathways for exploitation. Cybercrime complaints spiked above 90% during the MCO. Cybercrime stemming from online purchasing increased more than fourfold to 441.7% between March 18 and May 21 in the state of Penang[43] while Selangor recorded 128 cases of telecommunications fraud, 72 cases for non-existent loans as well as 136 cases of cheating from March 18 to April 16.[44] The rise in exploitation of e-commerce platforms utilized current COVID-19 conditions which included selling of masks online while merchants would disappear after payment is made.[45] In Penang, 13 were detained for such cases concerning e-commerce platforms while three were charged in court.

The increased use of cyber increased the canvas for incidences to occur. Such vulnerabilities impacting the security at various levels can be diverse. Malaysia's Computer Emergency Response Team (MyCERT) recorded various incidences in Malaysia such as intrusions, fraud, denial of service, cyber harassment and content-related issues. To protect Malaysia's cyberspace, Malaysia's National

---

[43] Basyir, Mohamed, Cybercrime in Penang shoots up 441.7 per cent since MCO, 2020 (accessed September 14, 2020). https://www.nst.com.my/news/crime-courts/2020/05/594436/cybercrime-penang-shoots-4417-cent-mco.

[44] Kit Yen, Ho, Selangor buyers lost RM1.9 mil to cyber criminals during MCO, *Free Malaysia Today*, 2020 (accessed September 14, 2020). https://www.freemalaysiatoday.com/category/nation/2020/04/16/selangor-buyers-lose-rm1-9-mil-to-cyber-criminals-during-mco/.

[45] Basyir, Mohamed, *op. cit.*

Cybersecurity Policy was launched in 2008. The document sought for protection of critical national infrastructure with the policy addressing legislation, regulatory, public-private cooperation and institutional areas. As Malaysia's online population grew, along with the diversity of threats online, an update of the strategy was announced in 2018. However, the policy was not launched in time to prepare society for the digitization amid the pandemic. This means that as state governments and the private sectors churn out applications to assist in the pandemic, the cybersecurity standards practiced may differ and may not adhere to high standards that would safeguard national interests. As states may prioritize the development of applications without considering security risks in the entire supply chain, weaker areas could open vulnerabilities for users. Lastly, as the National Cybersecurity Policy is aimed to address critical sectors, areas such as digital literacy are in its fledgling stages. Malaysia's cybersecurity apparatus hosting agencies such as Cyber999, MyCERT, MyCyberSecurity Clinic and CyberSAFE. Cyber999 is a mechanism for Internet users to report computer security incidents. MyCERT operated the Cybersecurity Malaysia Cyber Threat Research Centre which analyzes malware and computer security threats. MyCybersecurityClinic provides services such as data recovery and data sanitization while CyberSAFE conducts digital awareness programs. However, the impact of digital literacy efforts is not prominent.

Malaysia's use of technology was deemed as necessary to reduce the rate of infection in Malaysia. However, as use of technology grows, access to digital realms would expand. The collection of data to deliver services would grow. In other areas, cyber's multidimensional nature would bear economic and social impacts. Where governments become users of cyber, the issue related to national interests would be raised. The online and offline perils of digitization would be related to the use of technology. Thus, Malaysia would require assessments of failures, areas of concerns and successes to address future concerns over cyber.

https://doi.org/10.1142/9789811257896_0012

Chapter

12

Vietnam's Perspective and Policies toward Promoting Sustainable Development of Digital Platform

Nguyen Dinh Sach

Institute for Foreign Policy and Strategic Studies, Hanoi, Vietnam

nguyendinh.sach@gmail.com

Introduction

A digital platform can be defined as any type of platform that uses the Internet to connect dispersed networks of individuals to facilitate digital interactions between people.[1] Similarly understood, the work by Michael Cusumano, Annabelle Gawer and Peter Evans defines digital platforms as multisided digital frameworks that shape the terms on which participants interact with one another.[2] In more details, a digital

---

[1] The rise of the platform economy, Deloitte, December 2018.
[2] Kenney, Martin and John Zysman, "The rise of the platform economy," *Issues in Science and Technology*, 2020, 32(3) (accessed August 26, 2020). https://issues.org/the-rise-of-the-platform-economy/.

platform is any electronic tool for communication includes desktop, mobile, social and email software. This covers websites and social media — Twitter, Amazon, Wattpad, etc. Digital platform refers to the software or hardware of a website allowing for the interaction of its users.[3] According to recent research, digital platforms, as well as platform ecosystems, which are formed by them are capable of modernizing entire industries and various types of socio-economic activities, are becoming drivers of innovation, economic growth and competition.[4]

Recognizing the great potential to growth and development, the Vietnamese government is seeing the development and utilization of digital platforms and the digital economy as new drivers for modernizing its economy, especially in bringing the country into a higher-income country.

Vietnam has been transforming its economy from one of the world's poorest countries in the 1980s into the middle-income status by 2010 and is looking forward to becoming a higher middle-income country by 2035. To achieve further development, the government is focusing on innovation and promoting skills, improving market institutions and maintaining infrastructure investment under which digital transformation is set to be a key driver for the economic growth.

Digital Platform Development in Vietnam

The introduction of the Internet to Vietnam in early 2000s is the start point for the development of digital platforms in Vietnam

The adoption of high-speed Internet services, smart devices and mobile phones in Vietnam has been comparatively high since 2003. In 2017, more than half of the country had Internet access, compared with around 15% a decade ago.[5] Rural areas still lag behind urban

---

[3] IGI Global, https://www.igi-global.com/dictionary/digital-platform/55829.

[4] Digital platforms in the modern economy: The concept, features and development trends, January 2020 (accessed August 26, 2020). https://www.researchgate.net/publication/335829912_Digital_Platforms_in_the_Modern_Economy_The_Concept_Features_and_Development_Trends.

[5] World Bank, World development indicators, January 3, 2019 (accessed August 26, 2020). http://data.worldbank.org/.

areas, although the provision of satellite and wireless services is now boosting take-up rates in even the most remote provinces. The adoption of broadband Internet services is also increasing in the business sector. The share of manufacturing and services firms using the Internet for business activities rose to 71% in 2007 and 86% in 2011.[6] Around 500,000 Vietnamese business accounts had been created on Alibaba.com by 2016, and is growing by about 100,000 accounts per year.[7]

Vietnam has the highest number of registered domains in the ASEAN region.[8] In 2017 there were around 422,000 active ".vn" domain names, from a total of nearly 1 million domains registered for ASEAN nations. Vietnam also had also around 16 million allocated IPv4 addresses.[9] The development of high-speed Internet and its widespread have laid a strong foundation for the development of diverse Internet services, including the inception of digital platforms.

Utilization of ICT for economic development

The digital economy is booming in Vietnam with various sectors applying ICT in business. Emerging sectors and fast-growing industries in Vietnam include finance technology (fintech), telecommunications, electronics and computer manufacturing, and information and communications technology (ICT) services.

In mid-2018, Vietnam was home to an estimated 30,000 businesses spanning IT hardware, software, digital content and ICT services. The country has a thriving community of software developers and start-ups, developing digital products and services for use within Vietnam as well as undertaking software development

[6] Nguyen, H. and Marc, S., *Internet, Reorganization and Firm Productivity in Vietnam*, Washington DC: World Bank, 2015.
[7] Alibaba Group, OSB opportunity solution and business, 2017.
[8] Vietnam National Internet Exchange, "Internet resource statistics," Hanoi, Vietnam, 2017.
[9] *Ibid.*

offshored from advanced economies.[10] There are also training centers and technology parks for IT programmers and engineers in several locations, including the major cities of Hanoi, Ho Chi Minh City and Da Nang.[11]

ICT is one of the fastest-growing sectors in Vietnam. In 2018, the total ICT industry revenue was US$98.9 billion, 13 times the amount of the revenue in 2010 (US$7.6 billion).[12] The hardware industry is the largest subsector of Vietnam's ICT industry, contributing 89% of total revenue in 2018.

ICT equipment accounted for around 25% of total exports from Vietnam in 2016, up from less than 10% in 2011.[13] It was now the country's largest export sector in 2018, with telephone and broadcasting equipment particularly important.[14] The increase in ICT exports has come from leading Vietnam-located manufacturers such as Samsung, Intel, Dell and LG, who are expanding their businesses and increasing investments in the country.[15] Vietnam assembles electrical and electronic products, and increasingly exports sophisticated computing devices.

Half of Samsung's high-end S8 and S8 Plus phones and more than 80% of Intel's personal computer central processing units are produced in Vietnam.[16] As a result of foreign investment in ICT manufacturing, Vietnam has surpassed most regional neighbors in high-tech exports.

---

[10] Vietnam Information Technology Outsourcing Alliance, Why Vietnam? 2018.

[11] Ministry of Information and Communication and Vietnam Association for Information Processing, Vietnam ICT index 2016, Hanoi, Vietnam, 2016.

[12] Ministry of Information and Communications of Vietnam, ICT white paper, Hanoi, Vietnam, 2017.

[13] Vietnam Customs, Merchandise export and import, Ministry of Planning and Investment, Hanoi, Vietnam, 2018.

[14] *Ibid.*

[15] Oxford Business Group, The Report — Vietnam 2017, OBG Dubai, United Arab Emirates, 2017.

[16] Pricewaterhouse Coopers, Spotlight on Vietnam — The leading emerging market, PwC, Ho Chi Minh City, Vietnam, 2017.

The creation of platform economy

The digital economy has been facilitated by cloud computing platforms, the high rate of adoption of smartphones and Vietnamese consumer preferences for low personal asset ownership. For example, in the last 5 years, ride-sharing platforms have created competition for traditional taxi businesses. Vietnam was the first country in Asia to attract Uber, and, excluding China, was Uber's fastest-growing market globally in 2015.[17] In 2018, Grab acquired Uber's operations in the ASEAN region. Go-Jek's entry into Vietnam in September 2018 is set to increase competition.

Traditional taxi services are increasingly developing their own platforms and mobile apps to compete. Meanwhile, court proceedings are determining whether ride-sharing platforms will need to follow the same regulations as traditional taxis — which may reduce their competitive edge. Peer-to-peer lending is growing in Vietnam, with platforms such as Timma, Vaymuon and Mofin offering loans to individuals and Lendbiz offering business loans. Through the Lendbiz service, businesses can apply for up to 1 billion VND (US$44,000) loans without collateral, and these can be approved within 24 hours. The Lendbiz platform is attractive to investors. Only 500,000 VND (US$22) is needed to join, and there is the potential to achieve high returns with yearly interest rates up to 20%.[18]

Current digital platforms in Vietnam

Vietnam is having its own digital platforms which are operating in diversified areas. They are similar to a lot of platforms already created and being run worldwide, except for those in energy and heavy industries (Table 1). Those Vietnamese platforms have witnessed many successes and failures. Some have been enjoying rapid growth such as MoMo which provides e-wallet service that reaches more than 10 million users (in 2018) and successfully attracts an investment of more

---

[17] *Vietnam Economic Times*, Vietnam Uber's second fastest growing market, 2015.
[18] Lendbiz, Project selection criteria, Hanoi, Vietnam, 2017.

Table 1:   Digital Platforms in Vietnam

Areas	World platforms	Vietnamese platforms
Tourism	Airbnb, Tripadvisor	Asia Platform Travel, Tubudd
Transportation	Uber, Waze, Grab, Ola Cabs	Be
Retail	Amazon, Alibaba, Burberry	Tiki, Vatgia, Adayroi
Operating system	iPS, Android, Windows, Microsoft	
Social networks	Facebook, Twitter, Tinder, Instagram, Wechat	Zalo, Lotus
Education	Udemy, EdX, Doulingo, Coursera	Edumall, Kyna, Học mãi
Finance	Bitcoin, Lending Club, Kickstarter	Verig, Kalapa
Healthcare	Cohealo, SimplyInsured, Kaiser Permanete	Ecomedic, Vicare
Jobs	Upwork, Fiverr, 99designs, Sittercity	Vietnamwork, 24h
Agriculture	John Deere, Intuit Fasal	Nextfarm, Hachi
Energy and Heavy Industry	Nest, Tesia Powerwall, EnerNOC	
Logistics	Munchery, Foodpanda, Haier Group	Ahamove, Ship60

Source: Vietnam Journal of Science, Technology and Engineering.

than US$100 million from Warburg Pincus. MoMo is among 100 largest fintech companies in the world. Similarly, Zalo, a free messaging and calling app similar to Facebook's Messenger, has seen revenue growth at 20% in 2019 and its pre-tax profit increased 1.5 times, reaching VND641 billion. In contrast, many famous platforms appeared but quickly disappeared such as Lotus and Gapo. Those two social networks are expected to replace Facebook in Vietnam but finally performed under expectation.[19]

---

[19] Thi Hien, Nguyen, The road to build made in Vietnam digital platforms, *Vietnam Journal of Science, Technology and Engineering*, 2020 (accessed August 26, 2020). https://vjst.vn/vn/tin-tuc/3149/con-duong-xay-dung-cac-nen-tang-so-made-in-vietnam.aspx.

For cases of failure, the reason is that those Vietnamese platforms are built based on a format that already exists with no creativity or not being localized, making them less competitive compared with global firms. For example, in cases of social network, Facebook is almost a monopoly. Both Facebook and Twitter were developed to be friendly to Vietnamese users. Besides that, those global firms possess a huge amount of information from billions of users over the years which could be used to make their platforms more compatible and convenient to users while those of Vietnamese ones lag behind.

For the success cases, MoMo has been able to dominate over foreign platforms (such as Paypal) because the language system and the interface design are friendly and convenient to Vietnamese users. MoMo is also able to link its services with those of many domestic banks, for example, credit cards service that most Vietnamese have been using. Similarly, compared with Messenger of Facebook, Line, Kakao and Talk, Zalo is able to dominate the market thanks to its friendly function and design to Vietnamese people such as the language, interface and installation method.

From those experience of success and failure cases, it can be said that one of the keys for the success of a platform is through its creativity, friendliness to users and localization. From the policy perspective, the policymakers need to have a broader and long-term view for the development of domestic platforms. It is the work of the government to develop an environment that incentivizes the development of digital platforms.

Vietnam's Policy toward Developing Digital Platforms

The Vietnamese government views digital transformation across the broader economy as critical to continued growth and prosperity. At the moment, multiple agencies are charged with supporting and regulating different aspects of the digital economy in Vietnam. The current regulatory framework consists of commercial regulations and decrees issued by various ministries. Currently for telecommunications and ICT-related issues, the Ministry of Information and

Communication is the main agency. Having one single ministry in charge of ICT may contribute to the strong promotion, regulation and implementation of all activities related to digital economy development. This agency may be able to coordinate the development of the digital economy and create consistency, synchronization and feasibility in the amendment, formulation and implementation of the policies, programs and plans for the digital economy. The policies should be updated as new free trade agreements are signed and implemented. This will facilitate regional cooperation for digitalization, innovation, new global value chains and quality FDI. At the same time, creativity, openness and liberalization should be considered as principles of the digitalization process, starting from government and diffusing to the whole of society.

Create legal regulations and promote public's awareness on digital transformation

Over the years, the Vietnamese government has implemented a number of laws to regulate the digital economy. Detailed implementation of these laws is guided by decrees and decisions. This regulatory framework is further enhanced by Vietnam's free trade agreements (e.g., AEC, CPTPP) and bilateral agreements such as those with EU. Vietnam's commitment to digitalization is seen in the number of policies, master plans and directives published over the last 30 years. The main focus of these is to develop critical infrastructure, build the ICT industry, promote e-commerce and adopt technology as a means of lifting productivity. The main document guiding the development of digital economy policies and strategies is Directive 16/CT-TTg (2017), issued by Prime Minister Nguyen Xuan Phuc to strengthen capacity toward the 4th Industrial Revolution. The Directive 16 asked all heads of central and local governments nationwide to focus efforts on preparing the human resources and developing the infrastructure needed to implement the Fourth Industrial Revolution. The government also approved the Program on National Digital Transformation by 2025 with orientations toward 2030. The program aims to realize the orientations and policies of the government to develop the economy based on digital technologies. Accordingly, Vietnam will strive to become a leading digital country and economy in the ASEAN region by 2030 and allow comprehensive testing of new technologies in the digital economy. The main targets include improving competitiveness of the economy, with an average digital economy growth rate reaching 20% a year and labor productivity growth of at least 7% by 2025. The program also aims to build a transparent and effective government in order to be in the world's top 50 in terms of e-government.

According to Mr. Nguyen Huy Dung, Director of the Department of Information Technology (Ministry of Information and Communications), the key part in the Program is to promote the creation and development of digital platforms make in Vietnam (the slogan is Make in Vietnam).[20] Previously, any organization that wants to go digital must invest a lot in IT systems and have their own IT experts. This process is both long and costly. However, with the digital platforms in place, those organizations will not need to spend much money on IT but just play the role of users as those platforms will be able to provide most IT services.

Policy frameworks include other documents such as the National strategy on Transforming Vietnam into an advanced ICT country, the National program on IT application in the operations of state agencies, etc. Those policy documents are not limited to digital platforms but cover a wide range of issues related to digital transformation which are all important to the development of digital platforms. The main contents of those documents include:

- Focusing on developing new digital infrastructure and networks.
- Speeding up reform to encourage businesses to adopt new technologies — including implementing e-government across government agencies and reviewing related regulations and services.
- Prioritizing the development of the Vietnamese ICT industry in

---

[20] *Da Nang Newspaper*, Promoting digital transformation in Vietnam, 2020 (accessed August 26, 2020). https://baodanang.vn/khcn/202008/phat-trien-nen-tang-so-make-in-vietnam-thuc-day-nhanh-chuyen-doi-so-3604941/.

government policy and reform, and promoting the take-up of smart technologies across all industries.

• Building the innovation ecosystem through further funding for scientific and research infrastructure and institutions, creating international relationships and promoting tech start-ups.
• Building technological skills through a focus on STEM education and training from early childhood through to adult education.
• Raising awareness at all levels, and in all sectors, of the opportunities and challenges of Industry 4.0, ensuring all areas of Vietnam's society and industry are prepared for the changes ahead.

The policy and priorities set out in those documents are made on the foundation that the country is having a number of advantages in developing digital platforms. First, the digital economy is booming, creating the needs for digital platform development. Emerging digital sectors in Vietnam include finance technology (fintech), telecommunications, electronics and computer manufacturing, and information and communications.[21] The country also has a high rate of Internet and mobile phone use, specifically 145.8 million mobile subscribers out of total population of 96.9 million (150% of Vietnam's population), 68.17 million Internet users and 65 million social media users.[22] Second, the local software industry is growing steadily and starting to attract global attention. Local businesses account for the majority of the market, supplying low-cost software products. In mid-2018, a total of 9,500 businesses in Vietnam created digital software for sectors such as finance, telecommunications, smart agriculture and e-government. Vietnam has now been Japan's second-largest software outsourcing destination, behind only China. Third, the country has a thriving community of software developers and start-ups, developing digital products and services for use within Vietnam as well as

---

[21] Marvin, R., Vietnam's tech boom: A look inside Southeast Asia's Silicon Valley, *PC Magazine*, 2016.
[22] Anh Trang, Vietnam's advantage in digital transformation, *Vnexpress*, 2020 (accessed September 13, 2020). https://vnexpress.net/fpt-van-hanh-so/nhung-loi-the-trong-chuyen-doi-so-tai-viet-nam-4119734.html.

undertaking software development offshored from advanced economies. Recent research by the Ministry of Information and Communication shows that Vietnam has more than 955,000 workers in ICT sector and 80,000 graduates in information technology and communication industry. There are also specialist training centers and technology parks for IT programmers and engineers in several locations, including the major cities of Hanoi, Ho Chi Minh City and Da Nang.[23]

However, the country is also facing some weaknesses. According to Ms. Pham Chi Lan, economic specialist, digital platform development in Vietnam is faced with three challenges.[24] First is the data problem. Vietnamese users are employing foreign services every day, resulting in huge database for foreign enterprises while domestic firms are vastly lacking. Second, the regulation and policy documents are not transparent enough, not consistent between documents, creating some certain level of uncertainty and infeasibility. Third, Vietnamese enterprises are weak as most of them are mainly SMEs. There remain many limitations on scale, wholesale trade and retail with many scattered products, lack of necessary expertise, management and linkage between industries.

Prioritizing the "Make in Vietnam" digital platforms

According to Mr. Nguyen Manh Hung, Minister of Information and Communications, Vietnam must be able to create and possess its own digital transformation infrastructure and platforms for each industry.[25] One of the reasons behind this is that the country has enough

---

[23] Ministry of Information and Communication and Vietnam Association for Information Processing, Vietnam ICT index 2016, Hanoi, Vietnam, 2016.
[24] Anh, Hoai and Huu Tuc, Many opportunities for trade on digital platforms in Vietnam, Custom News, 2019 (accessed September 13, 2020). https://customsnews.vn/many-opportunities-for-trade-on-digital-platforms-in-vietnam-10198.html.
[25] *Da Nang Newspaper, op. cit.*

potential such as market size of 100 million people, rising middle-income class and young population.

Vietnam's Ministry of Information and Communications has determined that digital platforms must be developed first in the areas of pressing need. In details, Minister of Information and Communications identifies that domestic platforms such as those in the field of distance learning, remote health examination and treatment, online job, video conferencing, remote accounting services, electronic journalism platforms, network security and safety must thrive and keep data of Vietnamese users at home. Under the program on national digital transformation by 2025 with orientations toward 2030, government agencies at different levels have been tasked with related work in supporting the development of digital platforms.

The COVID-19 outbreak is indeed accelerating the development of digital infrastructures and platforms. Since April 2020, the Ministry of Information and Communications has continuously introduced Make in Vietnam platforms. For example, those in distance healthcare and online teaching play an important role in not only coping with the COVID-19 but also in easing the overload of hospitals. For business sector, a cloud computing platform has been launched. Stringee is the most recent Make in Vietnam, one that allows businesses to communicate with customers on existing mobile applications (or websites) without having to use third-party applications. Similarly, the National Payment Support Portal PayGov, a new platform has been put into practice to facilitate the online payment of public services. This helps reduce cost, time and prevent corruption.

Assessing the development of Make in Vietnam platforms, Mr. Dau Ngoc Huy, CEO of Stringee platform, comments that the past and current development of digital platforms proved that Vietnamese enterprises are fully capable of mastering technology and competing with similar international platforms through providing more added values such as new functions, data security and cost saving. In addition, Vietnamese cultural features can be integrated into new platforms to make them more friendly and convenient to Vietnamese users.

Developing Internet infrastructure

Vietnam is dedicated to providing universal connection coverage across the country. The first universal service program was implemented between 2005 and 2010 with a total investment of over 5 trillion VND (Decision No. 74/2006/QD-TTg). The program on the provision of public telecommunications services until 2020 was issued in 2015 and revised in 2018 under Decision No. 868/QD-TTg. Under this program, a total of 7.3 trillion VND will be devoted to investing in the development of broadband infrastructure nationwide, with a priority on remote and isolated areas, disadvantaged areas, border areas and islands.

The main objective of the program is to provide broadband access to 99% of the communities in Vietnam where have access to electricity. A critical part of this program is the scheduled rollout of 5G services by 2021.[26]

Human resources and R&D

Vietnam aims to enhance the quality of its workforce. Between 2005 and 2017, the proportion of state budget spent on education increased from 11% to around 15%.[27] Directive 16/CT-TTg clearly identifies human resources as fundamental to implementing digital transformation. The directive emphasizes the need to change policies, contents and methods of education and vocational training in order to generate human resources which are able to follow new technological production trends, including the focus on promotion of training in science, technology, engineering and mathematics (STEM), foreign languages; promote autonomy in higher education and vocational training; pilot regulations on vocational training and higher education applied to some specific fields.

---

[26] Onishi, Vietnam's viettel to roll out 5G service in 2021, *Nikkei Asian Review*, December 5, 2018.

[27] General Statistic Office of Vietnam, National account, GSO, Hanoi, Vietnam, 2017.

Directive 16 assigned two ministries to develop human resources — the Ministry of Education and Training and the Ministry of Labour, Invalids and Social Affairs. These ministries engage in several activities to build STEM skills. For example, through a public–private partnership with Microsoft, the ministries have increased digital skills training, created a new ICT curriculum, and promoted digital inclusion for rural students and ethnic minorities. The year 2019 was seen as a milestone for the implementation of the scheme Developing the Digitalised Knowledge System led by the Ministry of Science and Technology.

Promoting innovation and the digital ecosystem

The Vietnamese government has made a lot of efforts in linking innovation, including the development of the digital economy with increasing creativity. The country has adopted a number of policies toward facilitating research and development (R&D). Decree No. 95/2014/ND-CP, for example, requires state-owned enterprises to invest 3–10% of total revenue for R&D activities.[28] However, Vietnam's spending on science and technology is still low (0.8% of total national budget in 2017) and is decreasing (the figure was 1% in 2005). Vietnam also implements various programs to foster the start-up and innovation ecosystem. These include the National Agency for Technology, Entrepreneurship and Commercialization Development (NATECD), National Technology Innovation Fund (NATIF), Hoalac Hitech Service Centre and the Saigon Silicon City Centre. The country has also decided to build the National Innovation Center and National Start-up Center in which enterprises are put at the center through Resolution No. 1&2/2019/ND-CP in improving the country's business environment and national competitiveness.

In addition to enterprise-level initiatives, the government is also committed to various digitalization initiatives. The adoption of digital technologies across industries, including agriculture, healthcare, security and defense, is promoted in the National Technology Development

---

[28] *Ibid.*

Program up to 2020. Recognizing the importance of reform and digitalization, the Vietnamese government established a national e-government committee in 2018 (under Decision No. 1072/2018/QDTTg). The committee is responsible for researching and proposing strategies, mechanisms and policies, creating a legal environment to promote the construction and development of e-government, and facilitating the implementation of Industry 4.0.

Cybersecurity and data regulations

Cybersecurity in Vietnam is governed by two major legal frameworks: the Law on Information Security (Law No. 86/2015/QH13) and the Law on Cybersecurity (Law No. 24/2018/QH14). The cybersecurity law applies to domestic and foreign firms providing services on the telecommunications network or value-added digital services in Vietnam. The firms that collect, exploit, analyze or process personal information and/or data of users in Vietnam are required to establish a branch or a representative office in Vietnam. In addition, the law has articles on data localization for certain types of data, cybersecurity audits, handling illegal content and protection of children. The Vietnamese government also helps ensure cybersecurity through emergency response plans (Decision No. 05/2017/QD-TTg). Plans are informed by the National Steering Committee on Information Security, then decided and implemented by the Ministry of Information and Communication.

The Ministry implements the plans with assistance from the National Cyber Information Security Incident Response Network — which includes various state agencies (e.g., Vietnam Computer Emergency Response Team), and private firms from a range of relevant sectors (e.g., telecommunications, finance).

Taxation

Digitalization is imposing new challenges for Vietnamese taxation system. These include but are not limited to tax base erosion with new business models such as the sharing economy, the emergence of digital marketplaces and e-commerce platforms and new income sources such as data utilization. Vietnam, like many other countries, is trying to apply tax to digital transactions. For example, Official Dispatch 848/BTC-TCT (issued in 2017) requires foreign companies that provide online reservation services in Vietnam (e.g., Agoda. com, Traveloka.com, Booking.com) to pay income and value-added tax when signing contracts with accommodation establishments in Vietnam (hotels, hostels, etc.). It also requires the establishments to declare and pay taxes on behalf of foreign contractors.

Recommendations for China–ASEAN Cooperation in Digital Platforms

Based on the experience of Vietnam's policies toward developing digital platforms, this chapter suggests the following recommendations for sustaining the development and cooperation between ASEAN and China on digital platforms:

- *Educate stakeholders, especially the public and the youth about the benefits of digital platforms and services:* The private sector should inform governments about the latest innovations and co-operate with governments to deliver economic and societal benefits. Likewise, the public sector should educate potential users of e-business benefits.
- *Encourage government and private sector collaboration:* The public and private sectors must encourage mutual engagement to discuss current and emerging issues and opportunities as technology advances.
- *Increase digital adoption among all population groups:* To reap full benefits of the Internet economy, all population segments should be online and have access to high-speed broadband services.
- *Support ASEAN's SMEs to go online:* As the main engine of growth across ASEAN, SMEs need greater support to expand online, and across borders. Private enterprises have a significant role to play.
- *Support technology providers that help improve the performance of the economy:* E-commerce and e-tourism service providers are

particularly valuable in ASEAN, given the region's attractions and economic composition, with travel contributing an increasingly large amount of GDP in several countries.

• *Support digital economy program*: All stakeholders should support at the highest level the development and implementation of forward-looking digital economy strategies.

Chapter

13

ASEAN–China Digital Economy Cooperation and Its Prospects

Cao Xiaoyang

Chinese Academy of Social Sciences, Beijing, China

caoxy@cass.org.cn

The year 2021 marks the 30th anniversary of dialogue relations between China and ASEAN. After 30 years of development, China–ASEAN relations have achieved leapfrog development and the two sides have become the largest trading partner of each other. China–ASEAN relations have become the most successful and dynamic model of Asia-Pacific regional cooperation. Under the test of the COVID-19 epidemic, China and ASEAN have helped each other to overcome the difficulties, with bilateral cooperation deepened and political mutual trust strengthened. On November 22, 2021, at the 30th anniversary of the establishment of China–ASEAN dialogue relations, President Xi Jinping and leaders of ASEAN countries jointly announced that China–ASEAN relations will be upgraded to a comprehensive strategic partnership. The improvement of this bilateral relationship will create a better future for China–ASEAN cooperation.

Sustainable Development of China–ASEAN Relations

China–ASEAN relations have been through ups and downs for the past 30 years. The relations withstood the tests of the Asian financial crisis in 1997, the SARS epidemic in 2002, the Indian Ocean tsunami in 2004, the world financial crisis in 2008 and the COVID-19 epidemic, showing strong vitality and resilience. The sustainable development of China–ASEAN relations is mainly reflected in the increasing political mutual trust between the two parties, deepening of economic and trade cooperation, and frequent cultural exchanges. Firstly, the two sides have strong consensus and willingness to further deepen bilateral relations and cooperation. Secondly, China–ASEAN relations have a series of cooperation mechanisms to ensure the stable development of bilateral relations. Finally, the development of China–ASEAN relations benefits from geographical and cultural proximity of the two parties. The sustainable development of China–ASEAN relations also builds the foundation for both sides to deepen cooperation in the digital economy.

First of all, China and ASEAN have a strong consensus and willingness to cooperate

Since the establishment of the dialogue relationship between China and ASEAN in 1991, the relationship between the two sides has developed by leaps and bounds. The transition of China–ASEAN relations, from dialogue relations, negotiation partners, comprehensive dialogue partners, strategic partnership to comprehensive strategic partnership, reflects the deepening of the strategic relationship between the two parties, deepening of economic and trade integration, and the enhancement of political mutual trust.

After the Cold War, the eased situation in East Asia brought opportunities for the development of China–ASEAN relations.

In 1991, Qian Qichen, the then Foreign Minister of China, visited ASEAN to participate in the ASEAN Foreign Ministers' Meeting, which started the China–ASEAN dialogue. Maintaining regional stability and promoting economic development are the common aspirations of China and ASEAN. In 2003, China and ASEAN announced the establishment of *a strategic partnership for peace and prosperity*, and China–ASEAN relations entered a new stage of comprehensive development. In 2013, Chinese President Xi Jinping delivered a speech in Indonesia, proposing the initiative of building *the 21st Century Maritime Silk Road*. This initiative has injected new impetus into the development of China–ASEAN relations, and ASEAN have become China's priority partner in *the Belt and Road Initiative*. On November 22, 2021, at the 30th anniversary of the establishment of the China–ASEAN dialogue relationship, the two sides announced the establishment of a China–ASEAN comprehensive strategic partnership. This is an important historical milestone in the relationship between the two sides. ASEAN countries highly value the fruitful results achieved in the development of ASEAN–China relations and are full of confidence in China's development. They hope to further deepen cooperation with China in the fields of economy and trade, digital economy, climate change, cultural exchanges, and sustainable development, seize opportunities and deal with challenges together, to build a strategic, substantial, mutually beneficial and win–win comprehensive strategic partnership.

Over the past 30 years, China and ASEAN have taken care of each other's major concerns, respected their respective development paths, increased understanding and trust through sincere communication, and properly handled differences in order to seek common ground while reserving differences. Thus, bilateral cooperation has continued to deepen. In this process, despite the various versions of *China Threat Theory*, *Debt Crisis Theory*, *China Economic Coercion Theory* and other noises, ASEAN countries have always insisted on cooperating with China, hoping to realize rapid development and regional economic integration with the express train of China's economic growth. A strong willingness to cooperate and achieve consensus are the prerequisite and foundation for the sustainable development of bilateral relations.

Second, institutionalization of China–ASEAN cooperation has continued to improve

Since the establishment of the strategic partnership between China and ASEAN in 2003, institutionalization of bilateral cooperation has been continuously improved. China maintains frequent high-level exchanges with ASEAN, and Chinese leaders have attended all previous China–ASEAN leaders' meetings. High-level exchanges have enhanced mutual trust and laid a good political foundation for the development of bilateral relations. Within the *10+1 Framework*, China and ASEAN have established a dialogue and cooperation mechanism covering all levels of leaders, ministers and senior officials. The two sides have also established more than a dozen ministerial-level conference mechanisms for foreign affairs, economy, transportation, customs directors, attorney generals, youth affairs, health, telecommunications, news and combating transnational crimes. These institutional arrangements have not only promoted practical cooperation between the two parties but also strengthened the resilience of the bilateral relationship, enabling the relationship between the two parties to withstand external risks. The overall relations between China and ASEAN have not been affected by the dispute between China and several ASEAN countries.

In the field of politics and security, the two sides have carried out various exchange activities under the framework of China–ASEAN, ASEAN Regional Forum, ASEAN Defense Ministers' Meeting-Plus, 10+3 and ASEAN Summit. In 2003, China joined *The Treaty of Amity and Cooperation in Southeast Asia*, becoming the first extraterritorial country to join the treaty. In 2011, China and ASEAN held their first meeting for the exchange among ministers of national defense. In November 2002, China and ASEAN countries signed the *Declaration on the Conduct of Parties in the South China Sea*, demonstrating the determination of both parties to strengthen the partnership of good-neighborliness and mutual trust and to maintain peace and stability in the South China Sea. In July 2011, the two parties reached an agreement on the follow-up action guidelines for the implementation of the Declaration on the Conduct of Parties in the South China Sea. China and ASEAN are stepping up consultations on advancing the Code of Conduct (COC) in the South China Sea, striving to reach regional rules that comply with international law, meet the needs of all parties, have more substantive content and are more effective.

In the economic field, in November 2002, the two sides signed the Framework Agreement on China–ASEAN Comprehensive Economic Co-operation Area (CAFTA), marking the official launch of the China–ASEAN Free Trade Area. In 2004, the early harvest program of the China–ASEAN Free Trade Area was implemented, and the two sides lowered tariffs on agricultural products. After that, the two parties successively signed the trade in goods agreement, the service trade agreement and the investment trade agreement to further release policy dividends. On January 1, 2010, the China–ASEAN Free Trade Area was formally established. In 2014, the two sides launched negotiations on upgrading the free trade area. In August 2019, the *upgraded version* of the China–ASEAN Free Trade Agreement was officially implemented, and the institutional cooperation between China and ASEAN reached a new level. The agreement covers areas such as trade in goods, trade in services, investment, economic and technological cooperation, which is conducive to reducing transaction costs for both parties, promoting a higher level of openness between the two parties, deepening cooperation areas, and providing broad opportunities for the growth of trade and investment between China and ASEAN. On November 15, 2020, the leaders of the 15 countries of ASEAN, China, Japan, South Korea, Australia and New Zealand formally signed *the Regional Comprehensive Economic Partnership Agreement (RECP)*, marking the official conclusion of the world's largest free trade agreement. The signing of the agreement is of great significance to deepening regional economic integration and stabilizing the global economy. For China and

ASEAN, the most economically dynamic countries in the region, the signing of this agreement is *a win–win solution* for all the member states, and it will surely promote the rapid growth of trade and investment between the two parties and countries in the region. On January 1, 2022, RECP will be officially implemented.

Finally, China–ASEAN cooperation has geographical and cultural advantages

Connected by mountains and rivers, China and ASEAN have a close blood relationship and a long history of friendly relations. Since the establishment of the dialogue relationship, China and ASEAN have established cooperation mechanisms in science and technology, medical and health, education, tourism, culture, sports, media and other fields. The two sides have established China-ASEAN Education Exchange Week, China–ASEAN Center, Cultural Forum, Poverty Reduction and Development Forum, China–ASEAN Cooperation Fund, Elite Scholarship and other platforms, which have promoted the cultural exchanges and cooperation between the two sides. The proximity of the geographical location reduces transaction costs, and factors such as similar cultural customs provide convenient conditions for economic cooperation. Since China proposed and implemented *the Belt and Road Initiative*, China–ASEAN cooperation in connectivity and infrastructure has facilitated the in-depth development of bilateral relations. The China–Laos Railway, the Jakarta–Bandung High-speed Railway, construction of the Trans-Asian Railway, and construction of the China-Indochina Peninsula Economic Corridor have made China–ASEAN economic ties closer.

At present, the digital economy is booming, and the new generation of Internet technology has become a powerful instrument for optimizing resource allocation and realizing industrial upgrading. Under this trend of the era, deepening cooperation in the digital economy between China and ASEAN will not only become an inherent requirement for the economic development of both sides but also promote the further integration and development of bilateral relations.

Status Quo of China–ASEAN Digital Economy Cooperation

At present, with the development of a new generation of network information technologies such as cloud computing, big data, artificial intelligence and 5G, the digital economy is expanding at an unprecedented rate, promoting the transformation of the global industrial structure and business model innovation, and also profoundly affecting the intercountry relationship, ways of communication and people's daily life. As a new economic form, the digital economy is becoming a new driving force to support stable economic growth. The *G20 Digital Economy Development and Cooperation Initiative* issued by the G20 Hangzhou Summit defines the digital economy as: using digital knowledge and information as key production factors, using modern information networks as an important carrier, and using information and communication technology to effectively use a range of economic activities that are important drivers of efficiency improvement and economic structure optimization.

The China Academy of Information and Communications Technology believes that the digital economy is *taking digital knowledge and information as the key production factors, with digital technology as the core driving force, modern information network as an important carrier, and through the deep integration of digital technology and the real economy, to continuously improve the economy.* The level of digitalization, networking and intelligence in society *accelerates the reconstruction of a new economic form of economic development and governance models.*[1] Specifically, it includes four parts, namely digital industrialization, industrial digitization, digital governance and data value. Among them, digital industrialization refers to the information and communication industry, including electronic information manufacturing, telecommunications, software and information technology services. Industrial informatization refers to the increase in output and efficiency improvement brought about by the

---

[1] China Academy of Information and Communications Technology, *White Paper on China's Digital Economy Development*, April 2021, p. 1.

application of digital technology in traditional industries, including but not limited to industrial Internet, integration of industrialization and informatization, intelligent manufacturing, Internet of vehicles, platform economy and other integrated new industries, new models and new formats. Digital governance features *digital technology + governance* and digital public services. Data value, including but not limited to data collection, data standards, data rights confirmation, data labeling, data pricing, data transactions, data flow, data protection, etc. It can be seen that the coverage of the digital economy is very broad.[2]

In 2020, the COVID-19 epidemic spread around the world. In order to prevent the spread of the epidemic, all countries implemented social isolation and lockdown to varying degrees. The global production chain and industrial chain were at risk of interruption, and the world economy was hit hard. Digital technology is a key factor in our response to the global crisis brought by the COVID-19 pandemic. During the epidemic, the government can provide public services and companies can operate normally, all thanks to digital technology. Digital technologies are also critical to the sustainability of cities and towns around the world, especially as we enter a decade of action to meet the 2030 Sustainable Development Goals. Stimulated by the epidemic, China's digital economy has developed vigorously. The scale has expanded from RMB 2.6 trillion in 2005 to RMB 39.2 trillion in 2020.[3] The proportion of digital economy in GDP has increased from 14.2% in 2005 to 38.6% in 2020,[4] showing great energy and resilience. According to *the Digital China Development Report (2020)* issued by the State Internet Information Office, during the 13th Five-Year Plan period, the construction of Digital China has achieved important achievements. The scale of information infrastructure construction tops the world. China will build the world's largest optical fiber network and 4G network by the

---

[2] *Ibid.*

[3] Office of the High Commissioner for Human Rights, Digital rights during the COVID-19, 2019.

[4] *op. cit.*, p. 6.

end of 2020. The number of netizens in China has grown to 989 million, and the Internet penetration rate has increased to 70.4%. The speed and scale of 5G network construction ranks first in the world, as 718,000 5G base stations have been built, and the number of 5G terminals exceeds 200 million. In the global innovation index ranking, China has jumped from 29th in 2015 to 14th, and has become the world's largest source of patent applications. The total amount of China's digital economy ranks second in the world, and the added value of the core industries of the digital economy accounts for 7.8% of GDP.[5] China's *Outline of the 14th Five-Year Plan (2021–2025) for National Economic and Social Development and Vision 2035* announced in March 2021 lists the digital economy as a separate article, proposing to accelerate the construction of a digital economy, a digital society, and a digital government to transform digitally and drive the transformation of production methods, lifestyles and governance methods. For the first time, the outline proposed a new economic indicator, the ratio of the added value of the core industries of the digital economy to GDP, and clearly required that the ratio of the added value of the core industries of the digital economy to GDP should be increased from 7.8% in 2020 to 10%.

In 2017, the online transaction value of the Internet economy in Southeast Asia was US$50 billion. By 2019, the scale of the digital economy in Southeast Asia exceeded US$100 billion. The COVID-19 pandemic has contributed to the explosive growth of the digital economy in Southeast Asia. According to the 2021 Southeast Asia Digital Economy Report released by Google, Temasek and Bain & Company, since the outbreak of the epidemic, Southeast Asia has added 60 million digital consumers, with the fastest growing population coming from non-metropolitan areas. Online grocery and food delivery services have exploded, with food delivery the most pervasive. Compared with before the epidemic, food delivery and daily grocery online services in the six ASEAN countries (Malaysia,

---

[5] The release of digital China development report, https://m.thepaper.cn/baijiahao_13419897, July 2, 2021.

Singapore, Indonesia, Thailand, the Philippines and Brunei) increased by 65% and 62%, respectively. In 2021, new users in non-metropolitan areas of the six ASEAN countries accounted for 60% of new users. Digital consumers are 80% satisfied with online services. Digital consumption in Southeast Asia remained stable in 2021, and people took it as a new way of life. The report predicts that the digital economy of ASEAN countries is expected to grow to US$1 trillion by 2030 as millions of new Internet users drive online businesses in areas such as e-commerce and virtual finance.[6]

ASEAN countries have formulated Industry 4.0 plans and digital development blueprints, hoping to ride the express train of the digital economy by improving their digital capabilities, in order to promote post-pandemic economic recovery and achieve innovation in development models. For example, Singapore formulated the Smart Nation 2025 Plan as early as 2014, and put forward *the Research, Innovation and Enterprise 2025 Plan* at the end of 2020 to increase investment in talent training to attract and cultivate more digital talents. Malaysia formulated a national Industry 4.0 policy framework in 2018, and proposed a 10-year digital economy blueprint *Digital Malaysia* in February 2021, which will increase investment in digital infrastructure and encourage small, medium and micro enterprises to use e-commerce. Thailand formulated *the Thailand 4.0 Strategy* (Thailand 4.0) in 2016; Indonesia formulated *the Indonesia Manufacturing 4.0 Strategy* in 2018; and the Philippines formulated the digital transformation strategy in 2019. In June 2020, Vietnam issued *the National Digital Transformation Plan to 2025 and Development Direction for 2030*, which aims to develop digital economy, digital government and digital society while forming a globally competitive digital technology enterprise. Cambodia formulated the Digital Economy and Digital Society Policy Framework (2021–2035) in June 2021, aiming to achieve digital transformation by 2035.[7] According to the plan, the five development goals of Cambodia's digital economy in the next 15

---

[6] *Economy SEA 2021 Soaring 20s: The SEA Digital Decade*, Google, Temasek, Bain & Company.

[7] China News, Vietnam pushes forwards its digital transformation, June 18, 2020.

years are: developing digital infrastructure, building digital trust and confidence, cultivating digital citizens, building digital government and promoting digital business, and establishing a digital economy and digital society council to oversee the implementation of the policy.[8]

At the regional level, in November 2019, ASEAN released the Declaration on Transformation to Industry 4.0, emphasizing the importance of using advanced technologies to develop industries, taking care of different levels of development to maintain the momentum of inclusive growth and building the ASEAN community. In order to promote the transformation of the regional digital economy, ASEAN has successively issued *the ASEAN Economic Community Blueprint, ASEAN Digital Integration Framework, ASEAN E-Commerce Agreement,* and launched a smart city network plan, aiming to enhance ASEAN's competitiveness in the digital economy. In January 2021, ASEAN countries held the first series of digital ministerial meetings. The meeting adopted *the ASEAN Digital Master Plan 2025* to guide ASEAN digital cooperation in the next 5 years and build ASEAN into a leading community powered by safe and transformative digital service, technology and ecosystem. Actions set out in the ASEAN Digital Master Plan 2025 will prioritize ASEAN's recovery from the COVID-19 pandemic, improving the quality of fixed and mobile broadband infrastructure and expanding coverage, delivering trusted digital services, creating a competitive market for digital services, enhancing the quality and use of e-government services, providing digital services that connect businesses and facilitate cross-border trade, empowering businesses and citizens to participate in the digital economy, and building an inclusive digital society, according to a joint declaration issued after the ASEAN ministers' meeting.[9]

---

[8] Government of Guangxi, Cambodia launches long-term policies for digital transformation, http://swt.gxzf.gov.cn/zt/jjdm/jmdt/t9210652.shtml.

[9] ASEAN, ASEAN digital masterplan 2025 (accessed September, 2021). https://asean.org/wp-content/uploads/2021/09/ASEAN-Digital-Masterplan-EDITED.pdf.

China is an important partner of ASEAN's digital economy cooperation. Information interconnection is an important part of *the digital Belt and Road* between China and ASEAN. In order to promote digital economic cooperation, the two sides successfully held *the China–ASEAN Digital Economic Cooperation Year* in June 2020, and released *the China–ASEAN Initiative on Establishing Digital Economic Partnerships* in November. This initiative covers application in epidemic prevention and control; strengthening digital infrastructure cooperation; supporting digital literacy, entrepreneurial innovation and industrial digital transformation; promoting the innovation and development of smart cities; deepening cooperation in cyberspace; and promoting practical cooperation in cyber security, etc. In January 2021, the first China–ASEAN Digital Ministers Meeting was held. The meeting clarified the focus of digital economic cooperation between the two sides in 2021, and jointly formulated and adopted *the Action Plan on Implementing the China–ASEAN Digital Economy Partnership 2021–2025*.

At present, China–ASEAN digital economy cooperation is developing well and has broad space. First, the development strategies of the two sides are highly compatible and the willingness to cooperate is strong. Both China and ASEAN regard the digital economy as the focus of future development, and both sides hope to expand cooperation in the field of digital economy and cultivate new growth points. In 2021, on the occasion of the commemorative summit for the 30th anniversary of the establishment of China–ASEAN dialogue relations, the two sides decided to further strengthen cooperation in the field of digital economy and accelerate the implementation of the *Joint Statement on Synergizing the Belt and Road Initiative and the Master Plan on ASEAN Connectivity 2025* to carry out mutually beneficial and high-quality cooperation; and to explore the alignment of *ASEAN Digital Master Plan 2025* with *the China–ASEAN Initiative on Establishing Digital Economy Partnership* and the action plan.[10] Second, the areas of cooperation continue to expand. The scope of

---

[10] *Joint Statement of the ASEAN–China Special Summit to Commemorate the 30th Anniversary of ASEAN–China Dialogue Relations*, November 22, 2021.

cooperation between the two parties covers digital infrastructure connectivity construction, network security, cross-border e-commerce, smart cities, e-commerce, big data, 5G applications, digital transformation, digital finance, artificial intelligence and other fields. In addition to the consensus and strategic cooperation at the official level, Chinese high-tech enterprises have also continuously strengthened digital technology cooperation with ASEAN countries. For example, in September 2020, Huawei set up a 5G innovation center in Thailand to help incubate local SMEs and start-ups, and plans to promote the development of Thailand's Industry 4.0 by investing in the innovation center, which includes equipment and expert training. In April 2021, Tencent Cloud announced that its first cloud computing data operation center in Indonesia would be fully operational, helping enterprises and organizations in the region to quickly achieve digital transformation. Tencent plans to launch a second data center in Indonesia in 2021. Third, the cooperation mechanism is constantly being established and improved. The two sides have formed a multi-level and multi-channel cooperation mechanism that focuses on the China–ASEAN Leaders' Meeting, the China–ASEAN Telecommunications Ministers' Meeting, and the China–ASEAN Digital Ministers' Meeting, supplemented by the cooperation mechanism between China and ASEAN countries, industries, organizations and think tanks. For example, China and Thailand established a Ministerial Dialogue Mechanism for Digital Economy Cooperation, signed a *Memorandum of Understanding on E-commerce Cooperation* with Vietnam and Cambodia, and initiated the negotiation and signing process of a Memorandum of Understanding on bilateral cross-border e-commerce cooperation with Malaysia.

Challenges for China–ASEAN Digital Economy Cooperation

There is a huge digital divide

Due to the differences in the level of economic development and scientific and technological strength of countries, the digital divide has existed before the epidemic and is considered to be an important obstacle to global sustainable development. The digital infrastructure of developing and least developed countries lags far behind developed countries. As of 2019, developing and least developed countries lagged far behind in terms of mobile Internet penetration, Internet population ratio and Internet speed. In these countries, download speeds are slow and Internet access charges are high. In both groups of countries, the digital divide between urban and rural areas and the digital divide between genders are deep.[11] ASEAN developed countries such as Singapore have relatively complete network infrastructure. Cambodia, Laos and Myanmar are among the 47 least developed countries identified by *the United Nations Conference on Trade and Development*, and the construction of information technology facilities is relatively backward. The gender digital divide is also evident in the region, and there is a need to upgrade women's digital skills. The supply of digital infrastructure for interconnection among ASEAN countries is seriously insufficient. The lack of cross-border electronic payment platforms and the shortage of logistics supply chains make it difficult for ASEAN and Chinese enterprises to obtain large-scale operating benefits.

UNCTAD's 2021 *Digital Economy Report* argues that *the data divide is deepening the traditional digital divide related to connectivity, reflecting large differences between and within countries in the ability to harness data. Countries with less capability cannot translate data into digital intelligence and business opportunities and cannot use data for economic and social development. Thus, they are bound to be disadvantaged.*[12] The data divide have accelerated the traditional digital divide that already exists, and the differences between countries are widening.

---

[11] Luohan Academy, The pandemic will widen worldwide digital divide, https://www.luohanacademy.com/cn/insights/e6ab1b9228be78b7, August 27, 2020.

[12] UNCTAD Digital Economy Report 2021, Cross border data flows and development for whom the data flows. https://unctad.org/system/files/official-document/der2021_overview_ch.pdf.

There is a shortage of digital talents, and the digital literacy and skills of citizens need to be improved

Both China and ASEAN are faced with a scarcity of digital talents and the task of enhancing citizens' digital literacy and skills. Digital literacy and skills are a collection of a series of qualities and abilities that digital society citizens should possess, such as digital acquisition, production, use, evaluation, interaction, sharing, innovation, security and ethics.[13] Most ASEAN countries face a severe shortage of talents in the process of digital economy construction, and there are huge differences between countries. The lack of digital talents does not match the needs of the rapid development of the digital economy, which also makes it difficult for China–ASEAN digital economic cooperation to quickly improve quality and efficiency. Both China and ASEAN need to improve the education system, enhance the digital literacy and techno-logical level of citizens and cultivate high-tech innovative talents.

China–ASEAN digital governance capacity needs to be improved

At present, many countries in Southeast Asia are in the early stage of digital transformation, and the huge growth potential has yet to be released, and the lag of relevant digital governance rules has become a shortcoming for the rapid development of the digital economy. Digital governance rules mainly include two aspects: cross-border data flow and its governance; and the establishment of digital trade rules. In the era of digital economy, data have become an important strategic asset for creating private and social value. The raw data are processed into intelligent information, which can bring about economic value. The use of data affects not only trade and economic development but also human rights, peace and security.[14] Due to its economic value, data has become a new area of game for countries. At present, data protec-

---

[13] CAC, Improve people's digital knowledge and skills, http://www.cac.gov.cn/2021-11/05/c_1637708867754305.htm.

[14] UNCTAD Digital Economy Report, 2021, *op. cit.*

tionism is on the rise, and countries have introduced data restriction, protection and supervision policies, which are not conducive to the safe flow of data. The governance models of data flows and the wider digital economy differ widely among major economies, and there is no consensus at the international level.[15] China has not yet reached any bilateral or multilateral data cross-border circulation agreement with countries and regions along the Belt and Road. China and ASEAN countries have not yet formed uniform rules on data collection, personal privacy and data security.

At present, the connotation and classification of digital trade have not yet been uniformly and clearly defined internationally. There are still disputes between relevant international organizations and countries on digital trade and its classification, let alone the formation of globally unified digital trade rules.[16] Digital governance in the Asia-Pacific region faces issues such as digital transmission, cross-border trade facilitation, and emerging technology norms. The differences in national conditions and economic development levels of countries make it difficult to reach digital governance rules in the short term.[17] China and ASEAN should strengthen exploration and consultation in this regard, and build new rules for the digital economy that are mutually beneficial and win–win.

There is intensifying geopolitical competition among major powers

In the era of digital globalization, digital games have become the new focus of the game between China and the United States. Maintaining U.S. leadership in the world is an important part of U.S. national

---

[15] Ji Yenan, Hu Zhengkun, and Guo Feng, "Seeing China's position and measures in the field of global digital security and governance from the global data security initiative," *China Information Security*, 2021, 5, p. 31.

[16] Belt and Road research group of China Center for International Economic Exchanges, "Digital Silk Road focuses on rule building," *Economic Daily*, August 19, 2021.

[17] *Ibid.*

security after the end of the Cold War. To maintain its global leadership in the digital economy and counter China's influence in the digital economy, the United States' main measures include: First, to improve the level of export control, restrict or prohibit the export of innovative technologies, key technologies and strategic materials such as chips and high-tech materials to China; second, to increase cooperation with allies such as the European Union, Japan, Australia, etc., and to promote the decoupling of infrastructure, technology research and development, and industrial application to varying degrees to ensure their respective digital economic interests; third, to lead the formulation of new rules for digital trade and cyberspace governance together with allies; finally, to use American democratic values as the standard for digital assistance to shape *the digital future* of developing countries.

Southeast Asia is a key region for U.S. digital diplomacy. The United States has established *the Innovative Connectivity* program under *the US–ASEAN Connectivity framework* to carry out digital diplomacy with ASEAN countries. Relying on *the US–ASEAN Smart City Partnership Program*, the United States plans to strengthen cooperation with ASEAN countries in the fields of urban intelligent public transportation, network security, water resources treatment, data centers and other fields. The United States joins the European Union and Japan in an attempt to dominate digital governance rules in the Asia-Pacific region.[18] In October 2019, the United States and Japan signed *the Digital Trade Agreement*. The two countries restrict the government's supervision of cyberspace, oppose the government's requirement to localize data or disclose source code, and ensure that all departments achieve barrier-free cross-border data transfer. In April 2021, the G7 issued *the Ministerial Declaration on Digital and Technology*, announcing that they would cooperate in the supply chain of the information and communications industry, digital technology standards, and the free flow of data, so as to

---

[18] Minghao, Zhao, "America's perception and response to the digital silk road," *International Studies*, 2020, 4, pp. 53–54.

ensure the values of democracy and freedom and enhance digital competitiveness.

Future Direction of China–ASEAN Digital Economic Cooperation

Challenges and opportunities coexist in China–ASEAN digital economic cooperation, and opportunities outweigh challenges. It is the strategic consensus between China and ASEAN to strengthen digital economic cooperation and create a new engine of economic growth. In the future, we should promote the integration of various strategies and the implementation of plans; strengthen digital infrastructure construction and talent training, and enhance soft and hard power; continue to strengthen digital cooperation to fight the epidemic, and conduct consultations on China–ASEAN digital governance rules to establish digital economy rules conducive to equal and mutually beneficial cooperation.

First, we should accelerate the implementation of the China–ASEAN digital economy development plan docking and implementation rules

The China–ASEAN Leaders' Meeting has identified the main areas and priorities of future digital economic cooperation between the two sides. Next, we will accelerate the implementation of the strategic alignment and implementation rules of the two sides. We should specifically understand the strategic plans and needs of different ASEAN countries, analyze their strengths and weaknesses, formulate detailed cooperation plans and roadmaps, and conduct precise docking. For example, for countries with underdeveloped infrastructure such as Myanmar, Laos and Cambodia, the focus of cooperation should be digital infrastructure construction. For countries with better infrastructure such as Singapore and Malaysia, they can focus on areas such as smart cities, digital innovation, industrial transformation, cross-border digital connections and digital finance.

Second, we should continue to promote digital cooperation to fight the epidemic and ensure sustainable economic development

In the context of the continued spread of the COVID-19 epidemic, the two sides should continue to strengthen cooperation in digital epidemic prevention and anti-epidemic and vaccines. Digital infrastructure will ensure the accurate and efficient distribution of medical supplies and improve the efficiency of diagnosis and rescue of patients. China has accumulated rich experience in this regard, and sharing experience, measures and solutions with ASEAN countries in epidemic prevention and anti-epidemic is conducive to epidemic prevention and control and economic development in the entire region. President Xi Jinping said at the summit commemorating the 30th anniversary of the establishment of China–ASEAN partnership that China is willing to launch the *China–ASEAN Health Shield* cooperation initiative; to provide 150 million doses of COVID-19 vaccine to ASEAN countries free of charge, as well as US$5 million to increase joint vaccine production and technology transfer to carry out key drug research and development cooperation; and to help ASEAN strengthen the construction of grassroots public health systems and personnel training.

At present, the health and medical systems of China and ASEAN countries are still independent, and information sharing has not been achieved. We can explore the establishment of a regional public health center to exchange and share information, strengthen the detection and data sharing of public health emergencies, and improve the overall coping and collaboration skills.

Third, we should promote the construction of digital infrastructure and personnel training, and improve the digital literacy and skills of citizens

Digital infrastructure construction is the premise and foundation for the development of the digital economy. According to *the ASEAN Digital Master Plan 2025*, ASEAN will improve the quality of fixed and mobile broadband infrastructure and expand the coverage, which provides a broad space for China–ASEAN cooperation. China should rely on its own technological advantages to increase cooperation with ASEAN countries in the construction of digital infrastructure. China should also increase digital skills training for ASEAN countries. In addition to cooperation at the government level, Chinese companies should be encouraged to play an active role in talent training and skills training. Huawei's successful experience in Thailand is worthy of reference and learning for other companies. In March 2021, Thai Prime Minister Prayut Chan-o-cha awarded Huawei Thailand *The 2020 Digital International Enterprise Prime Minister Award*, in recognition of Huawei Thailand's contributions to promoting Thailand's digital transformation and economic and social development over the past 21 years.

Finally, we should actively explore and timely promote the establishment of a China–ASEAN digital governance framework.

In the era of digital economy, we urgently need to establish global digital governance rules to regulate the development of global digital trade and digital economy. In accordance with the principle of putting the easy before the difficult, China and ASEAN should actively explore the establishment of rules and standards for cross-border e-commerce, actively promote negotiations on digital governance rules, gradually form a consensus and rule framework for China–ASEAN digital governance, jointly create a more inclusive digital governance framework and facilitate new globalization of sustainability. China has applied to join *the Digital Economy Partnership Agreement (DEPA)* initiated by Singapore. In the future, China and ASEAN can discuss the establishment of digital trade rules. China should also actively participate in the negotiation of global digital trade rules. As the second largest digital economy, China should contribute Chinese solutions to the global digital economy development and cyberspace governance.

Printed in the United States
by Baker & Taylor Publisher Services